MISTER GUMBO

ALSO BY URSULA INGA KINDRED AND MIRRANDA GUERIN-WILLIAMS

*Sister Gumbo: Spicy Vignettes from Black Women on
Life, Sex, and Relationships*

MISTER GUMBO

DOWN AND DIRTY WITH BLACK MEN ON LIFE, SEX, AND RELATIONSHIPS

URSULA INGA KINDRED AND MIRRANDA GUERIN-WILLIAMS

ST. MARTIN'S GRIFFIN NEW YORK

www.stmartins.com

Library of Congress Cataloging-in-Publication Data

Kindred, Ursula Inga.
    Mister gumbo : down and dirty with black men on life, sex, and relationships / Ursula Inga Kindred and Mirranda Guerin Williams.—1st ed.
        p. cm.
    ISBN 0-312-32681-5
    EAN 978-0-312-32681-4
    African American men—Social conditions. 2. African American men—Sexual behavior. 3. African American men—Interviews. 4. Man-woman relationships—United States. 5. Sex—United States. 6. Sex role—United States. I. Guerin-Williams, Mirranda. II. Title.

E185.86.K564 2005
305.38'896073—dc22   2005042782

First Edition: August 2005

10 9 8 7 6 5 4 3 2 1

CONTENTS

CONTENTS

ACKNOWLEDGMENTS

Our sincere thanks to:

God, again, for inspiring us and blessing us with much success.

Our husbands, Wade and Jerome, for their continued love, patience, and support. We could not do this without their help, and words can't truly express how much we appreciate it.

Our children, Jazmyn, Alvin, Guerin, and Justin, for helping us stay grounded and focused. So what if this is our second book? As far as they're concerned, our world still revolves around them.

Barbara Dean Hilliard (Mother), who, by her own example, continues to teach us how important it is to be a lady and a good mother.

James Edward Harris (Daddy), who always was, and still is, a good example of what a husband and father should be. The way he treated us as young girls helped us know what to look for in our own husbands.

Our brother, Thomas Guerin, Jr., a.k.a. Tommy, a.k.a. T. J., the best brother in the world, and also a fine example of a husband, son, and father.

The men we interviewed: Thank you for sharing your stories, even though some of you had to be coerced a little. We truly appreciate your honesty, because this book would not have happened without you.

Our agent Jenny Bent, our editor Monique Patterson, and all of the wonderful staff at St. Martin's Press.

The African-American bookstores, our other family members, friends, and coworkers who continue to support us and spread the word about our books.

You, the readers. Thanks so very much for purchasing this book.

ACKNOWLEDGMENTS

We hope you will enjoy it as much as you enjoyed *Sister Gumbo* (if you read it). If you didn't, we know where you can find a copy! Seriously, your continued support of us and other African-American authors is invaluable. Without you, there would be no reason to write. Thank you again, and God bless!

INTRODUCTION

After we wrote *Sister Gumbo*, we began to get some feedback from our readers, both men and women, wondering when we were going to write a book from the male perspective. That's how *Mister Gumbo* came to fruition.

Upon conducting the interviews it quickly became clear that most men aren't always as open and talkative as women. A woman will tell a complete stranger the specific details of how a man broke her heart, but a man isn't going to do that. A man will say, "It wasn't working, so we broke up," whereas a woman will say, "He cheated on me with my best friend, I caught them in my house, in my bed, in the act. I was humiliated, and then he had the nerve to blame it on me."

It was difficult to find men who were willing to talk about personal issues like marriage, love, sex, advice, and so forth, but when we happened upon the few who were willing to do so, it was a real eye-opener.

Actually, it wasn't until we were both in the process of raising male children that we finally figured out that the thought processes of women and men are completely different. When men sometimes do or don't do certain things, it's not to be mean or hurt a woman's feelings, it's simply because they're being men. What's important to us is not always important to them, at least not important in the same way. That's the reason a guy will tell his girl, "I'll call you right back," but it may take an hour because he's watching a football game with his boys. On the other hand, a girl will fall down trying to get to the phone on the first ring when she thinks her boyfriend is calling.

We believe that women who read *Mister Gumbo* with an open mind will be in for a few surprises, and will come away with some knowledge of how men think and feel and why they do some of the things they do. Remember, they have to put ingredients into their gumbo just like we do, and none of us have the perfect recipe. But with time and patience, and some acceptance of each others methods, we can all cook up something the other will be able to enjoy.

1

RELATIONSHIPS

DUCE'S SHRIMP ÉTOUFÉE

SERVES 4

¹/₂ cup (1 stick) butter

2 green peppers, chopped

1 can of Rotel diced tomatoes and chilies

3 cloves garlic, minced

3 stalks celery, chopped

3 green onions, chopped

1 large onion, chopped

Tony's Cajun Seasoning

Worcestershire sauce

Salt

Pepper

1 (10-ounce) can cream of mushroom soup

1 pound peeled shrimp

4 cups cooked rice

In a large saucepan, melt the butter over medium heat. Add all ingredients except the soup, shrimp, and rice. Sauté for 10 minutes or until tender.

Add the peeled shrimp, and cook for another 15 minutes. Serve the étoufée in bowls over cooked rice.

1
PAST

DANTE
37, MARRIED, AIRLINE BAGGAGE HANDLER
AND PART-TIME MODEL

Dante, always one who's dressed to impress, comes flying into the library parking lot in a brand-new Humvee that he probably can't afford, and why he's wearing a burgundy leather suit in September is beyond my understanding. Oh, he's cute and everything, but it's only fifty degrees outside, not nearly cold enough for leather—unless, of course, your name is Dante Malone.

Look at him, talking on his cell phone. People walking past him are looking at him like he's crazy because he's got one of those little earpieces in his ear that you can't see. They're probably thinking, "Why is this man laughing and talking to himself, wearing a burgundy leather suit in September, and climbing out of a Humvee?" Then again, they're probably looking at him like he's a little strange because he's talking much louder than he needs to be, probably just to draw attention to himself and his new truck, which he's been trying to lock for the last ten minutes. Either he doesn't know what he's doing or he's just taking extra long so that more people can see him using the key to that massive box-shaped truck and think he's rich or something.

"Dante, boy, would you come on over here so we can go inside," I yell. But he looks at me over the top of his shades, which are trimmed in the same shade of burgundy as his suit and alligator shoes, and keeps right on talking—*if* he's even talking, that is. When he finally gets the door locked and crosses the street, he's chattering away, as usual. "That was my agent on the phone. You know I'm about to get back into modeling. See y'all don't know nothing about Dante Malone. I gots it like that. But enough about me—what's up, ladies? You two are looking lovely as usual, almost as good as me." He laughed as he gave us both a hug, even though we were looking upside his head like he had lost his mind. "Y'all know I'm just kidding—*damn*, stop looking all crazy. Come on, let me get the door."

Yep, he's still the same old Dante. Ain't nothing changed since high school. He's still cute, conceited, and loud. His hair is still jet black and curly, he's still got those thick eyebrows and long eyelashes the girls always loved, and his skin is still a flawless caramel color. Fortunately, one thing did change: he's grown maybe six inches since high school, which makes him about six-one.

The burgundy leather suit—and I know I keep bringing that up, but it's only because I can't believe he actually wore it—looks good on him because he's nice and slim. He stays in shape by running. He's forever saying he'll never be fat because he comes from "good blood," whatever that means. I'm not hating on Dante, I just think he's a trip. He's always been a trip.

We took the last private room available in the library, and Mr. "I'm Marvelous" finally took off his burgundy shades, and not a minute too soon, because he was beginning to look like a drug dealer or something in all that burgundy, and wearing dark shades in the library in the middle of the day. "Why are your eyes so red, Dante?" I asked, already knowing the answer.

"Wha— Now see, there you go, worrying about the wrong thing, but since you asked, I had to have me a little gin and juice on my way over here so I could be mellowed out for this little interview."

He picked up our sheet of questions, looked them over, and said, "Umm-hmm. Okay, let's get busy, ladies. Y'all know I'm wanted somewhere else as soon as I finish up here, so let me just run it down for you.

"I really didn't have a very eventful childhood, but when I was fourteen, I started hanging out with people who were eighteen or older, and people on the outside looking in said I was growing up too fast. My parents didn't like it, but I wasn't really out there being wild the way people thought I was. People thought I was a ho, but I wasn't.

"Around age sixteen, I started to become interested in cars and women, in that order, and the women I hung around were in their early twenties. I wasn't having sex yet, but I loved being in a fast environment and I loved being in the presence of women who were that old, just to see what they were about. They always thought I was older than I was, and I think that's because I'd been hanging with the older guys for so long. I already had a mustache, so I looked older than most guys my age, and I was already going to clubs. I had the clothes to wear wherever I went 'cause my friends bought them for me, but it wasn't a gay thing. My male friends just wanted to dress me up so I could look appropriate when I was out with them, and I accepted their gifts.

"My mother and father would complain and tell me, 'You growing up too fast. You shouldn't be hanging with older people,' because they were under the impression that I was out there screwing around, but it wasn't like that. I just hung out with them because they liked me. They treated me like I was their little pet. I had the freakiest and richest friends you could have when I was a teenager. I was in an environment where I met people like Grace Jones and Donald Trump. It was an eye-opening experience for me.

"I saw the drugs, the sex, the orgies, all of that at a young age, but I never participated. I could be sitting in a chair just like I am now, and a man and woman would start going at it. Even two women or two men might get busy right there in front of me, but I just looked and learned. That's why I say the assumptions that people make about another person are not always correct. Just because I hung around with people who were into drugs, sex, partying, and all that, didn't mean I was doing the same thing.

"During high school I had one girlfriend—well, only one I considered a girlfriend. We dated for a while, but I didn't really click with her, because she told me she wanted a baby, and that just threw me off. It was my senior year in high school, and I was like, 'Oh no, sweetie, we're not going to have no baby. Dante ain't ready for that.' Here I was only seventeen, and I hadn't even had sex yet, and she wanted a baby. I guess she didn't know I was a virgin and I didn't bother to tell her, but I was not interested in having a baby or being that serious about anybody, because I believe in God and I felt like he would let me know when the time was right.

"I can't lie. I didn't have a role model when I was growing up. I can't say my dad was a role model for me, because he was a whore and I never respected him as a man. The reason I say that is because when I was around sixteen, I came home from school early one day and caught him messing around with another woman. They were going at it on the living room sofa, the very same sofa that we weren't even allowed to sit on. When I walked in on them, nobody said a word. The woman just got up, pulled on her clothes, and left, but I saw her at the grocery store about a week later, and the slut had the nerve to proposition me. As I got a little older, I began to find out that he knew and had dated a lot of the same women I knew. Word was he'd sleep with anybody if she lay still long enough, and that made me sick because he should've had his ass at home. He didn't have any respect for women. None of the men in my family had a lot of respect for women from what I could see, and I always vowed that I wouldn't be that way.

"I left home and moved to D.C. with two buddies as soon as I graduated from high school, and I was out there trying to break into modeling and going to even more freak parties. I was like, 'Damn, I want to hit some ass like all these other guys,' but something in me just wouldn't let me do it. Something kept telling me I should wait, but because of the environment I was in, I had a lot of friends who were drug dealers. So they had money and gave me money—I mean paper, big money—and there were a lot of women who wanted to date me just because they knew that.

"I would take women on dates and kiss them and fondle them and shit like that, but that was as far as it went. They could kiss me and feel me, and get close to me, but they couldn't have me, and I enjoyed having that kind of control over myself. It always got back to me that some chick had said something like, 'Damn, he had me all horny and shit, then kissed me and left my ass at the doorstep,' because I did that a lot. I always had an excuse as to why I couldn't stay and hit it, because I felt like I should wait.

"When I was twenty, I decided to get into modeling seriously and I was still a virgin, for real. I mean, don't get me wrong, there were a lot of women I kissed and let give me head because I was modeling and hanging with all these fine women, so I couldn't say no to everything. But as far as having sexual intercourse with a woman, hitting the skins, no, I didn't do it. I even told one woman, 'I can't go to bed with you, because I'm not going to marry you. You're nice and everything, but you're not the type of woman I'd want for a wife, and I have more respect for a woman than to take a gift like that when it means nothing to me. I'm not going to play games with you or break your heart. I'm being real,' and believe it or not, she actually wanted to be with me even more after I said that."

G.G.
33, SINGLE, RESTAURANT MANAGER

I met G., as he chooses to be called, on a Friday evening while hanging out with a few girlfriends over dinner and drinks. He's the manager of a swanky restaurant in Dallas's upscale Oak Lawn area, and he'd stopped at our table to make sure we had everything we needed. When he approached us, we were laughing and chattering like magpies, and my friend Elise almost choked on the glass of wine she was sipping when she saw how extremely fine he was.

"Good evening, ladies," he said with a huge smile, causing all six of us to drop our forks and secretly hope that there was no smeared lipstick or misplaced salad dressing anywhere on our faces. "Y'all are having way too much fun over here, you make me want to take a seat and join you. What in the world are all you beauties laughing about? Are y'all over here talking about men?"

Casey, the only one of the group who wasn't married, ran her tongue across her teeth to make sure all was well, sat up straight, gave him a huge smile, and made herself the spokeswoman for all of us when she told him that the service was impeccable, but we could certainly use a refill on our water. In the process, she pointed to her half-full glass with her left hand, making sure that he noticed she wasn't wearing a wedding ring.

After giving all of us a friendly nod and promising to send our waiter over, he continued to work the room, and I told Casey that I didn't know why she was flirting with him, because he seemed like he was gay.

All five women clicked their tongues in the negative, Casey being the loudest when she replied, "Girl, you're tripping. That fine-ass man ain't gay. All this talk about black men being 'on the down low' just has women spooked, even you married women. You can't look at every black man and just assume he's creeping with another man just because that's the latest hot topic of conversation."

I sat back and kept working on my salad, but all the while I was thinking there was something about him . . . something about the way he moved or kept using the word *sweetie* that had me convinced. Since we had been unsuccessful at finding a man "on the DL" who would discuss his life with us for the book, I thought I'd try G. and see if he might be interested. I slipped away to the ladies' room and pulled him aside on my way back to see if he was game for an interview at a later date. I told him about *Sister Gumbo* and told him we were looking for a few interesting men to interview for *Mister Gumbo*, and handed him my business card, which included my phone number and e-mail address. Even though he gave me a wonderful hug and kissed me on the cheek before I left, I wasn't sure I'd hear from him, so I was pleasantly surprised when he called me about a week later and said he'd be willing to answer whatever questions I had if I would like to meet him one evening after the restaurant closed.

Sexy, slim, and standing about six-three, G. has a deep baritone voice, smooth golden brown skin, and long thick eyelashes. He had the bartender pour each of us a glass of white zinfandel before inviting me to follow him to his office in the back, where we could have some privacy. I noticed a picture of a beautiful young lady on his desk and thought that asking about her would be a good way to start off our conversation, so I did just that, and G. took it from there.

"That's Tia, my girlfriend, and for the record—since you've already said you're writing about life, sex, and relationships, and since you promised me that what we say is confidential—I'll admit that I'm one of those men who loves women, but I do keep a male friend to get with every now and then to keep things interesting. Even though I don't publicize the fact that I like sleeping with men and women, I don't consider myself to be one of those guys on the DL. Tia knows my sexual preferences, and she's okay with it because she's as open as I am about sex. I am definitely bisexual, but only the people I'm close to and intimate with know that, and that's how I prefer to keep it. I'm very private, and I don't believe what I do in the privacy of my bedroom is everyone's business.

"Growing up, I lived in a predominantly African-American community and attended private Christian schools before leaving home to attend college in California. My family is extremely conservative. I grew up in the church, my grandfather has been a Baptist minister for well over fifty years, and I'm one of the head deacons in his church.

"My parents have been married for forty years, and even though they haven't gotten along for most of those forty years, they are still together because they don't believe in divorce. They live in the same house but sleep in separate bedrooms, and they've been doing that for as long as I can remember.

"I have a sister and brother who happen to be twins. My sister is a doctor, but she's also an alcoholic. She starts drinking from the time she gets home in the evening and doesn't stop until it's time to go to bed, and she doesn't think anybody knows it. We all know about it; we just don't talk about it. My oldest brother was accepted to law school but got burned out and started running with a fast crowd. He recently got out of jail for dealing drugs.

"So as you can see, even though outwardly my background is conservative, if you look real close, you'll find that beneath the surface my family life is pretty interesting, to say the least.

"My father was always a very stern disciplinarian, and he was always on me about being too sensitive. I was the kind of boy whose feelings were easily hurt, and my father couldn't deal with that and he would chide me when I would break into tears when he would speak to me too harshly, while my mother would take me aside and hug or kiss me to take away the bluntness of his words. She never had to do that with my brother or sister, because they could hold their own with my father whatever the situation. They would nod their heads and agree with whatever it was my father told them to do but as soon as his back was turned, they would become children he wouldn't recognize in his wildest dreams. My siblings could outdrink, outsmoke, and outcuss anybody in their peer group.

"Coming up Southern Baptist, I wasn't taught anything about sex except that it was bad, and once puberty set in, I had a burning desire to know what was so bad about it, but was too scared to take the action and find out. The first time I had sexual intercourse with a man, I was nineteen years old and a freshman at UCLA. It happened in the apartment of a popular thirty-year-old radio and party DJ who was on the DL. I was nervous and excited at the same time, and even though I've dated women and have continued to have sex with women since then, for me the sex act with a woman is not nearly as intense as it is when I'm with another man.

"My mother and my sister know about my sexual orientation because I've told them, but my brother and my dad, who are also deacons in our Church, reside in the land of denial with their 'We're not going to ask, so don't you dare tell us' typical Southern Baptist crazy-ass mentality. I think they feel that if they really knew that I liked having sex with men, then they'd have to deal with it, and that might compromise their feelings about their own sexuality, so we don't even go there. And my brother was in jail, so I know he had to deal with that when he was locked up. When I'm back home and me and the fellas are just sitting around talking or whatever, I pretend I'm a womanizer like the rest of the men in my family, which seems like an acceptable way to be and the only thing they can be comfortable with. If it works for them, it works for me too, what the hell.

"I honestly feel I was born sexually uninhibited or bisexual. I can remember one evening during the summer when I was at church waiting to attend youth choir rehearsal. I was ripping and running all over the church because my grandfather was in his office working. I know he probably would have killed my ass and laid me out on the Communion table had he caught me all up in the pulpit, but luckily he didn't catch me. I eventually tired of playing in the pulpit and decided to explore some of the empty rooms in the long hallway and happened upon one of the Sunday school classrooms in the far corner of the church, where a muffled sound caught my attention. I peeked inside the dimly lit room, and my gaze fell upon the church's very married choir director and a teenaged boy kissing, and the boy wasn't fighting him off. He was acting as though he liked it. I knew instantly that what I was seeing was taboo, but I continued to watch because it excited me.

"I guess I was around ten years old at the time because shortly after that happened I remember having a birthday party and playing hide and go get it after all the adults went inside. This was a game that entailed catching a member of the opposite sex and then feeling that person up. The thing is, I was looking to "hide and go get it" from a boy rather than from one of the many girls at the party, and I think that's when I first realized that what I'd seen at the church appealed to me more than it should have. I never told my parents or grandfather what I had seen, because Lord knows I probably would have gotten a beating just because I'd witnessed something I shouldn't have and then to add insult to injury had the nerve to talk about it. But now that I look back on it, I must have known at that young age that I was maybe a little bit different than most other boys.

"I didn't consider that experience to be a traumatic one, because as I've said before, I was born sexually uninhibited. I have never felt that there was anything wrong with being sexually attracted to both men and women, even though the church has always taught me different. The thing I don't quite understand is that while the Bible says one thing and the preachers preach what the Bible says, why are there so many openly gay men in the church like the musicians, ushers, and so on who are accepted? My grandfather's church is huge, and his minister of music and several of the men in the choir are openly gay. I know for a fact that several of the deacons are DL, and while it is quite obvious that the gay men are gay, the church members must discuss this fact only amongst themselves in the privacy of their homes—because I have never been in one meeting or had one conversation with a family member or anyone else who would dare bring it up. It makes no sense at all, but that's the Southern Baptist way, isn't it? If you ignore it long enough, it doesn't exist.

"Outside of that, the most significant thing that happened in my life, that made me the man I am now, is when I was introduced to several glamorous, trendy, substance-abusing, self-righteous, but self-conscious, openly gay men at the age of nineteen, when I first left home and entered college. My roommate happened to be one of these characters, and that's how I became involved in the life, although I do remember innocently wanting to establish same-sex relationships as early as age ten."

JOE
41, SINGLE, SMALL BUSINESS OWNER

When we met with Joe, the first thing he said was, "I don't know if y'all really want to interview me, 'cause you know I keep it real," and that's the truth if I've ever heard it. At first he tried to act like he didn't want to talk to us, but as much as he loves to be seen and heard, we knew he was just fronting.

Joe is a Texan to his heart, and proud of it. If I'm not mistaken, he mentioned it at least three times during the interview. "My mama and daddy owned the first dry cleaners in the community, and they made a pretty good living, so I didn't want for nothing. That's why I'm so well dressed, my mama starched my clothes from the time I started kindergarten all the way through high school, and even today I won't wear a pair of jeans unless they're starched."

Today Joe wore a pair of blue jeans that had been starched to within an inch of their life coupled with a shiny black shirt and black eelskin dress shoes that had to be at least twenty years old but were shining like new money. Everything on Joe was shining. He wore at least six rings, a black square onyx, a couple of gold nuggets, and a few simple gold bands studded here or there with smaller diamonds, and when he smiled, the gold tooth with the half moon that capped his front tooth sparkled and glimmered as brightly as his rings. He's the type of brother who will show up at a wedding wearing a red suit, red socks, red shoes, red hat, and carrying a red walking stick if he can find one. And get this, if he's dating a woman and they're stepping out, you'd best believe she'll be wearing the exact same color he is and walking so close to him that all you can see is one big block of color as they approach.

From the first impression one believes, and rightly so, that Joe is stuck in the 1970s, but he is very much aware of what's going on concerning money, politics, real estate, and anything else that's happening in his community. You can laugh at him wearing that red suit all you want to, but don't try to run no game on him, because he's no fool when it comes to life, women, or how to make a dollar. Joe is barely five-eight and a little on the heavy side, has beautiful jet-black skin, dark brown eyes, and a Jheri curl that he has worn for the past twenty-five years. He's by no means handsome, but the way he handles himself makes him attractive, and the women certainly like him. Joe always has and always will drive the biggest, longest car he can find. In the eighties it was a gold two twenty-five (better known as a deuce and a quarter), in the nineties it was a gold Lincoln Continental, and now he drives a Cadillac and, you guessed it, it's gold too.

I first met Joe back in the early 1980s, when we all frequented a club called Panther Hall. I was at the bar ordering a rum and Coke when I saw him walk in, looking around like he owned the place, and politely ignored him because I was waiting for my ex-boyfriend to walk in so I could spend the night pretending to ignore him too.

Joe walked around to where I was standing, looked me up and down, and said, "Damn, you fine. Who you here with?" When I didn't respond, he kept right on talking.

"Say, cutie, I know you hear me talking to you with your fine self. Why don't you let me buy that drink for you?" When I still didn't respond, he got silly. "Oh, I see, I guess the cat got your tongue, huh? What, you can't talk? I bet you gonna talk to *me* tonight 'cause I'm gonna make it my business to bother you all night if you don't. You gonna dance with me too, 'cause you know you like me. Look at you, trying everything you can to keep from smiling with your pretty self. You even got pretty hands and pretty lips. What yo name is, girrrrl? Is you got a boyfriend? If you do, too bad for him, 'cause I'm gonna take you from him. I'm one of a kind—you can't resist me. Just look over here at this big smile I got on my face and tell me I'm not irresistible," and that was all I could take before I burst out laughing.

We've been buddies ever since.

For the interview, we met Joe at the BBQ Stand, a place he co-owns with a cousin. Joe said the BBQ Stand was known not only for the smoked brisket but also for the sweet tea his aunt made daily, so we both agreed to have a glass, and once the sugar kicked in, we were ready to roll.

"I grew up right here in Funky Town aka Fort Worth, Texas. My parents are from the north side and relocated to the south side right before I was born, so I've lived here all my life. Since they owned their own business, I had the opportunity to learn how to make money because I was always hanging around and watching them make decisions. Every time my dad made a business deal, even though all of them weren't legit, he'd say, 'See, son, that's why I like having my own business. I get to call the shots, and there ain't no glass ceiling unless I make one. Always remember that you can never be financially independent as long as you work for someone else.'

"My mom worked in the cleaners right along with my pops, but her main responsibility was keeping the money straight, and she did it well. She can hold a dollar tight enough to make Washington's hair sweat and curl up in an afro—that's the tightest damn woman I know—but I appreciate her thriftiness because if it weren't for her, Pops probably would have given all the money to some little hot-ass woman he was messing around with. I love him, I'm proud to call him Dad, and he taught me a lot, but I damn sure inherited his trifling-ass ways when it comes to women.

"I can't come right out and say I ever saw my dad with another woman, so maybe that's taking things a little too far, but from what I did see, I know he was a ladies' man. For years I watched the look on the different women's faces when they came by the shop to present Pops with one of their homemade pound cakes or sweet potato pies still warm from the oven. They'd always say, 'Brother Joe, I was just thinking I'd bring this by to make it easy on Mrs. Palmer so she won't have to do all that cooking when she gets home.' The funny thing is they never seemed to bring any of that food over when Mama was at the shop, and she never ate any of it either. I can remember her telling Pops one time, 'Keep on letting them little black-ass women bring you food. One day they gonna come up in here looking for your old gray ass thinking I'm not here, and I'm gonna get a stick and beat their asses all the way back out that door.'

"I did some crazy things as a kid, even as a young man, but I always had self-respect. I think your self-respect shows in the way you dress. In the late seventies and early eighties, you didn't go to school—or anywhere else, for that matter—with your clothes wrinkled. It just wasn't something we did. I don't know how many girls in my graduating class have messed-up feet to this day because girls even wore heels with their starched jeans when I was in school. We enjoyed dressing up, and we wanted to look good when we went to school, not like these bad-ass kids nowadays. The boys go to school with their pants hanging all off their ass, and now that those hip-hugger jeans are back in style, the girls got all their shit hanging out too. It's like the boys wear all their stuff two sizes too big, and the girls wear theirs two sizes too small. It's crazy. The sad thing about it is they think they look good dressed like that.

"People may say I'm a little eccentric with the way I wear my hair and the loud colors I wear, but that's me. That's my style, and I don't care if other people like it or not. They might not like it, but I'll bet they can't say they've ever seen me sloppy or dirty, or looking like I wasn't prepared to conduct business if the opportunity presented itself. I'm always up on my game, and that's the reason I've been successful in life, which to me means having money in my pocket 24-7, driving a nice car, wearing nice clothes, and owning my own businesses."

KEN
31, MARRIED, CHEF IN TRAINING

We met Ken at the *Essence* Music Festival during the Frankie Beverly and Maze concert in the Louisiana Superdome. He was seated in the row in front of us with a bunch of other guys and their women, and you couldn't help but notice him, because he was an extremely talkative cutie with cinnamon-colored skin, high cheekbones, and dreadlocks that reached the middle of his back. By the time Anita Baker was through singing, he had struck up a conversation with everybody in his immediate vicinity.

"Damn, this beer is too expensive to be lukewarm. I ought to take it back," Ken complained.

"Nigga please," the brother sitting next to him scoffed. "It's not like you can't afford it."

"That's beside the point," Ken replied. "You just wait until my wife gets back in town and I tell her how her cousin was all in my business." Before the other guy could comment, Maze had hit the stage, and why did they go and start off with "Southern Girl"? Everybody was on their feet immediately moving to the rhythm, and then the whole stadium full of people had the nerve to break into the Electric Slide and keep on beat. I'd never seen anything like it in my life.

"Go 'head, go 'head," Ken sang as he moved his shoulders and danced to the beat. When he went to raise his hands, he must've forgotten he was holding a cup of beer because what was left went flying out and landed right on my feet just as I was ready to go into my turn. I know he saw it happen because he stopped in the middle of his own turn and said, "Aw, damn, sister—I'm sorry." But I couldn't get angry with him, especially when he grinned at me.

I told him no problem; I had kicked my shoes off anyway, so at least my shoes hadn't gotten messed up, and instead of my feet just being sore from all that dancing, they were now sore and sticky.

"So, where y'all from?" Ken asked after handing me a clean

handkerchief so I could dry my feet. We told him we were in town do-ing a book signing, and he looked somewhat impressed.

"What? I've been telling my wife for the last few years how I plan on writing a book when I get finished with school, and look, I run into authors. Things always happen for a reason. I need to keep in touch with y'all. Once I get my restaurant up and running, I'm gonna write a cookbook. You're looking at a man who can cook his ass off. Right now I'm going to the Culinary Institute of New Orleans because I plan on being a chef, and my wife, Zonora, is going to Xavier and is about a semester away from graduating."

Because he was so personable, we asked him if he'd agree to an in-terview the next day. He said yes and invited us to his home.

Their house was located in the Garden District of New Orleans, and once we arrived it was obvious that spilling an expensive-ass beer in the Superdome and worrying about where he was going to get the money to pay for another one was the least of Ken's worries. Obvi-ously he or his wife came from a family with money—because prop-erty in this area of the city didn't come cheap. There was no way he could've afforded to purchase this property on his own, since he was barely thirty if that.

I pursed my lips and whistled silently as I took in the huge mahogany door inlaid with leaded glass, the well-manicured lawn, lush foliage, profusion of flowers, and the hundred-year-old moss-draped oaks sur-rounding the two-story house. The house wasn't as large as some of the others on the street, but it was still very impressive.

Ken opened the door and laughed when he saw our twin looks of surprise. After watching him carry on last night and seeing how down-to-earth he had been, I never in my wildest imagination would've thought he was living like this. I had been under the impression that he lived in some little garage apartment in the Garden District, being that he was so young and still in school, and here we stood in the foyer of this mini-mansion.

"I came into my inheritance when I was twenty-one; the house belonged to my great-grandmother," Ken explained. "I don't have to work for a living, but I do, and at least I got to choose to do something that gives me pleasure, unlike most people. Besides, my wife is not about to have a man sitting up on his ass all day, wealthy or not, and that was the promise I made to her when we got married six years ago."

He led us deeper into the house, and I stared in awe at the obviously expensive and original antique furniture. "Why don't we sit out in the sunroom. It's pretty comfortable. I fixed lunch and it just needs eating, so y'all are right on time."

Ken was about five-eleven and had a nice body. His wore a short-sleeved T-shirt that didn't reveal much, but it was tucked into jeans that outlined thick thighs and a slim waist, not too bad. Today his locks were held back with a bandanna.

"It's nice of you to take this kind of time with complete strangers," I said.

"Humph, I love to talk about me—tell me what man don't?" Ken asked, slipping into a Cajun dialect as we followed him into the sunroom. He already had the food warming in silver containers on the sideboard.

"I cooked y'all some shrimp Creole with my famous Ken's Creole sauce, and for dessert I fixed a white chocolate French custard bread pudding, and yes, it's fattening but you don' come down here to Nawlins expecting to be on no diet. Diets are for when you back in Texas."

"What prompted your interest in cooking?" I asked.

"I have to say my mama, because she loves to cook. Even today, all my mama watches on TV are cooking shows." Ken continued as we prepared our plates "I have a twin sister, and when my mama would show her how to cook something, I'd be right in there with them, and she was always able to make the lesson interesting."

"So", I said, "you're a down-to-earth kind of man, so that means you're going to be open, honest, and interesting, right?"

And with a sexy little smile, Ken replied, "Hey, all I got to say is be careful what you ask, because I'm ready."

SIMEON
38, SINGLE, ACCOUNTANT

Simeon flung open his front door and ushered us in, mouth running a mile a minute. "That's what I'm talking about—sisters who know how to be on time. When y'all said one o'clock, I was like, *Okay, in CP time, that means two.*"

Simeon said that he spends the majority of his time in the family room when he's at home, and apparently he shops at the same import stores that I do, because I have some of the exact same masks decorating my walls that he does his. I looked around and thought to myself, *Damn, this man doesn't need a woman. He's decorated this house, keeps it clean, and knows how to cook? Homeboy got it going on.* A flokati rug lay in front of the upright CD player and a zebra print rug was situated beneath the glass coffee table. In the center of the room was a pool table, and the far wall held a wide-screen plasma TV, a fully stocked bar, and a mini-fridge. Simeon pulled out a bottle of red wine and a corkscrew and poured equal amounts into the handblown wineglasses he'd set out for us.

He's six feet five inches tall with cocoa-brown skin and the build of a basketball player—nothing but legs and arms. In his ears he sports diamond studs that weigh at least two carats, and while he's not the pretty-boy type, his charisma and income go a long way to ensure that he has no problem getting or keeping a woman's attention.

When the first question out of my mouth was what he thought of women in general, he was quick to reply. "They ain't no good! But let me sip on this Rémy for a few minutes before I get into that," and it was clear he wasn't joking.

After handing each of us a glass of merlot, he sank down into one of the large chairs stationed in front of the CD player, took a sip of cognac, and began to talk.

"I grew up in a home with no father, and my sisters and I went to private school since my mom was big on education, but the majority of the kids in my neighborhood went to public school. Our neighborhood had a mixture of everything, and by mixture I mean some families had both of their parents living at home and some families just had a mom, and we fell into the latter group.

"Because our mom was a single parent, we understood at an early age that we couldn't have some of the things that kids with two parents living in the home had, and sometimes our not having a father around kind of made us feel left out. Back when I was growing up, it was a big deal for parents to be divorced and for a woman to raise a child by herself. It was almost like it was something to be ashamed of. Nowadays, it's the opposite.

"I learned and understood the essence of what was important, and even though we weren't poor, we definitely weren't rich. We never went to bed hungry or anything, but I did learn how to appreciate things. When I was growing up, it was like this: if somebody offered you a compliment or if someone gave you something, you appreciated it and said thank you. I was raised to never take anything for granted.

"My mom worked a lot, and because she worked a lot she required a lot from us. She was like, 'You know what, I'm going to bring the money home, but don't ever think that you're not gonna keep your room straight and keep this house clean.' It wasn't like we had a choice in the matter anyway. There was never an option. She'd never say, 'I would like you to clean your room and I would like you to make good grades.' No, it was, 'This is what I expect from you.' She was a true believer in that old saying, 'I brought you into this world, and I can take you out.' That was the kind of upbringing I had.

"My mom expected us to make good grades in school, and she also told us to be respectful because, as she said, 'It makes no sense for you to come in here with an A or a B and then get an N in citizenship. If you get A's and B's, that's fine, but you're still going to get an ass-whipping if you come up in here with an N in citizenship,' and I tell my nieces and nephews the same thing.

"My mom and grandparents instilled a good work ethic in me. It was like, screw what a person can *give* you—if you go out and earn it, you appreciate it, and I respected that. Even when my mom was disciplining us, she was going to give us an explanation for it."

Simeon turned the jazz music down some and placed the remote control on the glass tabletop.

"My sisters and I joke about it now. We would grumble amongst ourselves, but we made sure that Mom didn't hear us, because she didn't play that. You'd get a serious beat down if you caught yourself talking back after she said something. We'd be mumbling, 'Mom just whip us, we don't want to hear all that talking,' because when Mom talked to you, oh my God, it took forever. She would start off with, 'We going to have a talk.' Even to this day, those six little words chill me to the bone. I could come in thirty minutes after my curfew and she would hear the door open and call out, 'What time is it?' and I knew good and well she knew what time it was, and then she'd say, 'We going to have a talk in the morning.' I hated that shit, I hated the anticipation of knowing she was going to get on my ass about something and that I had to spend the whole night wondering what the punishment was going to be. Once she started talking, it seemed like she could go on for hours.

"But, really, everybody I knew worked to get what they wanted. If it meant working some overtime or whatever, that's what you did to get ahead. You didn't do no scamming, sell drugs, or try to beat somebody out of their money. You just worked real hard. When I got into accounting I was taught that it's okay to work hard but it's also okay to work smart. You can work from sunup to sundown, but the work's still going to be there, so if you can be more realistic about what you want to accomplish, then things kind of fall in line.

"I think the discipline Mom instilled in us helped me when I started working, because I was really young and I worked with a lot of individuals who were older than me, so I was always getting some kind of advice and I didn't mind it. I was used to listening to Mom and my grandparents anyway. It always pays to listen to people who are older than you and advice is free. It's up to you to take advantage of it and to use it as you see fit. I find that people who follow good advice and put a lot into life get a lot back, but if you don't put too much effort into life, you really shouldn't be expecting much out of it.

"My family didn't have a whole lot of material things, but truly speaking, when Christmas came around we were happy, and when birthdays came around we were happy. We had peace, friendship, love, and respect back then, and I feel like if I still got all of that now, I'm successful."

Simeon lowered his voice to a whisper and added, "Well that and a whole bunch of money too." Then he shouted out again like he wanted to make sure that we hadn't forgotten his earlier comment, *"They ain't no good, every color, every creed, every shade, ain't none of them no damn good!"*

QUINCY
36, DIVORCED, HIGH SCHOOL FOOTBALL COACH

"What's going on ladies?" Quincy said, greeting us. "Sorry there's not much room to park. Damn Mexicans and Asians got six cars in each yard and ten to fifteen people living in each house, just gets on my nerves." Quincy was sounding like a crotchety old man as he led us inside.

"I walked outside the other day and thought I was living in Chinatown, and the people in the house across the street had their music up so loud, I couldn't hear my TV. If it's not that, it's the Mexicans next door moving cars all damn night. One of the boys will come outside and start up one of those old buckets, rev the engine up as loud as he can, drive off real fast and return five minutes later, parking the car in the exact same spot he just pulled it out of like he ain't used to nothing.

"The black folk living in that house behind me ain't much better, 'cause they got a different group of people staying there every time I turn around, and they're partying every week, probably selling drugs. I swear, I probably should just sell this house and move, but I don't feel like buying a new house and being broke. I'm not one to try to impress the ladies with material things anyway, so I'm not getting into no debt just to keep up with the Joneses."

Quincy, a friend of a friend, is a young man from the old school. He's old-fashioned and down-to-earth, and he believes in things like hard work, commitment, and being true to your word. He's five-eleven, weighs around 190 pounds, has Hershey's dark chocolate brown skin, and a quirky little smile to go along with his sense of humor. A divorcé with two boys ages ten and eight, Quincy is a high school football coach. Except for the weekends when his boys are with him, he lives alone in one of the three modest two-bedroom town houses that he inherited from his grandfather in a neighborhood that used to be pretty decent but is now well past its prime.

The house is pretty neat for a bachelor and is chock-full of antiques on loan from his mother, even though he says he really doesn't like antiques.

"I'd been separated from my wife for a month before my mom found out, and the minute she found out, she demanded that I go to her storage room and get whatever I needed because she said she couldn't stand the thought of me being in an empty house with no furniture. She also made it very clear that if I up and married another sorry-ass woman, the furniture was not part of the deal.

"So I went and picked up that bench in the foyer, that armoire with the double doors that I remembered seeing in my grandparents' house when I was a kid, that Victorian bookcase in the corner which I converted into a gun cabinet, and this sofa and the wingback chairs. Oh, I also got a dining room set that consists of a china closet, sideboard table, and six chairs. Other than the sofa and chairs, nothing seems to really match, but I guess it's better than nothing at all, and it is quality furniture. I could have taken a few things from my house when I left, but my wife was such a bitch, I didn't want any reminders of her."

Oddly enough, the furniture seems to fit Quincy because of his old-fashioned nature. When you look around, it just seems like this is the kind of atmosphere he'd be comfortable in—if you exclude the neighbors, that is. He said that when his grandparents first moved here, the neighborhood was about 70 percent white and 30 percent "other," and the homeowners kept everything nice and clean because they realized the value of real estate. Now that the older people who were the original owners have either moved on or died, their children and grandchildren have turned the entire neighborhood into Section 8 rent city, and most of them don't even check backgrounds and references like he does before allowing someone to rent their property, which is causing the property value to drop and the homes to look run-down.

Quincy was dressed like he was prepared to go somewhere after the interview, and when we mentioned how nice he looked and asked about his plans for the evening, he replied, "I always dress like this, even when I'm not going anywhere. I like to be comfortable-casual just in case something jumps off, because you never know. Khaki pants and a button-down shirt aren't what I would call dressed up, but if I decide to go somewhere on the spur of the moment, I'll be ready. It's not that I don't own any FUBU, Polo, or Sean John, but I'm not really into faddish, name-brand-type clothes. I wear that stuff if it fits the occasion, but I'm a bargain shopper—and if I can't get my FUBU on sale, I'm not buying it. Besides, if a woman is looking for a hip-hop kind of brother with his pants hanging off his ass, I'm not the one anyway, because I'm not spending my hard-earned money on clothes that are too big.

"I've been through a lot in the past few years, and although I used to be very bitter about my divorce, I'm now at a point where I'm free of all the resentment and anger. Counseling and a few self-awareness courses really helped me understand more about myself: my likes and dislikes, and my feelings about women, love, and marriage. I think I may be ready for a serious relationship, but I'm not in any hurry to be committed again.

"I'm a by-the-book kind of guy. I follow the rules and expect others to do the same, especially where love and relationships are concerned, and that's one of the main reasons my marriage didn't work. I gave one hundred percent and then some, while she barely gave twenty, and she didn't want me to say anything to her about it. She turned out to be totally different from the woman she'd appeared to be the short time we dated, so after trying to make things work for three years, I finally gave up and decided that if I couldn't be happy with her, I'd have to be happy without her. I refused to raise my boys in an environment with fussing and cussing all the time, because it was unhealthy. I was just about to file for divorce, but she beat me to it and I wasn't mad at her. I guess she thought I was going to break down and cry and beg her to change her mind, but I was practically smiling when I signed those papers, and she's been pissed ever since.

"As far as growing up, I had a great childhood. I'm from San Bernardino, California, and grew up in the city, but my dad was a country boy and wanted us to experience the same things he experienced, so we did a lot of hunting, fishing, camping, and stuff like that when I was a kid, I had the best of the suburban and country life.

I'm the oldest of three boys, and me and my brothers are only like a year apart, so when we became teenagers and got inquisitive about sex, my dad started taking us to R-rated movies, and afterwards we would have a discussion about it. We didn't go see stuff that had a lot of low-down, dirty, rated-X sex in it, just good movies where sex happened to be included. Dad would ask us if we understood what we'd just seen, and that was our opportunity to ask questions.

"He always said that sex was a wonderful thing, then turned right around and said we should always remember that in order to play big-boy games, you had to be willing to pay the big-boy price. That meant if we got a girl pregnant, it was going to be our responsibility, and even though I had sex as a teenager, I was always very careful and I still am to this day. Actually, I was a little scared to start having sex, because I'd had that conversation with my dad so many times. His favorite saying was, 'If you don't want to see her face across the table from you every morning, then don't get her pregnant—because if you do, you're marrying her and you're gonna help raise that baby.'

"I sure as hell wish I'd had a little more fear and a lot more insight before I married my ex, because it seems like once we said, 'I do,' I wasn't looking at the same woman at all."

JARED
30, SINGLE, ENGINEER

We met Jared in a Mexican restaurant at the San Antonio International Airport during a short layover.

We'd just feasted on a bowl of charro beans that tasted homemade, the deep red ceramic bowl nearly overflowing with the hot and spicy mixture seasoned with onions, tomato, garlic, bacon, and jalapeño peppers.

Facing us were two wall-mounted, flat-screen TVs with the sound turned low as Mexican music played quietly in the restaurant. The walls were inlaid with yellow and cobalt blue Mexican tile and faux windows decorated with wrought iron. Small white Christmas lights brightened up the room. The floors were hardwood, the sheen dull, the tables stationed between thick round oak beams.

Jared had just finished his meal when he looked over and noticed our shirts; they never fail to get a second glance, but of course something that reads LIFE, SEX, AND MORE SEX will make almost anyone look twice. Catching our eyes, he flashed a smile and asked, "So what's *Life, Sex, and More Sex* mean?"

We described our first book, told him we were working on a sequel, and asked if he'd be willing to respond to a few questions.

Checking his watch, he shrugged slightly and said he had at least two hours between flights, so that sounded like a great way to pass the time. He picked up his Corona and walked over to our table where we sat nursing our own drinks. He was a tall, good-looking man and wore his long-sleeved white cotton shirt, blue jeans, and black leather boots with the grace of a male model. His hair was cut close, his eyebrows thick, black, and wickedly arched, and his only facial hair was a thin mustache and sexy goatee.

When we made mention of his awesome height, he said he was six foot six and that it had come in handy when he'd played ball throughout high school and college, and he had even been on track to becoming a professional player until he'd busted his knee.

"My parents were proud of my skills on the court, but they were even prouder when I brought home good grades. To this day, I'm glad I had the sense to listen to them when they stressed the importance of an education, or else I would've been up a creek because an uneducated black man with a bum knee who *used* to be good at basketball doesn't get very far in life." Jared flashed that perfect smile again. "After the knee injury, I put more effort into my studies and was able to graduate with my master's degree in engineering."

Jared shifted a bit in the wooden chair, stretching his long legs out in front of him and crossing his feet at the ankles.

"My dad is an engineer. He worked for the same aeronautics company until he retired, and my mom was a stay-at-home mom, so she was always around. Me and my brother didn't even think about getting away with anything. Well, let me take that back, we did make a few attempts to try and get away with stuff, but our mom would *always* find out. I don't know how she found out, but she did. She must've attended every PTA meeting, school outing, and anything else they needed parents to volunteer for. I swear, she should've been on the payroll she was around our school so much, and I mean elementary through high school. She probably would've hung out with me at college too, if I hadn't of gone out of state.

"I wasn't too fond of school early on, and I remember being in the first grade and my teacher, Miss Reese, teaching me how to write the letter of my first name over and over again. Apparently, I quickly got tired of that, so I issued her an ultimatum. As the story goes, or at least my mom's version of it, I told Miss Reese, 'Look, I'm going to write one more J. My mama didn't send me to school to write J's—my mama sent me to school to play.' "

Jared shrugged his broad shoulders as we stifled our laughter, and then he raised his bottle of Corona in a toast. "Here's to the innocence of youth."

GREG
38, DIVORCED, BEER COMPANY SALES MANAGER

Greg, a handsome chocolate brother who spent a lot of time in New York while he was married, is originally from Georgia. He's a senior sales manager for a large beer company and has four children by two different women. At five-eleven and 210 pounds, Greg is extremely well built because he works out faithfully six days a week.

He has nice dark brown skin, beautiful eyes, and is always flashing this sexy yet playful smile that seems to hint, "Be careful—there's more to me than you think." Judging from the way he carries himself and his mannerisms, it's obvious that he knows how to treat a lady, and because of that, he has no shortage of female friends. Greg was dressed in black cotton house pants, the type teenagers wear to the mall nowadays even though they shouldn't, and a sleeveless white V-neck T-shirt that showed off his muscular chest, arms, and stomach. He was also barefoot, and even his feet, which he propped up on the coffee table, were pretty.

Greg's apartment was immaculate. I'd already checked out his kitchen when we first walked in and noticed that there wasn't a dirty dish in the sink. The sink was chrome and had obviously been wiped clean because there weren't any water spots, and let me tell you, the smell of scented candles burning, his cologne, and that beautiful smile made for a superb setting. It was so cozy and inviting that it took me a moment to gather myself and get focused.

There is something sexy about an attractive black man sitting there smiling at you when you're trying to act like you don't see him smiling, because you're trying to be all about business. But the harder you try to keep your cool, the more you start to sweat because married or not you still realize that he's sexy as hell and knows it, not to mention the fact that you're on his turf.

Greg grinned.

———

"I'm not a shy brother, so if I get too talkative, let me know. Growing up, I had a pretty normal childhood. Both my parents raised me, and my father was a serious disciplinarian. He stayed on me, and now I realize that I needed that because if he hadn't, I probably wouldn't be where I am now.

"I was never crazy about school, but I wasn't no dummy either, and I should have gone to college. I had the opportunity to go, but I didn't want to, and that's one of my biggest regrets to this day. I didn't take the opportunity that I had available to me, because I felt like I would be missing something out in the streets. Fortunately I got with the company I work for now right out of high school, and I've worked my way up, so I make pretty good money.

"I just turned thirty-eight, and I'm looking to find the right person to settle down and grow old with. I've been married before, so I know what it's like and I know what it's like to be single, and I think marriage is a good thing. My parents have been successful at it, and I think I can be too if I can find the right woman."

XAVIER
24, SINGLE, FULL-TIME STUDENT AND ENTREPRENEUR

Oh Lord, here comes Xavier. He's late as hell for the interview and taking his sweet time getting off and parking that expensive motorcycle. It looks just like one of those bikes they call a crotch rocket in the movie *Biker Boyz*.

He finally strolls in, jeans hanging low on his narrow butt, and gives us each a hug and kiss on the cheek. When I look at him, smile, and say, "Boy, every time I see you, it seems like you've grown another two inches. You're just as handsome as you can be, you know that?" he grins and replies, "Yes, ma'am," showing all his big, white teeth. Looks almost like Tiger Woods, except he's taller and skinnier, and his teeth are not quite as big as Tiger's.

Did you notice that he said, "Yes, ma'am"? Well, we could have been offended, but Xavier was born and raised in Baton Rouge, and he, like many of the other young men he hangs with, was raised the southern way. That means he was raised to respect his elders, even though we don't consider ourselves elders. He still says "Yes, ma'am" to ladies and "Yes, sir" to men, because he was taught to do so.

Xavier is twenty-four years old and lives at home because he partied a bit too much when he went away to school in Houston, so he didn't graduate when he should have. Now he's made up his mind to stop playing around and to finish school, so he's attending LSU full-time, majoring in business management, and running his own car wash and detail shop that he started a year ago with money he saved while he was working full-time and not going to school.

Q's Qwik Wash and Detail Shop, appropriately named after Xavier's best friend and our *young* cousin Q, because that's where he got the idea from, appears to be a lucrative little business. He's open all day Thursday, Friday, and Saturday, but on Sunday he's open only from two until seven p.m., because, he says:

"You know black folks got to have time to go to church and then go eat before they do anything else, and I don't want them telling me how many stripes the Lord's gonna beat me with for not being in church myself. I used to open the shop every other Sunday at noon, but my grandmother got all upset and said the devil was gonna come driving up here one Sunday to get his car washed if I wasn't careful, and even though I didn't believe her, the thought of that scared me a little bit. You know how superstitious people in Louisiana are. Gram says the only people who would get their cars washed on a Sunday morning are heathens anyway, and that I already had two of those working for me, so that's enough."

Q's is a cozy little place with mismatched sofas and chairs scattered in front of a large TV so the customers can catch a basketball or football game while they're waiting. There's even a pool table and dartboard, and in a corner Xavier has a vending machine full of snacks and one of those old-time Coke machines where you have to open the door and pull your bottle out after you've inserted the proper amount of change.

The office has one of those glass windows where Xavier can see out but people in the front room can't see in, so he's able to keep an eye on things while he's doing homework, making phone calls, and handling other business. The office is just large enough to accommodate a love seat and a small desk, and this is where we decided to do the interview since it was private and quiet, but the building is old, so the heat wasn't working like it should. Xavier had borrowed space heaters from just about everybody he knew, but it was still cool, so we sat there bundled up in our sweaters and decided to jump right in.

"My childhood was all right, but my parents didn't get along too well. They argued all the time, and as a result I learned to talk really loud in order to be heard, and I believe that's the reason I'm so aggressive sometimes. Before they got divorced, we did a lot of family things together and went on some great family vacations, so I try to remember those times because those were the nice times. I was a pretty quiet kid for the most part, did okay in school and made friends easily, but once I got through high school and college, it was like I just blossomed. I left home and went to school for my freshman and sophomore year, but I partied so hard that I couldn't maintain my grades, so my mom made me move back home. At first I was pissed, but it's cool now because I've settled down and decided to go ahead and finish because I don't want to be in school all my life.

I want to be a successful man, which for me means happiness and having the ability to be free to do whatever I want to do with my life. That's why I want to eventually get into real estate because then I could be my own boss. I could set my own schedule and come and go when I want to, and I wouldn't have to be loyal to one particular company for so many years just to get a retirement. Working for the same company for thirty years is nice, but the way businesses are right now, they'll get rid of a person before they have to pay their retirement, and I don't want to end up in a situation like that. So, now that I've decided what I want to do, everything's cool; I'm a young, strong black man, I've got my head on straight, and I'm on my way to the rest of my life and I'm excited about it."

MALIK
41, MARRIED, POSTAL WORKER

When we arrived at Bennigan's to have lunch with Malik, we were running late because we had gotten lost—but he had no mercy on us. "Oooh, y'all ought to be ashamed to invite somebody to lunch then show up late. The waitresses have been looking at me like I'm crazy because I've been sitting over here for the past forty-five minutes by myself drinking homemade lemonade. I was going to order an appetizer, but after I'd been waiting for fifteen minutes and y'all hadn't shown up, I decided I wasn't buying nothing, and you know damn well I'm expecting y'all to buy me a drink for keeping me waiting so long."

We each gave Malik a big hug and told him how sorry we were, and even tried to explain that the reason we were late was because we had taken the wrong exit, but he wasn't even trying to hear no explanations. "So do y'all have everything? Do y'all need batteries? Need me to go to the drugstore across the street and get some tapes? Hell, did y'all even bring your recorders? I thought you would have at least called me or something. I got my cell phone right here," Malik said, holding up the phone for us to see. "Why didn't y'all call a—? Oh, damn, my bad." Malik squinted at the phone. "I see that you called six times but I had it on silent. Sorry."

"Uh-huh, you ought to be sorry," I said. "Just running your mouth and not even giving a lady a chance to talk. Now that your lips aren't moving, can I explain what happened? We got lost because the exit *you* told us to take was the wrong one. We passed this place thirty minutes ago and kept right on going, and now I'm about to starve to death." Before I could go any further, Malik looked me up and down, eyebrows raised, then stopped and stared pointedly at my hips.

"What you trying to say?" I challenged him. "Are you trying to insinuate that I'm a long way from starving just because I'm a little thick in the hips?"

Malik laughed and clicked his tongue against his teeth. "Woman, please, I know you pretty good and I know you ain't going to starve, because you'd hurt somebody first. So what's up, how y'all been living? But wait—" Malik held up a hand and beckoned for the waitress. "—before you answer, can we *please* order lunch because my ass is starving too. I'm going to order the country chicken salad with extra chicken and depending on how I'm feeling after that, I might just order dessert too."

Malik will tell you what's on his mind in a heartbeat. He's from Chicago and is flirty, friendly, and outspoken. He's short and stocky but not fat and has nice, smooth light brown skin and dark eyes. He's bald by choice and has a nice beard that he says makes him look young and sexy, to which I jokingly reply, "Okay, Malik, whatever you say."

He and his wife of fifteen years have a thirteen-year-old son, a ten-year-old daughter, and an eleven-year-old niece they're raising because her mom died and her dad, Malik's brother, is in prison. He's very much involved with the kids; therefore, he's a little rushed today because he has only two hours before he has to pick the girls up from school. We placed our orders and then listened intently as he started to talk about his life.

"Okay, you already know that I was born and raised in the Windy City. I had a pretty rough life because my father was an abusive, alcoholic asshole. We never referred to him as our father; we always called him our mother's husband because that's the only role he played in our lives. He moved us around a lot, most of the time back to his mother's house because whenever he did work, he'd find a way to blow all the money, and when he blew the money, he couldn't pay the bills or he'd just decide he didn't want to pay the bills, so we'd get evicted from a place every six months. He spent no quality time with us whatsoever and taught me nothing about being a man.

"I can remember getting several beatings when my mother's husband was drunk, and to this day I can't tell you why he beat me, but I finally ran away from home when I was sixteen because it was either that or somebody was gonna get hurt. I got tired of him hitting me for no reason, and I was trying to handle it the best I could. Then one day he came home sloppy drunk and jumped on my mom, and I couldn't take it anymore. I'm the youngest boy out of seven kids, so my three older brothers had already left home, and I felt like I had to defend my mom. When I tried to get him off her and she told me to mind my own business, something in me snapped, and I knew it was time to go.

"To this day she swears he never, ever hit her, but when I ask her if she remembers the day I left home, she can tell me exactly what the weather was like, what I was wearing, and which direction I headed. Denial is a bitch, and even though we were told never to discuss what went on in our house, I know that shit happened for real, and so do my sisters and brothers. I moved in with my aunt after I left home and finally, to some degree, had a normal life. I graduated from high school and went to college on a baseball scholarship, and I've been on my own ever since."

NEAL
55, DIVORCED, HIGH SCHOOL COUNSELOR

Neal was well prepared when we arrived at his home, typical for a man who was once in the military and is a stickler for things being done "on time and in order." He can easily be described as tall, dark, and handsome since he stands six-four, has dark brown skin, sports a slightly gray goatee, and has the cutest dimples in both cheeks. Although soft spoken, Neal is very direct when he speaks. It's almost like he thinks through everything he's going to say before he allows the words to pass his lips.

He was wearing navy blue Dockers, a light blue polo shirt, and navy leather Cole Haan house shoes, all in good taste, which was also reflected in his furniture, that appeared to be brand-spanking-new and gorgeous. We only went through the foyer into the dining room, where he'd prepared lunch for us, and that space was so beautifully decorated that I wanted to ask to see the rest of the house, but once I smelled what he'd cooked, I changed my mind.

He'd prepared a simple meal, which included a green salad with homemade dressing, crawfish étoufée with white rice, and sweet potato pecan pie. "Just a little something I threw together," he said, but of course we didn't care if he'd thrown it together or spent four hours cooking it. In case you haven't noticed it by now, we're always ready for a good meal, and today was no exception. When he finally announced that everything was ready, we almost got into a footrace to see who could make it to the crawfish étoufée first, but before we could take our first bite, he bowed his head to bless the food. "As soon as I say grace, you all can eat and we can talk at the same time," he said.

So we bowed our heads without saying a word so he could get his grace said and we could get our eat on.

Neal started off by telling us a little about himself and his life. He was born in Brooklyn, New York, but was raised on his grandparents' farm in Tallahassee, Florida. He said his father made the decision to move the family down South when he was about three because he could never find steady work up North. Fortunately, his grandparents owned fifty acres of land and a large house, so by moving back home, not only did his father ensure they had a roof over their heads and plenty of food to eat, he also had steady work on his father's farm.

The house he's living in now is the house he shared with his wife and children before the divorce, but he doesn't want to sell it, because he always told his children they could come home when they couldn't go anywhere else. His ex fought him tooth and nail, but when it was all said and done, she got all their other property free and clear and most of their savings too, but he got the house and custody of the kids, which was fine with him because he didn't feel like his wife would do a good job raising them. He felt she was weak and easily persuaded, and he wanted to be sure that his kids were raised in a loving but structured environment where they couldn't just do what they wanted to do, especially his youngest son, who he says is strong willed just like him.

"My parents made me the person that I am. They were highly religious individuals, and they were very strict and guarded, but the things they taught us as we were growing up made us very productive. There were seven children in my family—three boys and four girls—and I'm the third child. We were taught to have faith and trust in God, and to respect our elders as well as ourselves.

"I grew up in the Deep South, where you got baptized in an outdoor pond. It was a beautiful ceremony; the deaconesses of the church would be dressed in their white uniforms and white starched hats. The deacons wore dark suits and ties, and all of the candidates that were to be baptized would form a line. The girls went first, wearing long white robes with a sash tied around their waists and a white scarf around their heads, and the guys wore white shirts and dark pants.

"The pastor would have a deacon help him with the baptism because the pastor already had his hands full with having to pinch shut the nostrils of the person about to be baptized. Most of them couldn't swim a lick as it was, and it would've been a shame if someone would've messed around and drowned out there even though the water wasn't no more than three feet deep.

"After the baptism, we'd all have ice cream and cake, and I often wondered if some of those kids were being baptized and coming to Christ just so they could get that homemade ice cream and cake.

"My parents stressed getting an education, and that was the one thing that guided me throughout my life. We were told to stay in school and make good grades. You couldn't come up with any excuses like, 'Mama, the teacher doesn't pay attention to me, the other students are bad, I went to school hungry and couldn't learn, I didn't have time to study.' None of that worked. My mama's philosophy was, 'If it's being taught in that classroom and you're in that classroom, then you should be learning. You have no excuse for not learning.'"

PIERRE
30-SOMETHING, DIVORCED, PERSONAL TRAINER

Pierre had chosen a small intimate Italian restaurant as our meeting place, and since it was early afternoon the place wasn't extremely crowded. It was slightly misting outside, and the heat inside had caused the windows to fog a bit, offering a touch of coziness to our surroundings. We had arrived early for a change, so we sat down and ordered drinks and appetizers and gossiped about this and that as we awaited his arrival. At our request, the hostess had seated us at a booth in one corner of the restaurant, a bit removed from the other patrons, which would allow for some privacy.

From where we sat, we could see him when he parked his blue Jeep Cherokee and walked inside. He was wearing a gray wool jacket that zipped up the front, because it was kind of cool out, blue jeans, and brown Timberland boots. He's about six feet tall and high yellow, has beautiful, pink, full, kissable lips, pretty white teeth, and light brown eyes. As if that weren't enough, Pierre is very, very intelligent and well spoken and has a deep, sexy voice. His is the kind of voice you can listen to for hours on end and not digest a single word he says because you're too busy luxuriating in the rumble of it.

Pierre had initially appeared to be the strong, silent type when we'd met him a few months ago at his gym. He didn't say much at all during that first meeting, just offered a brief comment here and there and a fleeting smile. Now that our initial meeting was behind us and his comfort level had risen, he spoke more freely and we found out that the old saying, "Still water runs deep—and it's hell at the bottom," is true.

His hands were as nice, pretty, and manicured as the rest of him, yet they had the slight roughness that a man's hands should have. He took his cell phone from his pocket, turned it to VIBRATE, and placed it on the table in front of him. "I'm expecting a call from a friend of mine who's coming into town today. He's going to need directions once he gets here, so I don't want to miss his call, and I promise his will be the only call I'll take while we're talking." It was good that he had the forethought to turn it on VIBRATE—because he got so many calls, the poor phone danced all over the table the entire time we talked.

The waiter came around to take our orders, and Pierre asked for the calamari without looking at the menu, while we ordered pasta. He removed his jacket, revealing a fitted black shirt that only a man with a body like his could wear. The knit stretched across a muscular chest, broad shoulders, and flat stomach. Even if we hadn't already known that he was a personal trainer, it was obvious that he spent a great deal of time in somebody's gym.

Pierre took a sip of the Bellini he'd ordered and pretended not to see the hostess who had just found an excuse to walk past our table for the fourth time in five minutes.

"Women are always giving me things. I've never had to ask a woman for anything. If I spend time with a woman sexually and she gets to thinking that she's in love with me and wants to start giving me things like money, jewelry, clothes, or whatever, I don't feel bad about taking those things, because I feel like I've given her something of value as well."

Pierre laughed at our expressions. "Y'all looking at me like those women must be crazy or desperate or something. I don't know what it is—maybe ladies like you wouldn't do that—but it's been my experience that there is nothing a single woman, or married woman for that matter, won't do if she wants a man."

The waiter was back with our orders, and the food looked and smelled delicious. "I love coming to this restaurant," Pierre said. "It's one of my favorite spots. It's intimate, it's off the beaten path, and anything I've ever eaten here has been marvelous."

We consumed our meals over a bit of small talk, and after ordering a fresh round of Bellinis, we were ready to do the damn thing, I mean interview.

"I guess I had what some folks would call a normal childhood. My parents are still married, and we attended church regularly given that my father was a contract minister for the military. They were kind of old school: you had your chores you had to do, there was no talking back, what they said went, and all of that. I wasn't abused or anything, so I can't complain. I'm very thankful, and I think my parents did a wonderful job of raising us. Me and my sisters had a middle-class upbringing. I always lived in the suburbs and went to predominantly white schools where I was the only black kid in class, that kind of thing.

"There was no college fund set up for me, and I didn't get to wear the brand-name clothes. I had to wear my Chuck Taylors, jeans, and T-shirts, so I had a highly moral, very structured family life. Since my dad worked for the government, I'm not really from anywhere in particular, because we traveled all over. I've lived in New York, Atlanta, El Paso, Chicago, and lots of small military towns, which made me a more cultured person, but having a background like that makes it hard for me to settle down in one place. I got so used to moving all the time that even now, after living in a place for five years or so, I'm bored. Also, you don't keep the same friends when you move around a lot, so I don't have any childhood friends. I don't know what it's like to say 'I've known somebody since grade school.' But then I'll think, 'Why I want to know anybody that long anyway?' I know people from a distance, and that's cool with me."

COLLIER
50-SOMETHING, MARRIED, ELECTRICIAN

On a balmy evening in Baton Rouge, Louisiana, we talked with Collier while sitting on the tailgate of his customized, candy apple red, '55 Chevy pickup. We'd come down for a family reunion, so it was a perfect opportunity to interview him because usually it's impossible to get him to sit still for very long. He's always got somewhere to go or something to do, but because he's such a charming and witty man, we couldn't pass up the opportunity.

Collier is tall and thick, about six-three and 240 pounds, and he always wears a hat, starched jeans, a nice shirt, boots, and sunglasses. He's never without a cigar—either he's holding it between two fingers or it's sticking out the corner of his mouth, firmly clenched between his teeth while he talks. He smokes Swisher Sweets, and the scent is actually kind of nice and mellow if you like the smell of cigars. He usually looks serious and doesn't smile a lot, but when you talk to him or listen to him tell stories about his childhood, he'll have you in stitches and then he'll offer a brief smile because he was able to make you laugh.

When we first approached him and asked if we could talk to him, he looked at us like he wasn't quite sure. Then he took a sip of brandy, studied us again, and said, "Well, okay, you can ask me whatever you want 'cause I ain't got nothing to hide, but I ain't saying I'll tell you everything. You ever heard the old saying, 'Never let your left hand know what your right hand is doing?' Well, that's how I feel about telling some things, and my left and right hand are on the same body."

Collier had parked his truck across the street from the park where everyone else was gathered because he didn't want to take the chance of anyone parking too close and putting dents in the doors. He had a huge-ass cooler in the bed of the truck, full of ice, beer, and wine, just in case he ran across some of his friends and wanted to stop and talk for a while, so his truck was pretty much a bar on wheels because he even had a few folding chairs back there.

"I've got some wine back here, and even though it's got a screw-off top, it'll still give you a buzz. If you don't want that, I can make y'all a mean whiskey sour—what you say?" Collier asked, while taking out two plastic cups and filling them with ice. He mixed the drinks and handed them to us—and child, he wasn't lying. It was more whiskey than sour, but it was good. He pulled out a brown bag and poured himself some more brandy; then as the wind blew softly and the smell of rain hung in the trees, we sat on the tailgate. Collier unfolded one of his chairs, sat down, crossed his legs and said, "Let me tell y'all this little story first, okay?

"There were these two ladies who were girlfriends, right? One lived in the country and one lived in the city, but they were real good friends. The city girl was invited to a ball, so she called her country girlfriend up and said, 'Won't you come and go to the ball with me and meet some nice people?'

"But the country girl told her, 'No, I don't think I'm going. I never been to a ball before, and I might not know how to act or what to say.'

"So the city girl said, 'Look, girl, come go with me and say what I say and do what I do,' and she finally persuaded her to go.

"So there at the ball, a gentleman walked up to the city lady and asked her—he said, 'Excuse me, may I have this dance?'

"The city girl said, 'No, thank you. I'm concentrating on matrimony. I think I'd rather sit.'

"So he asked the country girl, 'Excuse me, may I have this dance?' and she say, 'No, thank you. I'm constipated on macaroni. I think I'd rather shit.'"

We fell out laughing, but he just smiled and cleared his throat and went right on talking.

"I'm from a big family, and I was the second to the youngest. My parents were very strict and very religious. In fact, my father was a preacher, and out of all six of us, I was probably the worst. I think I was the one who caught the most whippings, probably because of some of the things I used to do, like charging food on my father's account at the neighborhood store. See, I used to go to that store and get stuff for Daddy all the time. He'd send me, and I'd charge it.

"I know y'all probably heard the story before, but let me tell you how it really happened. I was mad because one of my sisters had asked me to wash dishes for her, and then wouldn't pay me, and on top of that I was hungry. When my daddy asked me to go to the store, I figured I would just have me a hootenanny. Man, I put on a raincoat and some boots, and it wasn't even raining. It was just cold, but I figured I would need that coat to store all the food I planned on getting.

"When I walked in the store, old Mr. Boudreaux looked up from his magazine and stared at me real funny and said, 'It ain't raining, Collie. What you doing with a raincoat on?'

"I say, 'You must ain't hear the weather. They say it's gonna rain a little later on.'

"My mama had plenty of food at home, and she had lunch meat, but I didn't want no lunch meat. I wanted me some pepper sausage, but back then you didn't tell your mama what you didn't want unless you wanted to get the taste slapped out your mouth, so I charged some honey buns, cheese, a whole loaf of bread, a big old cold drink, and about two dollars' worth of that pepper sausage, and it was sliced real thick, about like this."

Collier used his finger and thumb to measure a quarter inch of space. "After old Mr. Boudreaux sliced the sausage and got all the food rung up, I waddled out the store and went and ate until I almost knocked myself out. I weighed about sixty pounds, but I left that store weighing about eighty with my arms sticking out like this." Collier held his arms out horizontal to his body.

"I went to this little house right around the corner. It had a lot of bushes and stuff in front of it because didn't nobody stay there, and it was an old house. Child, I took everything out from inside that raincoat and laid it down on the front porch with my cold drink. Then I opened my bread, unwrapped my cheese and pepper sausage, and made me some sandwiches, but I couldn't eat more than two. I ate a few of those honey buns, and then I took all the leftovers and threw them under the house because I knew I couldn't take none of that food home.

"I skipped home, full, whistling and feeling good. You ever seen a little skinny boy with a big, tight stomach? Oooh boy, that was me. My stomach was 'bout to pop, but I didn't care. I was skipping because I just knew ain't nobody know nothing. I skipped up onto that front porch, and Daddy came outside and said, 'Collier, ain't I been good to you?'

"I said, 'Yes sir, you been good to me,' 'cause I didn't know where he was coming from.

"But then he said, 'Then what the devil you go round to Boudreaux's and charge—' and when he said *charge*, boy, I aimed to jump off that front porch, and he caught me while I was in the air and swung me back towards him, took my head, put it between his legs, and tore my butt up, and when he got through, my pants was smoking. He whipped me so until my mama finally had to come outside and say, 'Now that's enough, honey. You gonna hurt that boy.'

"That was the worst whipping I ever got, but it was worth it. See, back then the stuff Daddy would have me charge usually added up to about five dollars, but that day I charged about ten dollars' worth, so you know I had a lot. After Daddy whipped me, I looked down inside my boots, where I still had two honey buns stashed, but I was crying too hard to eat them.

"We had something we called a common in our neighborhood, and a common is really just a big old vacant lot. I went over to the common, hid between some trees, pulled them boots off, and threw those honey buns away. That one experience taught me something very important, and that's why I don't use charge cards. To this very day, I don't charge nothing.

"After I finished high school, I couldn't narrow down what it was I wanted to do, so I joined the Navy during the Vietnam War. Actually, the Army had drafted me, but I didn't want to go into the Army, because my brother had gone into the Navy. He told me, 'Man, if you go in the Navy, every port you go into has nothing but beautiful women. You can go to Hawaii and lay on the beach under the coconut trees and just let these beautiful women fan you all day long.'

"I was only nineteen years old, and of course that sounded good to me, so I went and joined the Navy, and at that time they had a four-year plan. I took a test and scored really high in electronics, so I ended up in the Operational Electronics Division, and I got shipped to San Diego and had a ball. I enjoyed the military experience because I got to see a lot of things I wouldn't have seen if I hadn't gone.

"When I finished serving my time in the Navy, I got out and because of the GI Bill, I was able to go back to school with every hope that I would graduate from college in a year, but my girlfriend got pregnant, so my plans changed. It was like seeing the flame of my life die out. I kept thinking about all the things I could have been and done had I not gotten her pregnant, and I was devastated. Back then, if you got a girl pregnant, the decent thing to do was marry her, so that's what I did. After all this happened, I realized that it don't matter how smart you are—you can have all the plans in the world, and something can always come along and change your life forever, and there's not a whole lot you can do about it. I kept telling myself, 'You should have kept your dick in your pants or put a raincoat on,' but it was too late for should have's.

"Even though things in my life didn't turn out exactly the way I wanted them to, I feel that I've been successful and the best is still to come, so I try to be positive about everything. I've had two major operations on my brain because I had seizures, and I haven't worked in almost a year, but other than my wife and my children, no one knows that because sometimes you have to keep things to yourself. Believe it or not, my bills are still getting paid even though my wife only works part-time.

"Look at this."

Collier pulled out his wallet and started counting the bills.

"One two, three, four, five, six, seven, eight, nine—that's nine one-hundred-dollar bills, and I'm not working. That's how I know that God is good. He gave me enough good sense to invest my money wisely, so that when hard times like this came, I could still take care of my family. So see, even in times like these when I'm down a little, I'm still not completely out of the game."

———

ANTONIO
47, DIVORCED, SPORTS BAR OWNER

We met Antonio in Reading Terminal in Philadelphia, Pennsylvania, and for those who have never been, it is truly a feast for the senses. You'll find freshly cut flowers, beautiful produce, seafood, all varieties of meats and desserts, and restaurants too numerous to mention. You can purchase cookbooks, jewelry, candles, freshly baked pastries, soft pretzels, and ice cream. You name it—this place had it. It was also interesting to see the Amish merchants—the men in their dark clothing, broad brimmed hats, long beards, and no mustaches—and the Amish women—free of jewelry, wearing long, modest, full-skirted dresses and aprons, with their hair pulled back in a bun and heads covered with white or black caps.

We were sitting at Pearl's Oyster Bar, trying to decide what to eat for lunch when Antonio sat down next to us and said, "Hello, ladies. I see you two trying to decide what to eat, so obviously you've never been here before. Where are you all from?"

We explained where we were from and told him that we were in town to do book signings at Robbins and Basic Black Books, as well as try to find a few guys to interview for our next book. He said he was free for the afternoon and would agree to an interview if we would let him buy lunch (which you know was no problem for us), and after we got down on the shrimp and oysters with extra tartar sauce that he recommended, we went back to our hotel lobby around the corner to get his story.

"I'm forty-seven years old, I'm half-Hispanic and half-black, and my mother's parents raised me until I was into my teenage years when I went to live with my mother. My grandparents put the *old* in old school; they were old, old, old school. My grandfather, by his very words and actions, defined the word *machismo*, which means a proud, Hispanic man with a lot of good characteristics like courage and heart and all the good things a man should have. That's the kind of man that raised me. He was always quoting things to me like, 'A real man—' Fill in the blank, 24-7. He was constantly teaching me things.

"I broke my nose playing baseball, and he popped it back into shape and held it in place with a Popsicle stick and two pieces of adhesive tape and said, 'Real men don't cry about getting hurt. Go out there and play baseball.' I broke my finger once, and he said, 'A real man don't cry about pain. Be tough.' Eventually I figured out that it was better to have too much guidance than no guidance at all, but as I got older, I was able to sort the good stuff out. Certain things like always being the one to pay when I took a woman out on a date—that's one of the things my grandfather taught me, that was part of machismo. He said it was a man's privilege to have a woman's company, so you always pay. 'It's a man's obligation to pay for a woman's company,' is how he'd say it, so I'm just used to paying for dates all the time. He also taught me to be honest, because he always said, 'Real men don't lie.'

"We lived in a tough neighborhood that was almost all black with only a few Hispanics. Then the few Hispanics that were there left and all that remained was the black people, my grandparents, and me. My grandmother gave me the tenderness I needed; she was the one who would save me from an ass-whipping. She'd tell my grandfather, 'Give that boy a break, give him a chance, he don't know, help him out.' I learned from her that everybody deserves a chance, everybody deserves this or that, and you have to have a little bit of tenderness mixed in with the toughness. I'd be like, 'God, he's so mean, Grandma,' and she'd say, 'Baby, people don't know what nobody's taught them, so your grandfather don't know, because nobody taught him not to be mean. He don't know.' She had a lot of empathy.

"A big turning point in my life was the summer of my eighth-grade year. I was always in trouble with the police for doing mischievous things. Shooting BB guns inside the city limits, lighting fireworks and pushing shopping carts down underpasses and hitting cars—this happened to be a sport of ours. One time my grandfather grounded me for the whole summer and made me read the encyclopedias from cover to cover, *and* do book reports. It's amazing how all of that reading changed my life.

"All of a sudden I became a great student, I knew everything; there was nothing they could tell me that I didn't know, *aardvark* to *zebra*, so I started doing well in school. Then I moved into a better neighborhood because my mother came and got me. I got to know her and then when I was eighteen she died. She basically worked herself to death.

"My father was an alcoholic when I was a young boy, but the lessons I learned from living with my mother taught me how to forgive and forget, and the reason I know how to shoot pool so well right now is because the rare times my father would come pick me up on Saturday, I'd shoot pool all day. There were many Saturdays that I would sit on the curb all day, till it got dark, and he never showed up. But when he did show up, he'd take me to the Tee Pee Tavern, give me a roll of quarters, and sit at the bar and drink while I played pool. I shot pool with the waitresses, and they'd bring me Cokes all day, from afternoon till it got dark.

"Now I take care of my father. He lives here in an apartment and I pay his rent and I take him to the store every weekend because he doesn't drive. Why hate him for what he did to me as a little boy? I let that go. I got him now, he needs me, and we're close. God changed my heart because I resented my mother at first—I actually hated her when I was a little boy because I always wondered, Why did she leave me? Then I realized it wasn't for me to know why she left me because I eventually found out that she was a wonderful woman. She took care of me and my sisters, so I didn't want to make that same mistake with my father and just throw him away because of what he did when I was younger. That's the mistake so many people make: they let what their parents did to them twenty years ago affect the rest of their lives."

EDWIN
54, DIVORCED, CONTRACTOR

Edwin stood on the front porch of his house puffing on a Cuban cigar in between sips of Grey Goose. He spread his arms wide open as we walked up the steps. "See, this is why I like living by myself: I can smoke and drink whenever I want to and I never get any complaints.

"I don't have to worry about a wife wanting to drive my car or truck." He motioned to a classic black Corvette and an ivory Cadillac Escalade. "It's not that I'm selfish, but that last wife of mine couldn't drive for shit. Every time I looked around, there was a new scratch or dent, but I couldn't keep that woman out of my car to save my life."

We followed him into the large, rambling, twenty-year-old house that he's renovated from the inside out over the past few years. He's replaced the roof, the light fixtures, the windows, and the plumbing, knocked out walls to enlarge some of the rooms and refinished the wood floors, which were highly polished and covered with expensive rugs. The house sits on a three-acre lot and is surrounded by pecan trees.

He placed his Grey Goose on the table and ran a hand through his curly, closely cropped hair that had a few strands of gray. "I'm fifty-four years old, and marriage is the last thing on my mind right now. I've already tried it four times. For now I'm just enjoying my space and living by myself. I'm finally learning how to be picky because now I know what I want in a woman."

He put out the cigar and stroked his thick black mustache. "Can I get you ladies something? If y'all want something to snack on, I got some tuna salad in the fridge." He patted his stomach. "I weigh about a hundred and eighty pounds, and the only way I'm able to maintain my weight is to be careful about eating the right kinds of food and besides that"—he winked—"I make a damn good tuna salad."

Edwin is fair skinned, but he's strictly a for-real brother. He has a dry sense of humor, is well read, cultured, and enjoys the finer things. I could be almost certain that the cigar he had just put out and the Grey Goose he was sipping were some of the best to be found, and his wardrobe is just as classy as he is. Whether the event is casual, social, or work related, he always has on the proper attire.

"I don't have a housekeeper," Edwin replied when asked who kept his house so spotless. "I clean my own house, I wash my own clothes, and I cook my own food. I learned how to cook when I was growing up, and I'm glad I did, seeing as how I can't seem to stay married."

The kitchen was well equipped and not just for show. A rotisserie and silver wok with a shiny red lid took up one portion of his kitchen counter, and in one corner he had a stack of cookbooks that included a *Southern Living 1988 Annual Recipes* book, a *Spoonbread and Strawberry Wine* soul food cookbook, and Mexican and Oriental food cookbooks. All four appeared to be well used, judging from the dog-eared pages.

After we settled in, Edwin began to reminisce.

———

"I grew up in a small country town and was raised by my mom and dad. I'm the middle child in a family of five with two sisters and two brothers, and my childhood was fun; I spent a lot of time playing with my brothers and what few neighbors we had in East Texas. Me and one of my brothers are exactly a year apart, so we grew up pretty close. My other brother is four years older than me, and of the three boys in my family, I am probably the most domestic because I would get in the kitchen and help my older sister out. Growing up in the country, it was always the girl's responsibility to take care of the cooking, the cleaning, and whatever but I'd get in and help a little bit wherever I could because I wanted to learn.

"I really didn't date until I was older because in small towns—you know how it is—everybody knows everybody, which means most of us were related. I spent a lot of time studying and playing basketball because I really wasn't interested in girls too much anyway, but I did attend all of the high school dances because my sister and her friends needed a dance partner. They used to dance my damn feet off, and that's probably why I don't dance now unless I've had a good bottle of liquor first.

"After high school, I went to college for two years and intended on majoring in electrical engineering, but instead of finishing my degree, I ended up getting married and got into a four-year apprenticeship program and subsequently got my journeyman's license. Then I got my master plumber's license and finally a contractor's license. Now, why I got married when I was so young, I don't know, but I do know that it was a mistake because it didn't last for very long, and I've been married three more times since then, so you know I got some stories to tell, and all of them ain't nice."

WARREN
50, MARRIED, CORRECTIONAL OFFICER

"Y'all just in time for some piping hot catfish." Warren spoke to us in a slow relaxed southern drawl as we rounded the corner of his house. He was taking the last bit of golden brown catfish out of a huge fryer. "I fry fish outside because I don't like grease popping all over the place and having the whole house smell like fish for days afterwards."

Warren is slender and about five-ten and dark skinned. He's a *real* black cowboy and wears the hat, the tight-fitting jeans, the huge belt buckle, the boots, the whole deal, and today was no different. We'd met him and a group of his friends and their wives at a club called Foxies one Saturday night. They're members of a swing-out club and get together the first Saturday of each month to drink and socialize and do this dance called the swing-out. Anybody is welcome to join them, and if you don't know how to swing out, somebody is always willing to teach you. The following Sunday, one of the members has a little get-together at his or her house, and it was Warren's turn, so he'd invited us over.

Warren wasn't a man to put on airs; he's comfortable with himself and with the life he leads. He's been married most of his life and is quick to say that if he had it to do over again, he'd choose the same woman—which is a pretty impressive statement, seeing as how his wife wasn't even within hearing distance of the compliment.

"I cook as a form of relaxation. Some folk like to bowl, some folk like to drink—well, I drink too," Warren said, sipping on a bottle of beer. "But you know what I mean. I do the majority of the cooking in my house, that La' Gay See fellow ain't got nothing on me," he said, mispronouncing the famous chef's name.

"See, the secret to my hush puppies is that I mix in a hint of sugar with the creamed corn, and I put in jalapeños but they're chopped up real fine. I also made the coleslaw but I use just enough dressing to coat the cabbage 'cause I don't want to drown it. Look at y'all, standing there looking all hungry. Come on, let's eat and then we can get to these questions y'all want to ask. There's nothing like talking about life when your belly is full."

Just as we finished eating, Warren began to talk about his past:

"I had a good time when I was a boy; we went to church on Sundays, choir rehearsals during the week, and on Friday night we had football games and parties—the usual stuff. There were four of us, three boys and one girl. I'm the baby of the family. I was raised by my mother and father right here in Louisiana.

"I wanted to play college football, but in my senior year of high school I broke my collarbone and couldn't play at all. I still went to Grambling for a semester, but then I quit school and went to work at the Angola State Prison, and I've been there ever since. When me and my wife got married, I was twenty and she was seventeen, and that was thirty years ago.

"We had some tough times, as young couples do, but we always managed to get by. I can remember when we were so broke that we ate spaghetti with tomato sauce and biscuits for dinner for a whole week— but shoot, we were so in love, it didn't even matter. As long as our bellies were full and we could make love, that's all we needed. It wasn't like it is now with some young folks who break up just because they wake up one morning and decide they don't want to be married anymore.

"We were young, but even at seventeen and twenty, we knew what a commitment was because we was raised that way. After she graduated from high school, she wanted to go to college and since I was the husband, it was my responsibility to put her through college, so I did that. She got her associate's degree, and then she wanted to be a paralegal, and

I supported her in that, and when she got pregnant I changed my work schedule so I could take care of the baby while she studied. So, I may not have a lot of money, and I may not drive a fancy car, but I feel like I've been successful because I've been a good husband and a good father.

"I'm a simple man and I live a simple life. I got me a piece of land with two horses on it, I go out there and ride them about once or twice a week to keep them in shape, and for the most part, I'm happy."

RUBEN
43, SINGLE, ACCOUNTANT AND MUSICIAN

When we pulled up, Ruben was just coming in from the golf course, with his tall, sexy Latino self. He slid his golf cart into one bay of the four-car garage alongside his Jag and the speedboat, which he confessed was his latest toy.

"You two are just in time—come on inside and let me freshen up." He motioned to his golfing clothes, which consisted of khaki shorts and a navy polo shirt.

He offered us something to drink and placed some sliced fruit and cheese on the black granite kitchen counter before slipping into his room to change. "Make yourselves at home," he called out over his shoulder. "I'm sure you can find whatever you need, and check out the new artwork in my living room. It's been a while since y'all have been over, and I've gotten some new pieces."

Ruben's house is custom built, about 4,500 square feet, with tiled flooring and modern furnishings. In the living room, he has a gleaming baby grand piano, which he plays well enough to make the ladies swoon—as if playing the saxophone and being successful and good looking aren't enough. We viewed his impressive art collection then returned to the family room and munched on purple grapes and strawberries as we gazed out of the massive floor-to-ceiling window at the well-manicured golf course, which was the main reason Ruben had chosen to move here.

He came back a few minutes later, wearing black linen slacks that tied at the waist, a matching shirt open to reveal taut abs that he'd earned from working out religiously, and black leather thong sandals on his feet. His shoulder-length, wavy brown hair was pulled back in its usual ponytail, and he looked a bit like Antonio Banderas, only his skin is more of a light honey-brown shade.

"My son has gone to the movies with some friends, so we got the whole house to ourselves." He sat down on the ottoman in front of us and stretched out his long legs. "It was nice seeing y'all at the club last night. Our band plays there about once a month, and I like the crowd because it's older and more sophisticated."

Ruben is an accountant by profession but plays saxophone with a local jazz band. He fiddled with the thick silver bracelet on his wrist then reached over for a slice of fresh pineapple, sank his teeth into it, and savored the flavor. "Mmmm, do I know how to pick good fruit or what? I sliced this fresh for y'all—much better than that stuff in the can." He flashed a smile. "So should I be nervous about the questions you going to ask me, or what?"

"I don't know, maybe we should be nervous about the responses you give."

"Y'all don't have nothing to be nervous about, I've kind of mellowed out in my mature years—just 'cause I date a lot of women doesn't mean I screw a lot of women. I'm not out there like that, but in my twenties— man, that was another story. I was like a kid in a candy store." He flashed another smile. "Are you guys ready, am I getting ahead of you?"

"Oh, our recorders are already running, Ruben," I laughed. "Since you're already talking, keep going. Just back up and start from your childhood, and we'll be right on target."

"Okay, cool. There are six boys in my family, and I'm the second to the oldest. My mom taught school for about five years, and when my dad got to a certain point in his career, she was able to stay at home and raise us. When we first moved into the house I grew up in, there were only three bedrooms, so that meant Mom and Dad had a room, and there were three boys in each of the other two rooms, which was a trip. Dad decided to add on to the house, and once mom stopped working, she actually became the building foreman on our house, and we worked on it every weekend until eventually each of us had our own room.

"My mom was strict, and she was running things because Dad traveled a lot with his job. We had a twelve o'clock curfew, and I don't care where you were or what you were doing, you better be home by then. I remember being seventeen and me and my friends had parked on one of those old country dirt roads and were out drinking, and it was after curfew. I saw lights coming down the road, and figured it was my friend Steve coming back with some more beer, but it was my mom. I had a cigarette in my mouth and I was holding this big-ass can of beer, and she let her window down, stuck her head out, and said, 'Get your ass home. Now.'

"When I got home, I said, 'Don't you ever do that to me in front of my friends,' and she let me have it. She slapped the hell out of me and said, 'Who do you think you're talking to?' And here I was almost six feet tall, and she was no more than five-one if that. Even to this day, when I go home to visit, I'm home by twelve. To me, it's a respect thing. They'll always be my parents, even though they're grandparents and great-grandparents now, so I give them that respect.

"During that time when I was out drinking with my friends, they were probably the wrong crowd for me to be hanging with anyway, but I had a chip on my shoulder because I wanted to date this girl and her parents said no because I was Latino. Then I got injured playing football and was told I could never play again, so I said, 'To hell with everything,' and forged my dad's signature and joined the Army.

"I turned my back on everything and just waited for the day I was scheduled to leave for boot camp. My mom told me that my dad wanted to contest the enlistment because I'd forged his signature, but she told him to let my ass go. I stayed in the Army for four years, but when I left home, I was a mess. Mom said that when the Army recruiter came to pick me up, I said good-bye to her, and once I got in the car I never looked back, and the thought of it still tears her up.

"I said, 'Mom, if I had looked back, I probably would've headed back. I had to move forward because my life was moving forward.' I left for the military a week after I got out of high school.

"Patriotism was ingrained in me as I was growing up. All of my great-grandma's sons were World War Two veterans, and she was always one to say, 'Serve your country.' So I decided that's what I wanted to do. But during the first week of boot camp, I was already asking myself, *What in the hell did you do?* Then I said, *All right, big boy—you thought you were a man, now you got to grow up and act like a man and tough it out*, and I turned out to be the number-one soldier in my training class. I scored high on all the tests, and after we went through three different platoon leaders who couldn't get the guys into shape, I decided to do it and I was put in charge of the whole platoon.

"When I got through all my security clearances and moved on to my new assignment, there were only sixty people there, so we did a lot of things together to pass the time. I started playing football again, and one of the colonels saw me. We'd been told when we took this assignment that the Army would work with us to get us a nice assignment afterwards because our current assignment was rough duty. While I was there, I saw people commit suicide, I saw people get hooked on heroin, I saw a lot of people go AWOL, which means 'absent without leave,' because they just couldn't handle it, but here I was, nineteen years old, and I'd made sergeant in two years. So when it was time for me to come back to the States, the colonel took care of me. He called one of his friends, a general, and said, 'You need this guy for your football team,' so I started coaching football, and I was the general's assistant.

"For eighteen months, I would just play tennis with the general in the morning, and I was defensive coach for his football team in the afternoons. At the end of my tour of duty, he asked why I'd quit playing ball, and I told him what had happened when I was in high school. He said, 'You've been cleared, you've seen the doctors here and you're fine, so you can still play. I'll write you a letter of recommendation to go anywhere you want to go.'

"By then I was twenty-one and I got out of the Army and went back home, and as soon as I got home, I ran into a guy who taught grad school in Arizona who had gone to high school with my parents. He asked me what my plans were, and I told him that I had a letter of recommendation from the general, so he made a phone call, and I got a meeting with the coach at Arizona State. He gave me a chance because he was a veteran, and that's how I got back into playing football. A week after I was there, they gave me a scholarship because I just got after it—I wanted it.

"I made the best of the military and used the experience to grow because I always felt like I owed my parents something back, and even though my mom wasn't happy about what I did, I can still say that the best relationship I've had with any woman is the relationship I have with my mom. She has been unselfish, loving, and nurturing yet still was able to make a clear distinction between what a mother's role was and what a son's role was, and even though she sometimes acted like a friend, at the end of the day, she'd remind you, 'I am not your friend. I am your mother.'"

LANDON
26, DIVORCED, MARINES RECRUITER

Landon swaggered into the restaurant like he owned it, bald head just a-glistening as he tucked the keys of his new Mercedes into the pocket of his baggy jeans. He wore a maroon mock turtle neck that set off his golden brown skin to perfection. Every female eye in the place tracked his glide, some covertly and some blatantly as he made his way to the table. One woman even put her menu down and licked her lips like she'd just decided what she was going to have for dessert, and her date was looking upside her head like she had just lost her mind. It just didn't make no damn sense for a brother to be as sexy as Landon.

He held a phone close to his ear and was speaking in Spanish in a low tone of voice. From the inflection, it sounded like he was telling someone where to get off—and none too gently.

"*Adios.*" He ended the conversation abruptly and placed the phone on the table before greeting us. "I apologize for my tone. I do my best to watch my temper, but some people know just the right button to push that will piss a brother off." Landon's English has a Spanish flavor to it. "I wish I'd inherited my mom's temper instead of her looks, but naw, I got a bad-ass Cuban temper just like my old man and my uncles."

Landon is the living, breathing description of the term *pretty boy*. He has full, pouty, bee-stung lips that a woman can spend hours kissing and nibbling. He has caramel-colored skin, soulful brown eyes, long eye-lashes, and ferocious black eyebrows that make him look like he's scowl-ing even when he's not. His only facial hair is a finely trimmed mustache.

"The woman I was just talking to, we broke up over a year ago, and she's still calling me and trying to hook up with me again, but I don't believe in going back. For me, once a relationship is over, it's over. Some women just don't get the message, and a lot of them are too damn easy. I can be driving my beat-up old truck, and they'll do any-thing they can to get my attention—and don't let them see me pull up in the Mercedes, they're really forward then."

His phone rang, and he scowled and placed it on MUTE—good thing too or we never would have gotten this interview done.

"Women have never been a challenge for me. I can be somewhere with my lady and get up and go to the bar to get a drink or go to the bathroom to take a piss, and I can guarantee you that three or four women will slip me their phone numbers.

"I won't lie—I'll be the first to say that I'm lustful. Sex is like a drug to me, and it doesn't help my habit knowing I can get a fix any-time I want one. Even when I was in high school, girls would send me notes and cards all the time; I have boxes of notes from high school back at my parents' house—they'll be something funny to look back on and read when I get old. My mom told me to save them because the first time some irate father came up to her or my dad talking about how I'd chased his daughter or how I'd done something to his daughter, we'd have evidence to the contrary that I wasn't the one doing the chasing.

"Women like the way I look, so it's just something I've become accustomed to. I don't let all that attention give me the big head. I had nothing to do with my physical features; it's just the luck of the genetic pool. Most of the men in my family are good looking, most of my cousins and uncles are pretty boys, so it's no big deal.

"I've never been a dog. I never had to be, because women are always up in my face. I listen to a woman talk, and I take the time to be nice to her if she captures my interest. Women fall in love without any provocation on my part. Most of the time I'm not even trying to go there with them. It's simple to make a woman fall in love with you. It starts before you even have sex—all you got to do is get inside her mind and listen to her and really hear what she's saying. All you got to do is show her a little attention and be yourself, and you're in there.

"I'm an only child, I grew up in a two-parent home, and my parents are still together. Even though I didn't feel that I could go to them for emotional support, whenever it came to getting material things, anything I wanted I got. I still do, surely you didn't think I was able to afford that Mercedes outside on my salary, did you? My parents are both professional. They're corporate lawyers and have been extremely successful in their careers, so they were always able to give me anything I asked for.

"The problem is, I've never been able to talk to them about things that really mattered, not even to this day. When you go that long without being able to talk, it's difficult to make a change. My dad isn't a man who's open for any type of discussion. He's a 'you do what I say and nothing else' type of guy.

"The only interaction I ever remember having with my dad was when he was telling me to do something, but growing up a boy needs emotional support. He needs a father who will say, 'This is how things should be' or 'I've been through this' or 'What's going on with your grades?' But it was never like that between the two of us. The only time he had anything to say to me was when he was getting on my ass about something I'd done.

"My parents always pushed me to do well, but a lot of times I didn't listen, because I never felt like they were there for me emotionally. I wasn't being rebellious, but in my mind it was like, *How can I take advice from people who don't understand the things I'm going through? I couldn't.* When they tried to give me advice, I brushed it off and said to myself, *They don't even know me—who are they to give me advice?* Yes, I realize that they brought me into this world, but where were they when I needed guidance on specific issues that concerned me?

"I learned to listen to advice from friends, compare their advice to what I thought I should do, make an educated guess, and stand by my decision. The way I've lived my life is that I don't want to do nothing I'll live to regret, but that doesn't mean I haven't made bad decisions.

"I was really into sports during my last few years of high school. That's where I got the team camaraderie and close friendships, things I was never able to get with my parents, because they were always too busy working and climbing that corporate ladder.

"My dad set the rules, and he would tell me, 'As soon as you turn eighteen, you got to get out of here.' He said, 'If you're going to stay in this house, you got to go to school or you got to have a job,' and at the time I wasn't sure that I was ready to go to school, even though I was a straight-A and -B student. School was easy for me. I was in honors classes my last three years of high school and graduated with a three-point-five grade point average. I had everything going for me, but by the time I graduated, I knew I wasn't ready to go to college, so I joined the military.

"I went into the Marines, and there was no privacy anywhere, and that was something I just wasn't used to. Open showers, open beds, open everything—you never did anything alone. Even going to the bathroom, you got five minutes to shit and pee. You got a line, and you got four guys standing there, watching you use the toilet, and they got to go bad, and they're like, 'Hurry up, you need to hurry up,' and all of this was a whole new experience for me. We had two gay guys in boot camp who would watch everybody shower. They were openly, flaming gay. You're dealing with all this, you're worried about your girl back home, wonder if your parents are all right, and then they got you doing four and five hundred push-ups a day and sit-ups and all this crazy shit. Man, I wasn't sure if I'd done the right thing.

"A few months after I got out of boot camp, I sat down and said to myself, *I got to start doing things that are good for me.* That's why I say I don't want to do nothing that I'll live to regret. It was a hard transition to leave home and go straight to the military because this was real—I was on my own, for real.

"I remember getting my first two checks out of boot camp. I got paid on the first, and by the second, I was broke. It only took two pay-checks for me to figure out I was doing something wrong. I went out clubbing, drinking, and doing whatever, and I wasn't worried about having money, because I knew I could eat in the chow hall and I lived in the dorm, but I realized that I couldn't go to the places I wanted and I couldn't meet the girls I wanted if I was broke, so after that first month I said to myself, *I can't keep doing this.* So I started saving my money, and I've been saving ever since."

2

DATING AND COMMITMENT

JOE

"Man, I've dated so many women, I don't even know where to start. Some were good to me, some were crazy, some were whorish—I've dated them all. Let me tell y'all about this girl I used to date named Donniece, and you got to know the shit was crazy already if she had a name like that, don't you? Donniece was a trifling-ass woman, but she was fine as hell and had some good pussy. She was so crazy about me that she was always trying to figure out a way to get with me. She'd buy me stuff, get me hookups, anything she could do to get next to me, she did it.

"One time she got a hookup on some meat, probably from some crackhead looking to make a quick dollar for his next fix, so she turned me on to it. She said she'd been getting meat from this guy for a while and supposedly he could get you anything you wanted—jumbo shrimp, steaks, baby back ribs, filet mignon, whatever. I told her to get me some jumbo shrimp and baby back ribs, and she was all excited because she figured I'd probably spend the weekend with her when I came to pick the stuff up.

"When she called me to come pick up the meat, she told me to meet her in a restaurant parking lot, and I was trying to figure out what was going on because she'd made me think the dude brought the meat to her house. I should have said forget it right then, but my mouth was set for those shrimp, so I agreed to meet her. I get to the restaurant and park, and here she comes about five minutes later, flying in that dirty-ass car she drives. I hate to see a woman driving a dirty car, because to me that says something about her, especially if her car is *always* dirty. Anyway, she pulls up next to me and says, 'Okay he just called me and told me he'll have the meat in a few minutes and then he'll be on his way,' and I'm like, 'What? What do you mean he'll have it in a few minutes? Ain't he the damn meat man? Why doesn't he have it with him, and where is he getting it from in a few minutes? This shit don't sound right, what's up?' She says to me, 'See, you worrying about the wrong thing. I got this—don't worry about it.'

"Then her cell phone rang, and her eyes got all big, and she said, 'Stay right here, Joe. I'll be right back with your stuff,' like the meat man was an undercover narcotics agent or something. So I'm sitting in the parking lot looking crazy, and she finally comes back with this wrinkled-up bag full of meat, but I didn't say anything. Donniece was smiling and shit, like she'd really done something. She parked and got in my car and handed me this wrinkled-ass bag and said, 'Go ahead, look inside.'

"I opened the bag, and inside was about five pounds of beautiful jumbo shrimp and four slabs of baby back ribs still in their original wrapper, and I started to smile myself.

" 'See, what did I tell you?' She grinned. 'Them some nice shrimp, ain't they. Now that's the hookup! All that meat for thirty dollars. Sheeiiitt, you can't tell me I ain't got the hookup.'

"I went over to her place for a few hours and handled my business, but I didn't feel like spending the night, so I had to stand up in the coochie and get her off real good so she wouldn't trip when I got ready to leave. I left at around one Saturday morning after taking my bagful of meat out of her refrigerator. When I got home, I put it in my fridge, then took a shower and went to bed thinking about who I was going to cook those shrimp and ribs for on Sunday evening.

"When Sunday came, me and my date were in the kitchen getting ready to prepare the meat for the grill, and she cut the package open on those shrimp, and the smell almost ran both of us up out of there. You know spoiled seafood smells horrible. I was like, *Damn!* The 'hookup' done sold me some bad meat. You can't be calling your hookup a *hookup* if the shit ain't straight. I was so pissed off, I didn't know what to do. I didn't care if all I'd paid for it was thirty dollars, the shit was rank. I had to change my plans and take old girl out to dinner because my kitchen smelled so bad and homegirl was hungry.

"The next day I called Donniece up and let her have it. I told her, 'God damn, Donniece, if you gonna get a hookup, at least make sure the shit is good. I had to run to the store and buy some meat because those damn shrimp were spoiled. Next time you tell me you got a deal for me, please make sure it ain't been sitting out for two days, will you? Better yet, just don't even hook me up, because you ain't never got your shit together.'

"I've dated a lot of women like that, and I've never been married, because I don't think I could be a faithful husband since I've always been such a whore. Truth be told, I used to be a lustful motherfucker. There wasn't nothing I wouldn't do with a woman if she wanted it, but I'm not nearly as bad as I used to be. Sure, a few of the women I've dated were everything a man could ask for in a wife, but I'd done so much dirty shit myself that I got to a place where I didn't trust anyone with my heart, so I figured staying single would be easier.

"A little while back I dated a chick named Maxine, and every time I hear that song "On the Down Low" by Brian McKnight, I think of her. She was a beautiful Creole girl with hair down to her butt, and she was so in love with me, she couldn't see straight. She actually moved to another state when we broke up because she said the thought of me being with anyone besides her just took her breath away.

"She used to cook for me, wash my clothes, send flowers for no particular reason, and come to my job and leave notes on my car. If I mentioned that I wanted something, she went out and got it for me.

She was a R.N. Supervisor, made about ninety-five thousand a year, had never been married, and didn't have any children, so money was no object for her.

"She took me to Jamaica, Alaska, and Cozumel, all in the hope of proving to me that there was nothing she wouldn't do if I'd just marry her, but I wasn't ready. It got to the point where there was no challenge with Maxine, because she was almost too good. She became too predictable, and it seemed like she was trying to buy me, and I wasn't comfortable with that. I started to feel like I was obligated to marry her because of all the good things she did for me.

"We started to argue a lot, and she was always going on about how she was getting older and so was I, but that wasn't what caused me to end it. What did it was when she said that she was the best thing that ever happened to me and told me it would be the worst mistake of my life if I let her walk away, because nobody else was going to love me the way she did. She told me that the type of women I normally dated might be able to fuck better than she could because that's all they knew how to do, but they could never take me to the places she could or give me the things she could, because they didn't have no money or class.

"I asked her, 'What the fuck do you mean? Are you saying that because I'm from the hood and my family is from the hood and all the women I've ever dated are from the hood that you're better than us? Are you saying that people in the hood don't have dreams and goals for a better future? Let me tell you something, baby, just because you have a little money and a college degree, that don't make you no better than anybody else. You might have more *stuff*, but your funky attitude and the fact that you've forgotten where you came from is part of the reason you're still single.'

"Homegirl cried and cried and told me she didn't mean it that way, but I hung up the phone, and when she kept calling back all night, I didn't answer. She sent me a dozen roses twice that next week, but I was through. There wasn't no looking back for me. I finally talked to her one time after that. She caught me at my mom's house about six months later and told me she'd taken a job in Atlanta and was moving."

G.G.

"I've dated a lot of women, and I'm currently involved in an open relationship with a young lady who is just as sexually uninhibited as I am, which means that she is bisexual as well and she doesn't have a problem with me being involved with men. I have dated several men on the DL—five, to be exact. The last one I dated over a year ago was single, three were married, and one was married but separated, but I don't feel that I honor myself in those types of relationships, so I don't seek them out.

"I personally feel that DL men are misled and that someone needs to pray for them because they don't know who they are or what they want. Either that or they're just afraid to be honest and say they enjoy being intimate with both men and women. Unfortunately our culture doesn't allow for black men to open up that way, because the black community places masculinity and fatherhood on a pedestal, and homosexuality is seen as something that only weak, perverted white men partake in, so that leaves DL guys trapped or at least more trapped than white men who are still in the closet. Being in the closet can be temporary because someday those guys plan to come out, but for DL men, who basically don't see themselves as gay or bi, there's nothing to come out to. There's no next step for them.

"There have always been black men who have had secret sexual relationships with other men, but this DL thing, which is made up largely of black men who normally live straight lives, has been on the upswing for the last ten years. Most of them date or marry women and only get sexually involved with men they meet in anonymous places like nightclubs, parks, and of course now on the Internet. Some of these men form romantic relationships with one another, but they are very careful to keep those relationships hidden from their spouses or family. They don't identify themselves as gay or bisexual, because they see that as a weakness and they don't want to be labeled as weak and would much rather prefer to remain appreciated as black *straight* men, which equates to being fundamentally masculine.

"You know how it is—masculinity is an effective defense and has been one of the few things that the black man has been able to hold on to and is still proud of. That's why DL men don't want to be called gay; they don't want to be associated with those they see as 'faggots' or 'sissies,' because it's another sign that they've let down the black community. You've never heard a black person say, 'He's gay, but he's still a hell of a man when it comes to his responsibilities.' Instead what you'll hear is, 'It's a damn shame for a fine black man like that to go to waste. All of us good-looking, hardworking black women out here looking for a man, and not only do we have to compete with other women, now we got to compete with men too. Hell, we already got enough strikes against us, and now this.'

"Still, I strongly believe that we are where we are at a particular time in life for a greater purpose, so I try not to condemn these men, but they need to make a choice or at least be honest and give the ladies in their lives the opportunity to choose whether they even want to be involved. I think that's part of the reason I'm bisexual; I'm okay with commitment in general, but I have unresolved commitment issues with males and almost always end up in a relationship with a female after ending a relationship with a male partner because most men seem to have such a hard time being honest with women or with themselves, for that matter.

"My first DL encounter with the DJ in Los Angeles lasted for about six months. We'd met off campus at one of the local clubs when I was outside smoking a cigarette. He came out for a break wearing baggy jeans, a do-rag, and an extra-large jacket. He asked me if he could borrow my lighter and then asked me if I was enjoying the music, which somehow led to him asking me if I wanted to hook up after the club closed.

"When I asked if he was gay, he said, 'No, man. I have a lady just like I'm sure you do, but I like to get freaky, if you know what I mean.'

"When I told him that I didn't have a lady at the moment, he moved closer to me and whispered in my ear, 'Well, then, that's even better, 'cause you look like a dude who's into women, so you're just what I'm looking for.'

"See, he was looking for a man who wasn't obviously gay, because he didn't want his image tarnished in case some of his 'boys' saw us together. He put his business card in my pocket and told me that he was strictly tops, meaning that he liked to play the masculine role during sex. He told me that the next move was mine and to call him if I was interested.

"I called him the very next day, and we got together at around three a.m. after he finished up at the club, and for the next six months we had sex at least once a week. We'd get together at his place during the day when his girl was at work, or at my place when my roommate was away, or sometimes if he called and just had to see me, we'd meet in a park and have sex in his car. There was never any kissing involved, because DL men usually don't do that, and sometimes we used condoms, but most of the time we didn't, because that takes away from that wild, uninhibited freaky sex. But after six months, that 'strictly tops' shit got old, and he started acting like I was his little bitch on the side, which completely turned me off, so I walked.

"Two of the married guys I dated, both at different times, were a trip, and for the life of me I don't know how in the hell either of them ended up married in the first place, because they both acted more gay than any gay men I knew. One of these guys used to be a hairdresser before he got married, and when he was doing hair, everyone knew he was gay, but all of a sudden he decided that he was straight and wanted to get married and start a family. His wife even knew that he used to date men, but she married him anyway and I was still having sex with him four months after he'd gotten married.

"All I can say is that women who marry men who are obviously gay must either be blind or desperate—because these guys, once you got to know them, acted as gay as Boy George. I slept with both of these married men for about six months each and finally broke it off because they were becoming too clingy, like strictly gay men usually do. Then one of them wanted to kick my ass for breaking up with him, and here he was, married."

KEN

"I met Zonora when we both worked at Ralph & Kacoos, here in New Orleans. She was nineteen and working as a waitress while going to school part-time. I was working in the kitchen, trying to learn all of the ins and outs of the food service industry because I knew I wanted to open my own restaurant one day, and I knew the best way to learn about the industry was to get hands-on experience.

"I was twenty-four when we met, and I was a serious player. I had so many women, it wasn't even funny, and what got my attention with Zonora was the fact that she treated me like I wasn't all that. She'd speak to me when she came in to work, but she'd speak to everybody else too. She didn't flirt with me, she didn't hang around after closing time to talk with me, she didn't make an excuse to be up in my face—she just came to work, did her job, and went home, at least that's what everybody assumed because she was so private, nobody knew her business. We didn't even know if she had a boyfriend, and plenty of the customers and male waiters tried to go there with her, but she wasn't having it, and I respect a woman like that.

"The only reason I knew she was going to school was because she'd have a book with her all the time and whenever she got a break, she'd sit in a corner somewhere and study. If I tried to interrupt her with some flirtatious small talk, she'd just smile at me and roll her eyes as if to say, 'Negro please,' then go back to her book without saying a word. After a few months I was crazy about her, and she hadn't even given me the time of day.

"I finally asked her out, and she said no, which was another first for me, but then I really couldn't blame her, because she would see all of the women who came through that restaurant looking for me, and it was obvious that she didn't want no part of that. I even let it slip, on purpose, that I was pretty well off, just in case none of my coworkers had thought to tell her that I was only working because I wanted to learn the business before opening a place of my own, but all she said was, 'So that's why all those women are after you—they're gold diggers. I thought it was because of that pretty face of yours. Well, at least you won't have a shortage of customers once you get your own place,' and then she turned her attention back to her book.

"She was one of the prettiest, most self-confident women I'd ever met, and it was a challenge for me when she didn't fall for me like every other woman did. I actually had to chase a woman for a change, and that was another first. Here I was, twenty-four years old, and I'd never had to chase a woman in my life. So I set out to wear her down. I sweet-talked the girl in payroll into giving me Zonora's address and sent flowers to her house weekly, and I asked her if she would at least give me her phone number, seeing as she didn't have the time to talk to me at work, so she finally relented and gave me her number but told me not to be calling her mama's house after eleven because she still lived at home and she didn't want me calling and waking her mama up at all times of the day and night. I even offered to buy her a cell phone, but she refused my offer and told me that her phone at home was good enough and that she didn't like talking on the phone all that much anyway. Now that really impressed me because a lot of women I dated would've taken me up on that without a second thought.

"When she finally agreed to go out with me, we went to dinner for our first date, and she told me that I seemed like a real nice guy and everything, but she wasn't looking to be one of many. She told me that she liked a man who had goals in life and that she was impressed by the fact that even though I had money, I was still willing to work for a living. So over the next few months we got to know each other really well, I cut out the other women in my life, and Zonora and I got married a year after we started dating."

SIMEON

"Women get possessive way too quickly," Simeon said. "I've been dating this shorty just a couple of months." He pointed out the large eight-by-ten picture on the mantel above his fireplace.

"I didn't ask her for that picture, by the way. She brought it by, frame and all, but she ain't gonna be around much longer, 'cause she's too jealous of the time I spend with my family. She doesn't want to be bothered with my nieces and nephews, and my family is close. Her family don't even like each other, so she doesn't understand. I look at it like this: if she don't have time for my family, then she don't have time for me. She's already telling me she loves me and wants to know if I love her."

Simeon sucked his teeth.

"I didn't lie. I flat out told her no. Ain't no way I'm going to be in love with a sister I've known for all of two months, and here she is already showing me her bad side. That's why it's important to take time in a relationship. A woman can only keep up a facade for so long. It's just a matter of time before her true self comes out. Shorty wants to occupy all of my free time, and when I'm out of town on business, she calls my hotel room every thirty minutes, getting on my nerves. I don't have time for no insecure woman.

"The biggest factor that has influenced my life when it comes to relationships is a lack of honesty. As a matter a fact, I don't even think I've had what you would call a great relationship, because I've never been married."

Simeon paused a few seconds as he thought about it.

"Wait a minute. There was one in college, and her name was Crystal Baker. Even when Crystal and me broke up, the breakup wasn't bad. It was the first time I was away from home, and I didn't have to answer to anybody. That was my first real relationship—you know where you spend the night over at the woman's house, and she's cooking for you, doing your laundry, and all that? Wait, you know what?" Simeon stopped in midsentence. "There was another good one, Juanita James. Her nickname was Nita. Nita and Crystal were my best relationships.

"Crystal and I were in college together, but Nita, that relationship happened about six or seven years ago, and I just wasn't ready, but she was cool. I messed that up; I ain't going to lie. She was older and I just—" Simeon paused again as he gathered his thoughts. "—she just caught me at the wrong time. She had been married, had a child, been through a divorce, and she lived far away, and being far away was a big factor, but she was one black woman who had her shit together. She was a strong woman. Nita and Crystal.

"We never got into arguments or confrontations; we never let it go there. It's easy to meet nice women, but it's more convenient to sleep with a woman you don't know nothing about, because then you don't have to get to know her. You can't assume a person is nice just by saying hi to them. You got to really get to know a person first. Some people feel like, 'Oh she talks to her parents every day, so that makes her a nice person.' That doesn't automatically make her nice, and you don't even know for a fact that she talks to her parents every day, and if she does, she could be cussing them out, for all you know. In order to figure out if a woman is nice, you got to get to know her, and that takes time."

QUINCY

"I'd been dating this woman for about a month, and things seemed to be going pretty good until she felt the need to ask me, 'Okay, where is this relationship going? What do I mean to you?' We'd only gone out a couple of times even though we talked almost every day, but as far as I was concerned, it was way too soon for her to be asking me about where the relationship was going. What relationship? We'd only been dating for a month. If I truly care about a woman, she'll know it, and she won't have to ask me a question like that because I make it clear how I feel about her. This woman didn't even give me time to do that, and I was immediately turned off because she was acting like she was desperate, like if I didn't hurry up and tell her that this relationship was heading towards marriage, then she was wasting her time and she didn't have that much time to waste.

"Interracial dating never came up in my household while I was growing up, but I grew up around people of all cultures, so white women were never a mystery for me. Maybe I'm wrong in saying this, but I get the impression that some, not all, but some white women have this attitude that the world considers them beautiful just because they have long straight hair and white skin. They have this mentality that black men are crazy about them solely based on the fact that they are white, and that turns me off.

"I mainly prefer dating black women versus women of a different race because black women can relate to me. Black women think like I do. They've experienced some of the same things that I've experienced—things like discrimination. I can talk to a black woman about things I experienced while I was growing up, and she can relate to those things because she grew up the same way.

"Now I ain't going to deny the fact that black women can be a trip too. I had a date with a woman that my cousin set me up with. When she asked me for the second time where I worked, and at that time I was the lead security officer at an upscale nightclub, she got this stupid look on her face and said, 'Oh, so you're in *security*? I thought you were in securities, like in banking. I don't think I've ever dated anyone in security.'

"I think she was a little taken aback that my line of work didn't meet up to her expectations, and I thought to myself, *Ain't this some shit?* Here she was, a thirty-five-year-old woman with her biological clock ticking like a damn time bomb, and she was so concerned about my job that she couldn't even sit back and enjoy the rest of the evening.

"There are a lot of positives and negatives to dating. You meet a lady, and then you got to decide if you like her, and if you don't like her, you got to figure out how to get rid of her, so it's almost a chore. It can be exciting at the very beginning, but then all the shit starts coming out, and then you got to find a way to end it."

GREG

"The best part of my relationship with a woman seems to be at the beginning, when we are just discovering each other. I enjoy getting to know a woman: learning what she likes and dislikes, what makes her laugh, what makes her sad, what turns her on. That seems to be the most fun and interesting part of a relationship for me, and I think you should always keep that interest going.

"I had a relationship with a girl named Nika who I dated for about three years, and it was always interesting because she wasn't just a lover, she was a friend—a real good friend. Right now, we're still friends, even though the relationship didn't go in the direction that we wanted it to. I'm the type of man who enjoys being with someone who has a good sense of humor, and she had a very charming sense of humor. She was the type of person who could always pick you up if you were feeling down, and she was a great inspiration to me. I probably would have married her because she would have been a wonderful wife, but I messed up.

"I was still running the streets and chasing other women when I knew Nika was ready to get married. We'd talked about it many times, and even though she said she would wait for me, I couldn't tell her how long it would be before I was ready to make a commitment like that, and I didn't think it was fair to ask her to wait, so I had to let her go.

"I hate to say it, but I know I broke her heart and she didn't deserve that. It's been about five years since we broke up, and I can still remember the day it happened. Two months later, she got married, and she says that she got married because she wanted to hurt me. The marriage didn't work out, though, and we still talk because I always called her at work and we keep in touch that way. We'll always be friends, but I don't think we will ever be more than that because I'm involved with someone else now. She sort of has the same personality that Nika had, and she's a very spiritual person, which is what I need in my life at this point in time. I hope to marry her when the right time comes, but I can't say for sure when that will be, because I've got this great big ego, and I'm kinda set in my ways.

"My damn ego is what normally messes up my relationships because I just get so relaxed and full of myself sometimes that I feel like I don't need to give as much as I did to get that person in the beginning of the relationship. I just get laid back and say, 'Whatever,' and that's when the relationship seems to go downhill, so for the most part, I'd have to say most of the breakups I've had were my fault.

"I've dated white women and Hispanic women, and I've even taken them with me when I stopped by my parents' house. But I couldn't marry one, because I couldn't take her to my mother and say, 'Hey, this is going to be your daughter-in-law,' after the things she's had to struggle through as a black woman. I just couldn't do that to her. I don't tell a woman that while I'm dating her, but for me, there's no prospect for marriage if she's not black.

"As far as women of other races being different from black women, I don't think that's true. They have the same issues, and the guys who say a white woman is better than a black women and that he likes white women because he can do what he wants when he's dating one, that's just foolish. It's all the same, exactly the same.

"I don't have a problem with interracial dating, even with black women who date or marry white men. That's their choice, and I don't have to live with it. I don't know what that woman has been through, and I can't judge her just because I see her with a white man. As long as he's treating her right and fair, that's fine because I don't have to live under the roof with them, but me personally, no, I couldn't do that. We go through enough dealing with people who are prejudiced that we know about, and I wouldn't want to go to a restaurant with my white wife and some ignorant person is cooking or serving my food and I don't know what they're doing to it behind closed doors, just because they don't like seeing us together. So I don't need that unnecessary drama in my life.

"When I did go out with a woman who was white or Hispanic, it was very uncomfortable because you attract all this attention and you can hear people mumbling. Then you might get a group of white boys who are hanging out together, trying to impress each other, and when that happens, that N-word always comes up, and I have to retaliate. So I had to stop dating outside my race because I didn't want to go through all that. I was dating the ladies I dated because they were nice and they were attractive; it had nothing to do with the color of their skin. I don't feel a need to date a woman of another race in order to feel like I've achieved something. Any black man who feels that way is a fool and doesn't really know who he is as a man.

"Let me tell you about this relationship I had with a young lady that turned bad, and it really wasn't my fault. Tanji was a very giving person; anything I wanted, she would get it for me. But then she got too possessive and wanted me to drive all the way to her house every day when I got off, and she lived about forty-five minutes from where I work, if there's no traffic. I stand on my feet all day, so I didn't feel like driving to her house every day.

"Just because I couldn't or wouldn't see her every day, she started acting insecure, and that got on my nerves. When I would go over to her house to see her, I'd have to spend the night to keep from hearing her mouth, and then she started going through my things when I was asleep. If she found something that she thought shouldn't be there, she'd ask all kinds of questions, and I didn't feel like she had the right to do that.

"I'd spent the night at her house several times, and during this particular time, I carried a pager and drove a company car. I'm a heavy sleeper, so I didn't hear her when she got up one night and took my pager and called every number in there. She told any woman who answered the phone that I was her man and that we were dating. It didn't matter who the woman was, and as a matter of fact, most of them were clients, but she didn't know that. I don't have set office hours since I'm a manager, so when she would leave for work at six thirty a.m., she'd leave me there, and I would lock the door behind her. Well, one morning when I got up to go to work after she'd left, all four of my tires were flat, and I had no clue who did it.

"Well, after that happened, the phone calls started. Someone called my job and told them I was using the company car for personal business, that I was an alcoholic and smoked weed during work hours. I had to go through a bunch of shit with my employer after the phone calls kept coming, and then I lost my company car and my position as a manager and was demoted back to salesman because I couldn't prove I wasn't doing all these things.

"Then when I thought all that mess was over, someone called the apartment complex where I lived and told them that I was living under an assumed name and selling drugs out of my apartment. I had to go and prove to them that I was the person who was renting the unit and that I did still live there, and they had to verify my employment so I could prove that I was really employed and not sitting around all day selling drugs. As if that wasn't enough, I stopped spending the night at her place because after my tires got cut a few more times, I figured I shouldn't stay over there anymore. But when I started staying at my place again, my tires were still getting cut. Every other day I would get up, and three of my tires would be cut, and this went on for about another month.

"I finally stopped seeing her completely because the relationship became too strained and there was too much drama going on in my life. I started dating another lady, and we went on a trip to Cancún. "While we were there, her cell phone rang. When she answered, the woman on the other end said her name was Tanji and told her that I was her man and we were engaged and all this bullshit. I grabbed the phone from her, and Tanji was running off at the mouth so much that she didn't even realize I was on the other end. That's how I found out what she'd been doing.

"When she figured out I had taken the phone, she got so pissed off, she told me everything. She said she had a girlfriend who worked for the phone company who would pull up all my bills, so that's how she got the phone numbers of all my friends. Then she had another friend who worked for some credit bureau, and she pulled up my credit card information and found out what I was buying, where I was buying it from, and everything—this woman was crazy!

"After all this was over, my neighbor told me that he'd seen my girlfriend cutting my tires one night, but didn't want to get involved, so he didn't say anything. I'd set up a camcorder to try to find out who was cutting my tires, and I'd told her about it, so she knew what time I turned it on and off and everything. That's why I never caught her in the act. Of course, I confronted her about the tires but she denied it. I was so pissed off for being played like that, I didn't know what to do, but I just had to get her back so she could see how it felt. I have a friend who delivers bread to grocery stores, so he's out early in the morning. I had him pick me up in his work van, and we went by her place early one morning and cut her tires, and of course she called me and I denied knowing anything about it, just like she'd done. After that, I never heard from her again. I did see her about two years later at the mall, but she didn't see me 'cause I was hiding behind a clothes rack. It scared me to death to even cross her path.

"See, women like that, the ones who will give you anything you want even though they may be crazy, make it hard for men like me. I think the reason some of us are so afraid to commit is because there are so many distractions out here—you know, so much temptation. If I commit to one person—not that I can't commit, but if I make that commitment today and then walk out my house—the temptation is still there, and it's hard. It really is hard. Every day I get propositioned, and some of these women are hardworking, good-looking women. I know I have a nice lady now, and she's a very giving person. She would give me anything I want, and I know I probably couldn't find another woman like her. She's thirty-eight, has no kids, only been married once, and has a good job. It's almost like I hit the lottery, but I'm still tempted. It's a daily struggle for me, just like alcohol is for alcoholics.

"I've dated lots of married women, and the married women seemed to be more controlling than single women. One in particular was always accusing me of doing things and didn't want me to see anybody else, even though I'm single and she's married. She always wanted to know if I was seeing somebody else. If she was at home, she'd be calling me all the time, trying to control my house and her house. Most of the time when I was dating a married woman, she didn't know I was also seeing someone else, because it was just too much of a hassle when she found out.

"The last married woman I dated knew I was seeing someone else, and she had a problem with it. I couldn't go to the town she lived in, because people knew her and her husband, but she felt like if she came to where I lived, I should take her out in public in front of everybody. I tried to let her know that just like I was willing to be understanding of her situation, she needed to understand mine. I have a lady, and even though we're not married, people know we're dating, so I tried to tell her she had to respect that just like I respected her and her husband. She felt like I didn't have as much to lose as she did, but I felt I did because the lady I was seeing was a very good woman, and I didn't want to mess that up. So my take on that is that married women are too controlling. They feel like you should always be available to talk when they want to talk, but I have a life too, and if she doesn't understand that, I'm sorry.

"I don't really think there are any positive things about dating a married woman. You're not getting anything out of it except sex, because the relationship can't go anywhere. There are only certain places we can go, and even then we're looking over our shoulders, afraid to run into someone we know. Then, if she and her husband divorce, I wouldn't want her. As a matter of fact, if she's this controlling with me and she's married to someone else, I can't even imagine being her husband—I'm not going to go through that.

"Right now I'm ready to be married because I'm older and I'm tired of running around and there's too much out there sexually that's not safe. I've done all the running around, partying, and clubbing I want to do. Now that I've gotten older, it's time for me to settle down and raise my kids. I know that marriage won't stop the temptation, but I'm going to do my best to fight that. I'll just have to pray about it because I think that's the only way for me to stay away from it.

"Don't get me wrong—being single has its advantages too. If I have a hard day at work, I can come home, close my door, and leave the world on the outside, and I love being able to do that. I can't say I've ever been lonely, because I always have someone I can talk to, or who will drop by and see me. Now, I do have my moments where I just don't want to be bothered, and being single allows me to do that if I want to. But I never have to be lonely unless I really want to. I always try to keep somebody around so I don't have to be lonely."

DANTE

"Interracial dating was never an issue in my house; my parents never said anything about us dating outside our race. I always dated internationally anyway, so color never mattered to me. I believe in equal opportunity. I do believe there are differences between black women and women of other races. For one, I think black women are more aggressive, but that's not a bad thing. Black women speak their mind much more, but I don't have a problem with that.

"My wife is Asian, but I didn't choose an Asian woman over a black woman. God chose her for me. I married her because I loved her—it had nothing to do with her race. As a matter of fact, when you talk to my wife, you forget what race she is because she has such a big heart. When I brought her home to my mom, my mom said the same thing. You don't see an Asian girl when you talk to her, you just see a good person, if you allow yourself to see past her color.

"As far as commitment goes, most men are afraid of commitment because the average man is out to conquer. He's not out to find that one true love or anything like that; he's out to get another notch in his belt. Now, notice that I said *average* because *average* is ninety percent. There is that other percentage that will commit, but even some of them are scared to death because they feel like they got to give up too much. You can't be a whore if you're married. Well, you can, but it's harder. I could be a whore if I wanted to—any man probably could— but the challenge in being a mature man is being true to one woman."

XAVIER

"Guys don't define dating the same way women do; dating is just having a good time with a certain person, and it's not an intimate or committed relationship. Now as far as a committed relationship, if we're dating and in a relationship like that, I'm just as committed to her as a man is to his wife. We're just not living together. Then again, that can be kind of hard, because although you're committed to her, you're still single and there are things you will want to do that will cause problems.

"Nowadays, there's no difference between what men and women expect in relationships. Older women are different because they came up during a time when the standards were different, but these young women—shoot, their point of view is almost equal to a man's, so it's hard to trust them. They're out for themselves, and a lot of them don't want to be in a committed relationship, just like a lot of men don't. I'm not sure when they started being that way, but it's like that. Even though I'm young, I wasn't looking for a young lady who just wants to kick it; because I'm not into changing women every three months like a lot of my friends are. I really wasn't even looking for the girl I'm with now. She just ended up being someone I liked to spend time with, and she's cool, but her morals are totally different from what you find in most women her age. It's a quality that I haven't seen, and I think it's because of her religion.

"It's like young women are out there trying to be video hos, and they don't realize that they're not supposed to dress that way. I mean, come on, some of the stuff you see on these videos is ridiculous. What man in his right mind would take someone dressed that way home to meet his mama? I know I wouldn't. But they think the nastier they look, the shorter the skirt, the more titties they have showing, the more a man will like them, and they're right, men like them, but not when they're looking for a wife. Sure, it's cool to hang with a girl like that and have fun with her, but then by the time she's ready to stop having fun and stop moving from man to man, when she gets ready to settle down and come out of those streets, it's too late because she's been around, and she's made a lot of mistakes that can't be corrected.

"I don't want to marry a woman who's been around. The young lady I'm with has high standards, she has good morals, she wants something in life, so I feel like she's someone I could spend the rest of my life with. I'm not saying she's all business and doesn't like to hang out and have fun, but she won't compromise what she believes in, no matter what.

"It's not hard for me to be monogamous, even though I'm single. I don't put myself out there like that when I'm involved with someone sexually. I have a lot of women who flirt with me and make comments, but I treat them just like a woman would treat a man she's not interested in: I smile and laugh and say what I need to say without hurting their feelings, and keep on moving, because I'm involved with somebody right now, and I don't want to get involved with somebody else and hurt her. I'm in school and I'm busy, so any extra time I have, I'm either with my boys or I'm with her, and that doesn't leave much room to mess around with anybody else. Besides, having more than one woman is too much trouble; it's not worth the headache.

"Race really didn't come up when I was growing up, but my step-brother, who's older, is hooked on white women, and I do mean hooked. He's an Uncle Tom to his heart. As for me, I don't like white women. I've never been attracted to them, because I don't like their pale skin. I like women of color because they have that brown, soft skin, and that's beautiful to me. I've never even dated a white girl, and I'm not even attracted to high yellow girls, for that matter, but I did date one girl who was mixed. I'm not that dark myself, and if I married a high yellow woman, my kids would be too light, and I wouldn't want that.

"My girl is Panamanian, and even though her skin is dark, there are things about her that are different from the African-American girls I've dated, simply because of the way she was raised. I mean, things that went on in my neighborhood probably didn't go on in her neighborhood. She didn't have to deal with prejudice, because where she's from, there are more blacks in power and they run the country, so she has no clue about the struggle African Americans have gone through except what she's read about in books. Therefore, she's different in that way because she's naïve to certain things, and she doesn't understand why African Americans feel the way they do about certain things.

"Her parents aren't really fond of me, so we don't hang out around them too much. We hang with the younger people in her family, which usually isn't a problem for me until the holidays or something like that. I know they don't want me there, but I want to be there because I know that's what she wants, and I know that if we ever get married, she would want me and our children to feel comfortable around her family. She wouldn't want to have to take the kids to her parents' house and leave me at home, that would pose a dilemma for her and put her in an awkward situation. Hopefully if we do decide to get married, they'll accept me when they see how happy I make her, but that's down the road.

"Let me just say this as far as commitment goes: A man doesn't consider himself committed until he's married. If his tax form says he's single, then in his mind and heart he is, even if he's engaged. But speaking for myself, I'm not afraid of commitment. I just want to know when it's the right time. I'm afraid that I won't do it at the right time in my life, or that I may wait too long and then miss out."

NEAL

"What is dating? That's a good question. I know from a female perspective, dating usually means the beginning of the ultimate date, which is the wedding, but from a male perspective, it doesn't.

"You have to be truthful and up-front with your partner, no matter what the situation. I've always stated from the beginning, 'At this time, marriage is not in my plans, but I respect the institution of marriage, and one day I will probably return to that because I think it's a beautiful place to be.' I've never said I don't want to get married again, and I never will say that, and you will never hear me say negative things about my previous marriage or my ex-wife.

"I don't talk bad about her, because she is the mother of my children. I always say, 'Don't say things that hurt—say things that help,' and that applies to any person or situation, even an ex-spouse. If we can get to the point where we stop saying things that hurt and say things that help, can you imagine what type of world we'd be living in? The tongue is a very powerful tool. It can put you in the grave or it can put you on top of the world; it can get you fired from a job or help you get employed; it can bring about sickness; it can bring about joy, love, and peace—the tongue has even caused us to be at war. The power of life and death is in the tongue, so people need to be careful of what they say.

"Marriage is about two people, and until both individuals reach the point of wanting to be married, there should be no marriage. The pressure that females place on a relationship is unfair because I have the right to take my time in deciding if my wants agree with your wants.

Why get into something that's not going to work because you're push-ing in one direction and I'm pulling in another?

"The more you state that we need to be married, the further apart it pushes the relationship. A man is not going to be forced to do any-thing he doesn't want to do because of that macho nature. You may find a wimp who has no self-esteem at all, who will do exactly what you want him to do, but a real man won't let you force him into any-thing. There are a lot of sisters who would accept a brother saying, 'I love you,' even though he doesn't do anything for her, but *love* is an ac-tion word. If a man says he loves you, you don't have to push him to do things to prove it, marriage included.

"If I'm true to you, I'll do things with you and for you, but if you can't see from my actions that I'm true to you and you prefer the verbal side of the relationship over the action side, then we got a problem.

I didn't realize that there weren't many real quality guys out there until some of my lady friends asked me to introduce them to some of my male friends. I'd say, 'No problem, I have lots of guys I could in-troduce you to.' But then I would come home and really think about it and discover that there were very few of my male friends that I would be willing to introduce my female friends to because I knew how these guys were. I kept trying to think of one guy I would introduce one of my friends to, and I couldn't think of even one.

"It's really sad that the pool of eligible, quality men is so small, es-pecially when at one time we had many men who would have made good husbands for our black women. Some of those men have been convicted for crimes they didn't even commit, and others did commit the crime but the punishment was much too harsh to fit the crime. So often there are obstacles placed in the way of black men that make it really hard for them to be available, productive citizens in our country. I'm not saying that's always the case, because sometimes brothers just make bad decisions, but a lot of the time that's what's happening.

"In this day and time women need to be aggressive. Once they find a brother who is all of the above on their list, they need to be aggressive because the entire situation has flipped. A lady can't wait for a brother to come to her and ask her name and phone number anymore, because there aren't enough brothers out there. The thing about it is a lady needs to learn how to be positively aggressive. If a woman comes up to a man, with everything open, giving him all she has and leaving nothing to make him wonder and no reason to make him want to keep the relationship going, then she's going to end up being a one-night stand.

"It's almost like what you have to do when looking for a job. You have to know something about that job. So when you're looking for a relationship, you can be positively aggressive when talking to a brother, and you can ask certain questions to find out what he's about.

"From that point on, you two start talking more and dating or whatever, and if something happens, it happens. But you don't just come in and—*bam!*—give up the panties. That's being negatively aggressive, and you lose everything, including your chance at a relationship because he's probably thinking, 'How many other brothers has she jumped into bed with this quickly?' That's not to say that if you're positively aggressive you'll win all the time, but at least you will have your self-respect because of the way you went about it. At least he can't say you just gave it away without even really knowing him."

PIERRE

"About two years ago I went to Miami to see Gina, my ex-girlfriend, and we hadn't seen each other in a few years. I didn't know how it was going to be since it had been so long and we both were kind of nervous because we didn't know what to expect. We didn't know if the way we felt about each other had worn off or not, but I always say love never ends and it doesn't die. The people involved may change a little, which may change how they feel about each other, but they still love each other, although they may not be in love anymore. People change, but love doesn't change, so I thought maybe she had changed to the point where I wouldn't be so crazy about her.

"She never got married, and I think it's because once you've been in love, it makes you dysfunctional for other potential mates. You may find someone you really like, but you're always comparing that person to the person you loved, and it's like that for the rest of your life. You're gonna end up settling unless you can fall in love again with someone else.

"When I got to the airport, I didn't see her until I got to the baggage claim area, and it was like the feelings had never stopped. I'm a witness to the fact that chemistry is a motherfucker—I ain't lying. I got turned on right there at the airport, my dick got hard, my heart was beating a hundred miles a minute, and I was like, *I cannot believe this.* I wish we could get together, but we can't see eye-to-eye on some things, like where we'd want to live, for instance. I need to be close to my son, so I can be in his life, and for a while she resented him because of my ex-wife, and I couldn't deal with that. I won't deal with that.

"Even though she accepts my son now, I don't think we should force it. It's just going to have to happen. She told me a little while back that if I moved to Florida, she would fly me back twice a month so I could see my son, but I wouldn't agree to that because I don't like to depend on a woman for any type of financial support. I felt it was easy for her to say she would do that, but then it's another for her to actually do it.

"As far as dating, my definition of dating would be just hanging out, which means since I'm living with my girlfriend, that's not happening. This thing with her doesn't even include dating anymore, and that has kind of messed things up. *Dating* is such a general term nowadays, almost as general as friends are. You can go out with somebody one time and it's like, 'That's just a friend of mine' you know? And then you can go as far as having an intimate relationship with someone, and it can be called the same thing. A person you're dating is just somebody you go out with, and it doesn't have to be on a regular basis. It's like the beginning of a relationship, where you're kind of developing a friendship, and for me it's usually platonic, for the first couple of dates anyway.

"I don't like the part of dating where you have to get to know a person. It's like every time you start dating someone, you have to start all over again. You have to find out what kind of baggage they're bringing with them, and sometimes that just ruins the entire situation. That's one of the biggest problems I find in dating. You know, there's nothing wrong with a person having baggage, because your past experiences, relationships, marriages, dates, whatever, mold you and shape you into the person that you are. The bad thing about it is when you can't let that baggage go, or when you start taking those issues and applying them to the next person who's completely innocent, just because maybe one little conversation you have with them reminds you of your ex. When you place that dark cloud over the next man in your life and start taking things out on him because of something your ex did, that's bad, that's not fair. You go through that a lot when you're dating because initially they hide this baggage. They wait and keep it tucked in their back pocket. After you're in there and you think everything's cool, all this shit starts coming out, and you're like, 'Whoa, where is this coming from?'

"I had a situation with one friend of mine where we were playing in bed. I wanted some, but she didn't want to give it up, so I asked her to just give me a kiss. She wouldn't kiss me—well, she acted like she was going to kiss me, but she kept teasing me by getting real close to my lips and then laughing. So I held her face in my hands and pulled her lips to mine, but we kind of bumped lips, and her lip started to bleed a little, and she went off.

"She got really pissed and just flipped out, and was like, 'Okay, now I see. You don't like to hear the word no, so I guess that's how it would be if I was in a relationship with you, right? If I told you no, I guess you'd hit me in the mouth.'

"I apologized over and over again and asked her to please forgive me because I really didn't mean to hurt her. I don't really like nobody touching my face either, so I understood where she was coming from, but for her to go off like that, I knew there had to be more to it than that. I told her, 'I think you're overreacting a little bit, don't you? You know I didn't mean to do that—you know it was purely accidental. Don't trip like that.' Then she got mad because I said she was overreacting, and at that point I was through. I knew I'd never see her again after that."

ANTONIO

"I have a list of rules that I follow when dating, and one of my first rules is called Rotation." When asked to explain, Antonio replied, "Let me show you a diagram," and he took a paper napkin and started to write as he talked. "I love sports, baseball especially, so if you know a little bit about baseball, you know about the starting pitcher, right?" He wrote down the word *start* and underlined it. You're looking for one good one, but until you get one good one, you've got to beat the bushes every day, so you have to rotate.

"Once you get a good one, you drop the rotation." Under the word *start* he listed three names. "Here's your starting lineup. These are the main three or four girls that you like best. They're classy, you're not embarrassed to take them anywhere, they're attractive, they're smart, and you enjoy spending time with them.

"Now—" Antonio wrote down the word *inactive* and underlined it and listed two or three different names.

"—what you got is here is your inactive list. These women are on the way out. You've known these women for a while, you've probably slept with them, and they may cause you grief or they're trifling, but you keep them around because you can call them anytime.

"Like this girl Nikki. Nikki is a, 'Sho could use some help with that light bill' kind of girl. She's pay for play. You help her with the light bill, and you get to spend the night.

"Then there is this white girl, Lauren, who will do every kind of freaky sexual thing you want to do, except she failed to tell you that she had multiple partners. So after you've done all kinds of freaky shit and put it in every hole but her ear, you find out that she was also messing with some guitar player in a band, so she's on the inactive list. *Totally* inactive."

Antonio went back to writing.

"Then you have the up and coming. These are women that you just met, like Rose, the girl I met at the bar. She's star material, she's got some potential, she could be the number one, she could be the girl, and could move everybody off of this list.

"Most of these women started out as my friends because being friends with a woman is important. Get to know her and be her friend first, and that way you can break it off anytime because she hasn't really invested anything in you. I think you really get to know a person's character if you start out as friends, and if something blooms from that, then good, but what's the harm in just having a lot of friends? I have a lot of female friends because we always start off without any anticipation of it going any further than that.

"There is a saying that men just want to be friends until they get in, and that's true even for me, even when I know we're just friends I'm still thinking, *Okay, one night it might happen.* You like all of this woman's characteristics, you like everything about her, but you know if you cross that line, it's going to ruin that friendship. That other head starts thinking, *Boy, I sho would like to get some of that.* You hug and kiss at the end of a date, you cuddle, but you don't cross that line because if you do, things will change, so you just don't go there.

"Also, I've learned to listen. My grandfather would always say, 'You got two ears and one mouth, so you can always listen twice as much as you talk.' If you listen, a woman will tell you at the very beginning what her issues are. Then you can look out for those issues and decide whether you want to get involved or not.

"Like my grandmother said, 'The reason people don't know something is because nobody ever taught them.' People are the way they are because of their upbringing. It's their character. I have a friend who was very negative when we first started hanging out. We'd go out to dinner, and I'd ask her how her day had been, and she'd say, 'Oh God, it was so bad I'm thinking about slitting my wrists and killing myself. Why even get up tomorrow?'

"She would always say stuff like that and I'd be like, 'Girl, what's wrong with you? Don't you know that every day God gives us is a blessing? Don't you know that every day that you're dancing on the dirt and the dirt ain't dancing on you, that's a good day?'

"And she actually listened. She told me, 'I've learned a lot hanging out with you. I was never really around positive people before.' But she didn't know how to be positive, because nobody ever taught her.

"There was this one Hispanic girl I used to date by the name of Julie. Julie worried my ass to death. She looked to me as her savior, so I knew I was going to have to get out of that. We had sex too fast. It happened on the second date, and after that she got all clingy and would call me all day every day, like she didn't have any kind of sense. We couldn't have a normal conversation and talk about current events or anything, all she could talk about was, 'Baby did you like the way I did my tongue last night?'

"I'd be in my office and say, 'Hey, I'm in a meeting right now, and there are a lot of people here,' so I could get off the phone because sex was the only thing she could talk about. And once again, she didn't know any better, because nobody taught her any different."

Antonio pulled out his wallet and flipped to a picture of a beautiful dark-skinned sister.

"This is the girl who broke my heart. She's the one I was absolutely in love with. She'd make me laugh all the time. She was a PR person, and when she met me, she had it in her mind that it would be a business relationship.

"Eventually we started dating, and she says, 'I'm thirty-two and I want to get married and have kids. If you're not interested in that, if this isn't going anyplace, if there's no end to this, we can keep going as we're going, but I'm looking for a man to get married to and have children with.' As I said before, listen to a woman, and she'll tell you what she wants, the way it starts is the way it's going to end. She was honest and I respected that. She was like, 'We can be cool and everything, but if you don't want marriage then we won't be having sex,' and we dated for a year and a half and never had sex.

"One thing that I've learned throughout all this that you don't date outside your class. I know me, and I know that I don't need to date some blue-blooded rich woman that don't like to shoot pool or go to baseball games. What's the point? She's used to the finer things in life that I can't give her. Nothing I'm gonna do is gonna impress her, nothing is going to make her happy—she's out of my class, she's out of my league. She's champagne and I'm beer, so why try to date her? It's not that you're selling yourself short. You're just increasing your chances of being happy.

"I'm from the ghetto, but I got an education and I got out of the ghetto so I do all right. I don't think someone from the ghetto is out of my league. I'll date a hood rat in a minute because she still has the potential to do better—she still has the potential to educate herself and get out. But if a woman is so much further advanced than me and has these big-time degrees like doctorates or whatever, sometimes that makes a big difference and sometimes it doesn't, it just depends on the person, but you have to look for that stuff.

"Many educated African-American women over the age of thirty are single, and that's because there is a limited pool of men for black women to choose from. Either he's married, in jail, gay, or on the down low. It's a damn shame that women have to compete with men for other men. I meet single women everywhere—in fast food restaurants, at the mall, in line at the movies—and if I see a black woman over thirty, there is a pretty good chance that she's single, and when I get to talking to her, nine times out of ten she'll say something like,

'I haven't been in a relationship in a while, because there aren't any good men,' and that's a shame.

"See, there's dating, and then there's *dating*-dating. Dating is going out and having fun with no set destination. We go to the movies, we go to a concert, we go to the club, and I don't expect anything from you at the end of the night. I don't expect no booty. I'm going to hug you and kiss you at the door, say, 'Great date,' and be gone.

"Dating-dating or serious dating is when you get further down the line. You started out as friends, you started dating, then you start serious dating or, as I call it, dating-dating. That's kind of defined as, 'We're exclusive, we're a couple, we might get engaged one day. We might get married one day, we might live together, and I'll get some booty.' You expect that every time you go over there to see her, you're going to get some booty. That's dating-dating, serious dating, exclusive dating, or whatever you want to call it.

"I got my heart broken in that last serious relationship, and it affected me so much that I don't have a current relationship. But it's not because I'm afraid to get hurt again. It's because this woman who hurt me, this woman who I actually loved, I compare everybody to her. Nobody is as fun as her, nobody laughs like she does, nobody dances like she does, nobody smiles like she does, nobody kisses like she does, nobody understands me like she does. Until I met her, even after being married, I'd never experienced real love. I got married out of convenience. So she is the woman who allowed me to experience love. She taught me the difference between lust and love.

"Interracial dating was never an issue for me. Look at me—I'm mixed. My mother was Hispanic, and my father is black. A lot of my uncles married white women, and my ex-wife is white, but it never was an issue. Being half-Hispanic and half-black in an all-black neighborhood was never an issue. I liked black girls when I was growing up and I dated black girls, and I learned that there was a difference between white women and black women, and eventually I started dating black women more than I did white women. Black kids are raised differently than white kids. Their values are different, the things that they find important are different, and so are their qualities. Black women have different smells and scents than white women do, and I think it's the things that black women use on their bodies that makes the difference like the cocoa butter and the lotions and the hair products. Black women just smell warmer to me.

"I think I made a conscious effort early in life not to date Hispanic women, because Hispanic women reminded me of my mother and my sister, and it's hard to get excited about somebody that reminds you of your mother or your sister. You know how people will say you're looking for your father or you're looking for your mother in a person—well, what you're looking for are the qualities. You're not looking for somebody who looks like them. My mother was beautiful, and my sisters are beautiful, and I've since loosened up a bit about that. I've gotten more mature, but as a young guy that was an issue for me.

"My goal now is to find the one quality woman to be in a committed relationship with even though our view of what a committed relationship is may be different. I'm thinking that her idea of commitment is going to be living in the same house, being married, having kids, and having me take care of her. But my idea of a committed relationship is one where she'll live in her house, I'll in my house, she's the only woman I date, she's the only woman I sleep with, she's the only woman I call, she's the only woman I do for. I'll do anything she needs or she wants, she can depend on me and I can depend on her equally, *but* it's like the old Monroe Doctrine, 'separate but equal,' until at some point I might change my mind about marriage. Right now I'm 'living la vida loca.' I like living at my house. I like being by myself."

EDWIN

Edwin laughed when asked about his definition of dating.

"Dating is a sustained relationship, so if I had to go down the list of women I've had a sustained relationship with, I'd have to say there were no more than six in my lifetime, because I'm talking about a relationship that lasted more than two weeks.

"There is a woman I date exclusively now, but I also have a lady friend I've hung out with for about three years, and I've got some other women I can call up and go to a movie or out to dinner with, but we're just buddies.

"The majority of the men I know think differently about dating than women do. Women are looking for a long-term relationship that will end in marriage, and you may have a few guys who think that way as well, but I think overall it's the women who are more drawn to that long-term relationship. Most guys aren't really looking for commitment, because they're afraid of it.

"I've got stuff in my closet right now that women bought for me, and I'm like, "I don't need you to buy that for me," because I don't want to feel obligated. I don't want somebody to feel like they're getting their claws in me. When I meet a woman and I feel like, *Yeah, this is it, this is the one*, and she buys something for me, that's fine if we're doing things for one another, but if it's just somebody I'm hanging out with—no, I don't want that. Buying stuff for me is the quickest way to push me away because I'll be thinking that she's trying to put that extra pressure on the relationship while I'm just trying the relationship out to see if it has a chance to go any further. I don't want to feel like I'm using a woman, because I got a conscience and I believe in the old saying, What goes around comes around. I don't believe in using people.

"My ideal date is going out to dinner and then to the theater. I have season tickets, I like going so much, but I also like being spontaneous. One time I had a woman meet me in New Orleans for the weekend.

We flew in on Friday and stayed Friday and Saturday night and flew out on Sunday and had a wonderful time.

"I like having a woman I can hang out and have a pleasant conversation with. It's nice to have a friend to talk over your ideas and share life experiences with, but I don't want any more commitments until things feel right. I'm leery of commitments.

"Back in the day, I would go out with one woman on Friday, a different woman on Saturday, and another woman on Sunday, and I did that over an extended period of time until I finally told myself, *This has got to stop*, because it got old.

"I only date black women. There are plenty of fine sisters out there, and sisters are what I've always liked. My brother and my sister are married to Hispanics, but I don't date Hispanic or white women. I've slept with some in the past, but I won't even do that now. I'll look at a white woman or a Hispanic woman and say, *That sure is a fine ole girl there*, but that doesn't mean I'm attracted to them physically. There's just something about the way a black woman carries herself that I love.

"When I lived in Corpus, I was in my early twenties and I drove a Corvette. One day I was at the car wash cleaning it up, and a white guy looked at me and told his friend, "I bet he got him a white woman." He was saying this because he'd bought into the stereotype that successful black men only dated white women, and I didn't like being put in that category. I don't even like the way white girls giggle and carry on. They got that funny little laugh about them, and truth be told, I'd just rather be with a sister. A sister holds herself together better as she ages, and we just have more things in common, so that's my preference.

"There is a difference in having sex with black women too. A sister goes at it like there ain't no tomorrow. With a white girl, you have to say, 'Do you need to read a book? Do you want to look at a movie or something?' I might be overexaggerating but overall I just enjoy a sister with that beautiful brown skin. I want something with some color to it. You look at a white girl's body compared to a sister's body, and the differences are obvious. I've seen some white girls with nice shapes, but not like a sister—it's totally different."

WARREN

"Men are afraid of how women change once they commit. Women seem to get selfish once a man commits. He commits to this woman, and automatically he's committed to paying her bills and then he looks up and she just went and got a credit card over here and a little loan over there, and she's acting like she don't have no responsibility at all. Men get committed and end up with more bills and less sex, so that's what makes men afraid to commit. Women get selfish and start thinking, *Well, that's what he's here for,* but it's a two-way street. A lot of women do that; they're only concerned about what that man can do for them."

RUBEN

" People always say to me, 'Why do you only date white girls?' Well, that was all I was used to when I was growing up. When I was growing up in Arizona, you couldn't date. You had to hide even with the Latino and black girls, because their parents were so strict. I was like, *Why hide? Dating is part of life, it's normal.* But I was always looked at as an outcast by my Latino peers because the friends that I had were all white people. Other Latinos at my school didn't play football, and I did, so that's the reason my friends were white. They were too busy smoking weed and didn't give a damn about school, and I wasn't into that.

"Every relationship I've had with Latino women has been very, very bad. The attitude they had about wanting total control and not trusting me ended every relationship. I was engaged to a Latino girl once. I dated this girl for two years, and my mom once again said, 'This is not the one.' I didn't listen to her this time though. I figured I was going to do this, so I gave her a ring and asked her to marry me. A week later we went out to dinner, and when we got back to my house her pager went off. She'd gone to the bathroom or something, so I picked it up and it said nine-one-one, so I took the pager to her 'cause it had to be important. Then I started noticing some things like her phone ringing and her going into another room to talk or she wouldn't show up when she said she would, and when she did show up she'd have all these flimsy excuses, so my thoughts went back to what my mom had said about her not being the one, and I eventually found out she was seeing another guy.

"That really hurt me, so since then whenever I date somebody, and I tell them I'm committed, I don't step out. But if I'm dating somebody and I'm not committed, like when I was in college, I would always tell them, 'Look, we can date, but I'm not ready for a serious relationship,' so if I dated somebody else, I never felt guilty.

"I don't date married women at all, no matter what, because they're already committed. Now, if a woman tells me she's divorced, I got to take her word for it, but if I find out that she's just separated, I cut it off because from a spiritual standpoint, she's still married. Even though in man's law it's only a piece of paper, in God's eyes, you're still married, so I'm not interested.

"So many of my friends who have been married have gotten divorced, and the divorces were supposed to be amicable, but after they signed the final papers, they told me they had this bad feeling that they did something wrong. One guy said he was thinking, 'I must not have done anything right, and that's the reason it didn't work.' I guess that's why I'm still waiting. I want to do it right the first time.

"I've dated two types of Latino women. The first type is the controlling type because she's seen so much unfaithfulness in her life. It's either unfaithfulness amongst her peers or it's unfaithfulness in her family—men just weren't faithful. The second type, the Latino woman who goes to college, feels like if she marries a white man, that's going to get her instant success. As a professional Latino man, I don't want somebody like that. She sees a white man as a status symbol, and that points to the shallowness of her character, so to me she'll always be lacking.

"I want a woman who doesn't want to be without me. I've had a few situations like that, but then I see some things that I know I can't change, so I cut it off. It's hard, but that's what you got to do—you got to keep moving, you got to keep living. If you don't live, you don't learn. It's like a scar. You fall and scratch your knee, and it's going to bother you—but you got to keep walking, you got to keep moving. Then that scratch will scab over and will eventually heal, and a scar will form and you'll remember. If you keep making the same mistakes, what are you learning? To me, a wise man learns from his mistakes, but a wiser man learns from his mistakes and the mistakes of others. You got to be smart enough to look around you and see how other people go through certain things, and stop doing the same old shit over and over again.

"I've dated about every race you can think of—Indian, black, Asian, even one woman from Guam. Women aren't any different, only the features. Women are all women. I don't know what more beautiful blessing God could give a man than a woman, but the bottom line is, I haven't found my missing rib.

"I watched my mom and dad a lot, and I saw where her strengths complemented his weaknesses, but he was still in charge. It's hard for me to deal with a weak man, because traditionally in the Latino machismo community, Latin men are not supposed to show their weaknesses. I treasure my mother for giving us that delicate balance growing up. It was good to know that it was okay to be nurturing and sensitive as a man. Unfortunately, when you meet some women and you show that sensitive side, she thinks you're weak and she'll try to take advantage of you. That's why some men try to appear hard.

"Men by nature don't know how to manage their emotions, so they try to show no emotion at all. He fears that if he demonstrates his emotions that he'll be thought of as a lesser man. A good example of that is my dad. I've never seen my dad shed one tear, ever, not even when his mother died, when his father died, when his brothers died, or when his sisters died. I have not seen him shed one tear. I don't want to be that way; I want to have that balance."

LANDON

"If I'm sleeping with a woman, then we're dating, automatically. She's with me. If I go out and screw another woman, that's how it is, but if my woman goes and fucks another man, I don't put up with it. Yeah, I know it's a double standard, but I don't want to have to deal with the pain. She can deal with whatever she wants to, but I'm not going to deal with it. If she finds out that I've fucked around and she chooses to stay with me, that's her choice.

"Dating is hard because a man is not going to stop messing around until he finally finds that one woman who will make him stop. Still, some women don't know how to let go even when it's obvious that she's not that woman and he's told her that the relationship is over and done with.

"There was this one chick I dated, and we saw each other every day. We had sex all the time, but then I got bored with her. She was a beautiful girl, but we didn't have anything in common except sex. I could just pick up the phone and tell her I was horny or I needed my dick sucked, and she'd leave work and come take care of me. No matter what I wanted her to do sexually, she'd do it, but I got bored with her because she acted like she didn't have a mind of her own.

"I told her I couldn't see her anymore, and I stopped calling her—then she started stalking me. She'd leave notes on my car, she'd call me on the phone all times of the day and night crying about how much she missed me and how she couldn't see herself not being with me sexually—the whole nine. I kept telling her it was over and that she needed to move on, but I finally had to take action to get her attention. Me and some of my boys were at the club on base one night, and she was there with some of her friends, but I ignored her and started talking to this other chick. That pissed her off, so she started drinking and flirting with one of my boys, hoping to make me jealous, but I'd already told my boy that I wanted him to take her home that night because I was going to set her up. I'd given my boy the signal to make his move on her, and because she knew he was my friend, she felt comfortable flirting with him and leaving with him. She made sure I was looking when she grabbed her purse and headed out the club with him.

"Now, me and this dude were roommates, so I gave him time to do what he needed to do before I headed to the room. When I got there, I unlocked the door and walked in, and she was lying in bed with him, butt-ass naked, trying to grab for a sheet or a towel or anything she could find to cover up with, and I could tell by the look on her face that she was embarrassed. I just stood at the foot of the bed, shook my head at her like I was disgusted, then turned around and left. She never bothered me after that, because there was nothing else she could say to me. What else was there to say? Just the other day she'd been telling me how much she loved me and couldn't do without me, and next thing I see, with my own two eyes, is her in bed with my boy. It wasn't no 'he say, she say.' I witnessed the shit firsthand.

"The first place I was stationed was in Korea, and it's easy to approach women in Korea because of their culture. The Korean father raises his daughter to take care of her man. That's her only job in life, so it was so easy for me. I'd walk into a club and see a Korean girl and I'd say, 'Hey, how you doing? What's your name?' and she'd reply, 'My name is Miuki,' or some shit like that. Then I'd say, 'I don't feel like chilling here, do you want to go to my room?' And we'd go back to my room and have sex the same night. For at least a year, I was getting with four to six women a day. I would start about two or three in the afternoon. I'd go to the gate because they couldn't come on base by themselves, we'd take a cab back to the barracks, we'd go inside and have sex, be there like an hour, I'd take her back to the gate, and when I dropped her off at the gate, I'd be picking up another girl.

"Four to six women a day, and my dick would be sore, but that didn't stop me. Most people don't know this, but after the third time, when a man ejaculates, blood comes out. Sperm doesn't come out anymore. Blood comes out, and your dick is sore, but I kept doing it out of lust. I wanted to do as many women as I could. I did that for like a year and then I got burned out. I finally said to myself, *You know what, I'm going to leave all these women alone and settle down with one woman.* When I went from Korea to Japan, I met Kiara and I fell in love with her. She was the first decent-looking sister I had even seen in like two years, and I've always loved the sisters, but we broke up because I fucked up. It took me about two months to get over her, and that's when I met my wife. I was looking for somebody to get serious with when I met her, and I was looking for a sister.

"It takes a strong man to deal with a black woman. I've found that in general black women bring baggage into a relationship, but I'm willing to deal with that baggage because I love black women. If it's not kids and baby daddy drama, it's mental baggage or a negative attitude. You have to be strong to be able to deal with that, and you have to actually want to be with that woman, and a lot of brothers either can't or don't want to put up with that shit.

"Some black men hold a grudge against black women because they don't understand her or what her needs are. First of all, the man can't deal with his own shit, and that's where the problem is—it ain't the woman. He can't handle his own issues, so he don't know what the hell is going on. If he were a thinker, he would understand.

"The reason it's not a problem for me is because I exist in my mind. Other people exist in their bodies, they exist in the world, what's the going thing, what's the new dance or whatever. I exist right here."

Landon pointed to his head.

"That's what puts me a couple of steps ahead of everybody else. That's what puts me on that level with thirty- and forty-five-year-old people, because I *think*.

"A lot of black people raise their children the same way that white people treated their slaves. All they knew was, 'Nigga, you did wrong, so I'm going to beat you.' Have you seen *Antwone Fisher*? It's that slave mentality. You got a different type of black folk today. You got black people who are wanting a better quality of life, but you also got black people who have found contentment in their misery, and they ain't gon' change—they don't want to change. Some people are content with living in the projects. Some people are content being in gangs, and some people are content doing bad and struggling their whole life—that's all they're used to, so that's all they know. So when women grow up in all these fucked-up homes, they come out with fucked-up ideas. I'm not saying I don't have any baggage—I do, and I'm willing to admit it. But some sisters got some real baggage and don't even realize it. Then when you try to say something to help them out, you get, 'Fuck you, nigga. I ain't got no problem.' "

3

LIKES, DISLIKES, AND PET PEEVES

KEN

"When I was dating, it used to piss me off when me and a woman were only on the second date and she was already planning a trip to the jewelry store to look at engagement rings. That kind of shit turns a guy off immediately. I don't know why women don't understand that and why they're always in such a hurry for a commitment. At least try to get to know a man first. You can spot a single woman a mile away: she'll be standing there having a conversation with her girlfriend, but her eyes are on every man that steps into the room. She's looking at each one of them like, *Is he the one? Is that my potential husband?* and it's so damn obvious, it's embarrassing.

"I also don't like it when a woman thinks something is wrong because I'm not talking. Sometimes I just want some quiet time. It's not a bad thing to just be quiet and watch the game on TV, but a lot of women will assume a man is thinking about breaking up with her because he's not all in her face, running his mouth. If I don't have nothing to say at that moment, I'm not going to try and make up something just so we can have a conversation.

"One of my big pet peeves was always women who would give it up on the first date, then lie and say, 'Oh, I've never done anything like this in my life. I don't know what got into me.' I know what got into her. Her ass was as horny as I was, and women are just as dirty-minded as men. I've heard women talk, and they can be downright nasty, but they always want to act like men are the only ones with dirty minds.

"I guess most women I've dated would say I had a lot of nerve to be so picky, but single women need to understand that there are more of them out there than there are single men, so men who are looking for wives have a lot more options. I'm not saying women should settle, but those who are desperate to get married may have to settle faster than a man will because he has more to choose from. I know when I was out there, I was dating at least three or four women at a time, and most of them would have done anything if it meant I might ask them to marry me, so I know how the game is. I know that the dating scene is messed up, and I know that men can pick and choose, but that's just the way it is, and women know it too."

SIMEON

"My worst relationships were with women who were very possessive."

Simeon grimaced.

"I've been through some ordeals. I've had women stalk me, hide out in bushes in front of my place, and all that stuff. I talked to my dad about it one time, and he said, 'If a person is always accusing you of something or has a lack of trust in you, then they're probably up to something. And maybe they aren't doing anything shady; it may just be that this was the person they used to be in a past relationship.'

"Like if I tell my woman that I'm going over to my mom's house instead of hanging out with her, she might interpret it to mean that I'm going to go spend time with someone else because that was something that she used to say and do in another relationship. But that's not fair, because I'm not her. That's her issue, not mine.

"Take strip joints, for example. I'm not really into them, but I'll go. I didn't even bother going to strip joints until I moved into corporate America. I soon learned that when you go on those out-of-town trips and you get through with all those meetings, that's where all the men go—to the strip joint. I really don't care for that environment, but I do like the male bonding aspect of it. I enjoy going and hanging out with the fellas to have a good time, but I'm not out chasing skirts or anything like that. Now that's not to say that I won't go along with the crowd and say, 'Oh yeah, homegirl's got a bad-ass body,' but nine times out of ten, I'm not going to do anything except look and go back to my hotel room. Believe me, men *can* go to a strip club and just hang out with the guys and nothing else has to happen, so if I tell you I'm going to a club with the guys, don't interpret that to mean I'm going out there to chase other women.

"Some women are basically insecure. They have this mentality that the only reason a man is going to the club is to meet another woman, or the only reason he's going out to dinner or has two women come over to his house to interview him is because he's trying to push up on one of them—that's the only reason. At first, it seems kind of cute when a woman acts like she's jealous. She'll have you thinking, *Oh, she really cares about me*, but when a person is overly possessive, things can get bad real quick, and you start to feel smothered.

"When I first got out of college, I moved into some apartments on the west side of town, and I'd been working long hours. One Friday evening, I just wanted to get some rest, so I turned the phone off and went to sleep.

"There was this girl I was dating, Toya. I woke up after I kept hearing all of this loud knocking and loud talking. I got up to answer the door, and I hear, 'I see your black ass. Open this door.'

"Now, I'm halfway groggy because I just woke up, and I'm thinking to myself, *How you going to see me through the peephole?* but then I look over my shoulder, and there she was standing on my balcony like that crazy female straight out of the Martin Lawrence movie, *A Thin Line Between Love & Hate.* I slid open the balcony door and asked her what she thought she was doing. I couldn't believe that she had climbed up to my balcony on the third floor, and she was acting all angry and crazy and saying things like, 'Who you got in here?'

"To this very day I am still amazed that she did something like that. I told her, 'I have no one in here, but you know what, if I could convince the police that I didn't throw your ass off this balcony, I'd make you climb back down the same way you climbed up.' I hadn't done anything to make her feel insecure; I think she had just been in some very bad relationships and she was taking it out on me."

Simeon sighed heavily.

"Needless to say, after that, the relationship was over. See, game recognizes game. Take the relationship I'm in now, for instance. She asked me what would cause me to end this relationship, and I told her, 'The only thing that would cause me to end a relationship is if you cheat, because I ain't dealing with that. If you want to bounce around and you want to see other people, then bring it to the forefront, and maybe we can try to have that type of relationship. If you lie and tell me we're going to be exclusive, and then you cheat, then I'm going to start thinking, *Okay you lied about this, so what else have you lied about?'*

"I guess I need to start clarifying what I want a little better because my definition of dating is where we're seeing each other but it's not that boyfriend-girlfriend type deal or that, 'Well, where are we going from here?' You've got different types of relationships. You can say, 'Where do you see us in the next five years?' and to me that's a relationship that builds upon itself. We may get married, we may do this, we may have kids, and we're making career decisions together. That's different than the girl that you go to dinner and the movies with, and she's never met your parents and you don't intend for her to. She doesn't know anything about your family, you don't know anything about her family, and if you were asked her middle name, you might not even know it, but you've probably known her for years. That's just 'kickin' it' to me.

"That kickin'-it thing really goes on a whole lot more, the older you get. When you're in your late thirties and early forties, there are a lot of people who already have kids, and they've given up on relationships. They may just want a companion; they don't want a commitment. They want somebody to have dinner with or go to a play with, and that's cool.

"I've never been in love. I can love someone, but being *in* love with someone is something totally different. If I was in love, I'd probably be married. If I was in love with a woman, I would've asked her to marry me, but I know I've never been in love because the difference between loving someone and being in love is that you have no insecurities.

It might sound crazy, but the thing that really makes me afraid of being in love is that she could *die* on me. There would be nothing I could do, and the thought of losing someone I love enough to marry really bothers me. It's not the same as if she ended the relationship; it would be like I became one with this person and now part of me has died.

"If we broke up, I could come up with all kinds of reasons as to why I'm better off, but if she died and I truly loved her . . . I'd be like, man . . . I don't know if I could deal with that. That's what happened with my uncle Paul and aunt Love when I was a kid. He died after they'd been married forty years, and she seemed so lost without him. You walk into the room, and you see a person just sitting there crying for no reason, and then she says, 'I miss him so much' and there's nothing you can say. There's nothing you can do except hope that time is going to heal it. I remember telling myself then that I'd never let myself get that deep. I'd like to get married and have a bunch of kids, but it's about taking chances, so that may be the reason why I've never been in love.

"I got a whole lot of partners my age who have never been married

and don't have kids, but if you watch TV or read newspapers and maga-
zines, you don't get that impression at all. I don't know if it's media
propaganda or what, but they're always giving the impression that black
men got babies all over the place. You know what, that ain't all true.

"I'm looking for the right one, but I guess I'm kinda picky. One
thing I don't find attractive in some women is their expectation or
need to be taken care of financially. She expects to be taken care of,
and what I mean by that is she's saying, 'If you date me, you need to
kick in on the rent.' A relationship like that is based on things that really don't matter, and that's one of the things that I really dislike about
some women.

"I went to school with this girl who became a flight attendant because she wanted to see the world. I helped her move to Sacramento,
and she said, 'Okay, because you helped me move, I want you to come
to Provo with me and a couple of my girlfriends, and we can go see
the Tyson fight and go to a couple of other places.'

"I started noticing something when I hung out with her at these
different places. I started seeing the same group of women at all of
these events, and I thought, *It's cool that these females like sports but it's
strange that all of them are always at the same functions. I make decent
money but it would be quite expensive to do this all the time, so what's up?*

"Here I was being naïve and thinking they must have very good careers until my flight attendant friend pulled me over to the side when
this one girl was trying to holla at me and said, 'No, Simeon, you don't
want to mess with her.' I asked why not, 'cause she was a pretty girl.
My friend said, 'Most of the women you're seeing here are flight at-
tendants. That's how they can afford to fly all over the country. But,
they're trying to get hooked up with a baller. They're after the
money.' At that time I was pretty buffed, and I guess the woman
thought I was a professional ball player. My friend said, 'That girl
right there is getting fifteen thousand a month from Such-and-such
because she had a baby by him, and she planned the whole thing.'

"I'm not a cheap man, but it's the principle of the thing. There are some things that are called upkeep, and upkeep, to me, are those essential things that *you* should be handling. Things like your hair, your nails, bathing every day, brushing your teeth, getting up and going to work, food and shelter. If you're dating a guy, expecting him to provide shelter for you, get your hair done, get your nails done, my question is, 'Do you want the guy or do you want his wallet?' because to me, that ain't a relationship.

"You got some guys who will take advantage of a woman the same way. He'll be bragging about how she's paying him, and you know what it boils down to when you sit down and think about it? It's called low self-esteem. When your self-esteem is low, you let people take advantage of you."

QUINCY

"I've dated a lot of women, and it took me a while to find out what I really like. I'm attracted to women who are witty and intelligent but down to earth. They have to be genuine and not fake, have a good value system, and be ambitious. As far as appearance, there are many things I like. Eyes are the first thing I look at, and I love women with high cheekbones. As far as color, I would have to say I like anything from medium-brown-skinned to dark-brown-skinned women, but I'm not attracted to light-skinned women for some reason. She can be anywhere from a size six to size twelve, and her height could be four-eleven to about five-six, but not much taller than that, and I don't care if a woman has long or short hair, but I don't like fake hair. I don't like nothing fake, period. I don't like fake breasts, long gaudy nails, thick makeup, or any of that.

"I like a woman who is independent. I can't stand lazy women who don't want to go to work and expect you to buy everything for them. An independent woman will meet you halfway. Sometimes she'll take you out and pay for the dinner, and I like that. As long as a woman is not too headstrong, there's nothing wrong with her being independent. I expect a woman to have her own ideas, but I hate it when I'm dating someone and she turns everything I say around to make it sound like I said something else. You know, always reading into something and making it more than it really is. I used to date needy women because I felt that if I helped out and made her life better, she'd really love me, but people like that drain you.

"I got tired of being the rescuer because I found out if you constantly rescue a person, they're not ever going to help themselves. I don't need someone like that; I need a woman who is willing to meet me halfway so we can help each other. If I can see that a woman has some potential and just needs me to help her a little so she can get on her feet, that's fine. But I don't want to have to keep on bailing her out, because that gets old. I've dated several women like that because I didn't recognize the signs. But now, I just move on if they even act like they're going to be begging all the time, 'cause I can't help them.

"I actually have standards when it comes to the women I date. There does have to be some kind of physical attraction, but the most important thing is her personality. The way she carries herself and if she's friendly—that's an attraction to me. If a woman is stuck up and tries to act like she's all uppity, I'm turned off and won't even try to talk to her—I don't care how she looks. But if I like the way she looks and then I like her personality, I go on to find out if she's working or if she's just looking for a handout. I want to know how many kids she has, and if she doesn't have any kids, does she have a crazy ex-boyfriend or ex-husband? Is that ex in jail and why? 'Cause I don't need to be dating no woman if her ex is a convict who might come looking for her when he gets out.

"On the flip side, even though I like intelligent women, I don't like it when a woman is so educated that she's a damn idiot. I dated one woman who knew a lot of famous people because she was an events planner for a large hotel in Los Angeles. She was always name-dropping, which made her appear shallow and immature in my eyes, so I finally asked her, 'Why are you always talking about who you know and what they have like you think it makes *you* look important? Those people aren't giving you any of their money, so what's the point? I could care less about who you know or how much money they make, because that doesn't make me like you more. To tell you the truth, it turns me off because you obviously attach your self-worth to what other people have.' Of course, her ego couldn't take my being real, so that was the end of that relationship, but I didn't give a damn.

"I'm also a stickler for good hygiene; I think a lady should always make her best effort to be clean, *always*. The reason I say that is because I've come across women with bad hygiene a couple of times, and it is a total turn-off. I can't get past that, no matter what a woman looks like. One lady I dated was beautiful, but she was so damn musty that I found myself sniffing my underarms more than a few times to see if it was me. I just can't deal with a funky-smelling woman.

"Another thing that turns me off is women who don't wear the right color makeup or don't know how to put it on right, or women who wear the wrong style of clothing for their size. You know, everybody can't wear everything. One girl I dated used to wear white shoes *all* the damn time, even in the winter, and she always wore the wrong clothes for the occasion. No matter where we were going, her outfit was either too tight or too short, because she had this big, fine ass that she loved to show off. Yeah, I liked her ass as well as the next man, but she dressed like she was trying to put it on display, and it got to be embarrassing.

"I tried to tell her in a nice way that she needed to tone it down a bit, but no, Miss Ghetto Fabulous said she hadn't had any complaints before and that she knew how to dress. I decided that since she wanted to dress like a hood rat, there was no point in wasting my time. After all, there are some men out there who like their woman to dress like that. I'm just not one of them."

GREG

"The worst thing a woman can do is nag. I don't feel like every woman has to be clean to the point of being anal, and she doesn't have to cook a five-course meal seven days a week—I can cook myself, and we can do that together. But constantly nagging and constantly checking up on me for no real reason—that drives me up a wall. I can put up with anything else, but I can't stand a nagging woman.

"Women miss out on a lot of good relationships because they think a man may be intimidated by how much she makes or how many degrees she has and stuff like that, but that doesn't bother me. I feel like all the money goes towards the same cause—to pay the bills and enjoy the rest—so I don't have a problem with that. The lady I'm dating now makes twice what I make, and it doesn't bother me. She never throws that in my face, and we always share the bill. You know, if I get paid this week and we go out, I pay the bill, and the next week if she gets paid, she pays. When we go out of town, we split the cost, so it's never like she has to take care of the whole bill or vice versa.

"Also, I wouldn't want a woman who is insecure and needy and wants constant praise. If the lady is pretty and fine, I'll let her know that, but if I have to constantly do that to make her feel good about herself, then we have a problem. I don't have time for that. There are some men who like women who are dependent on them for everything, but I don't need that.

"I like a woman who is petite, her hands and toes are well manicured and polished, and her hair is well groomed. And those little sun dresses and wraparound skirts that women wear—oh my goodness! . . . Those outfits do something to me! I love to see women wearing those kinds of outfits, and that makes it hard for me to stay focused on my woman, especially during the summer. I like a woman to be aggressive—I like for her to come on to me instead of me being the aggressive person all the time. That's also a big turn-on once we're in a relationship. You know at the start of a relationship, it seems like you're both being aggressive, but the longer you stay in it, it seems like the man is always the aggressive one. I think it turns a man off when he always has to be the one to initiate things, because personally, I feel like if you want it just as much as I do, show me, flirt with me, tell me what you want."

DANTE

"Being jealous, being insecure, and pushing the wrong button—those are the three major things women need to work on in any kind of relationship. If you know what sets him off, you should know not to go there, but—" Dante threw his hands up and shook his head.

"Women insist on doing it anyway. A woman won't stop at *A* once she starts pushing your buttons—aw, *hell* no. She will push every button between *A* and *Z*, and that's when you get to the hell zone, which means fighting, cussing, saying 'I hate you,' and all that. Then when you up and call her a crazy bitch, she tries to act like she don't know why you went off.

"You may even make an attempt to try and walk away, but most women won't allow you to walk away. If you go to marriage counseling, they always say you should sit down and talk, but talking isn't feasible when you're upset. When you're upset with someone, that's not the time to talk, because you're not in the right state of mind. You just need to walk away. Get in your own space and cool down before you talk. Sometimes, when I get really angry with my wife, I think of her in a coffin, and that makes me realize that what we're arguing about isn't even worth it. Shit like leaving a coffee cup on the table or forgetting to put a new roll of toilet tissue out after you've used the last piece—it's just not worth it. Minor stuff like that shouldn't cause big arguments.

"You got to know what you want when you're out there looking. You need to know what you like, what you don't like, and what you can tolerate, but you've also got to be willing to compromise some-times. When I was looking for a wife, I was looking for a woman who was honest, big-hearted, and God-fearing. Looks were important, but not so important that I'd overlook a woman if that was the only area she was lacking in."

XAVIER

"I hate it when a woman asks me the same question over and over and over again—that drives me crazy, especially when I've already an-swered her once. Then, she gets pissed off when I answer her that sec-ond time, but I fail to use the same exact words I used the first time. The worst thing a woman can do is nag and drag things out too long.

"I don't want to stereotype young women, but a lot of them feel that if they have a baby by a guy, that means he has to take care of that baby, which in turn means he has to take care of her, and that's bull-shit. Then she gets mad when the guy gets a new girlfriend and won't make any commitment to her, and I don't think that's fair. Getting a baby to trap somebody is the oldest trick in the book: it didn't work then, and it doesn't work now, so women may as well stop trying to use it as a hook.

"Yeah, you might get him to be in your life for the next eighteen years because of that baby, but at the same time, he'll probably resent you for it, which means there won't be a chance in hell of a relationship between the two of you. A woman who has a child out of wedlock these days will find it much harder to get someone to marry her than a man will, because the pool of eligible black men is smaller than the pool of eligible black women. Add a baby to that equation, and the woman has put herself in a whole different category because there are some men who will not date women with children, especially if they don't have any themselves, and I'm one of them.

"Young women today are just out there, they're so willing to try things without even giving it a second thought. Right now, there are girls in high school who are perpetrating that they're bisexual. They watch the movies or the videos and find out that some guys think it's a turn-on, so they go for it. It's just all messed up. The trends these days are much more dangerous, especially when it comes to sex and drugs, and a lot of that is due to the music and what they see on TV.

"I hear kids say the music doesn't have anything to do with the way they dress, or the words they use, or even their mind-set, but that's not true, because if all they see and hear men say to women is 'bitch' and 'ho,' and 'Gul, you look good—won't you back dat ass up,' and then they see women backing it on up like they enjoy being talked to that way, then they think that's the way a man and a woman are supposed to communicate with each other. If that's all they see, then it becomes acceptable for them to relate to each other that way. It's all just a big game—everybody is saying what they think the other person wants to hear, so they can get what they want, because there's no longevity to relationships now. There's no real commitment."

MALIK

"It's a turn-on for me when a woman makes a move on me rather than me having to be the one to initiate everything. I'm not saying I like for a woman to be too aggressive, because I don't like overly aggressive women at all, but a woman who is very affectionate towards me and lets me know in a subtle way that she wants to be with me is very nice. If a woman comes up to me and says, 'Damn you got some big-ass hands. You look like you could be packing. Why don't you take me somewhere so we can fuck?' Whether she's my woman or not, that turns me off. It may be okay to do that every now and then with a woman I really like, but I like romance. I love a woman who is sensual. There's something about a woman being too direct that doesn't sit right with me, especially if all she wants is sex—that scares me. If tha   all she wants from me, how many other men has she done that with? For me, there's more to it than that.

"Don't get me wrong. Sex is important to me just like it is to any other man, because in a man's mind, sex is a natural part of a relationship. Sex is not always an intimate act to some men, but when I have sex, it's an intimate act to me. I can't have sex with someone I don't know nothing about. So, because of that, it's important to me to have sex with someone I'm involved with, because that's part of how we bond with each other.

"My wife and I are having problems right now because we only have sex once every two or three months, and I always have to be the one to initiate it. She tells me, 'All you want from me is sex,' but that's not true. She's my wife, and I want to make love with her, but that's not all I want, and if I don't want sex from her, that's when she should be concerned. I want my marriage to work, but just because I do romantic things for her doesn't mean my ultimate goal is to get sex. Sure, we might eventually end up making love, but that's not always what I'm after when I do something nice for her. The bottom line is this: Sex is very important to a marriage, and it's crazy as hell to think otherwise."

NEAL

"One of the common mistakes that females make is not believing in and trusting their mate. Another mistake is when a married woman goes to a single woman for advice, not realizing that birds of a feather flock together. Most of the time when a single woman gives her married friend advice, it's the type of advice that will end up making her single as well. Another thing women do is gossip too much, and that's a turn-off for most men.

"I've met some of the most successful, beautiful women in the world. One of them wrote me a check for ten thousand dollars and told me to cash it because she said she was in love with me and wanted me to have anything I wanted, but I gave it back to her. She'd come to visit me—it was an hour drive each way—two and three times a week, but I finally had to tell her that I didn't feel right spending time with her, because I was dating someone else. See, women think we're bigger dogs than we actually are, but all men aren't that way. Mostly we're just talk.

"Another time I was at a convention and met a woman who was a full-bird colonel in the Air Force. This lady had it going on, and she was really nice. She'd been married before, her children were both in college, and she was looking for a serious relationship, but she lived in D.C., so I knew there was no future for us. After I returned from the conference, we talked frequently, and she even came down to visit me a few times when she had to attend a meeting near my area, so we became friends, but I could tell she wanted us to be more than that.

"I'd planned to take a weeklong vacation just to get away, and I was telling her about it, but I hadn't decided where I would go. So she told me about this nice house she owned in Saint Thomas that she'd bought with the money from her divorce settlement several years ago. She'd had it remodeled, and she offered to let me stay there for as long as I wanted.

"She told me that all I needed to do was schedule a date, get my airline ticket, and let her know when I was going so she could have the property manager get the house ready. She said that she would even arrange for me to have a maid and a cook.

"Well, all of that sounded good to me, so I did just like she said and made myself a reservation for the very next week and told her when I'd be leaving. I told her the maid would be nice to have, but I didn't need a cook, since I'd invited a buddy of mine to go with me and he was a caterer. I was happy as I could be. I went to work the next day and told my staff that I'd be on vacation the following week and even did some shopping during my lunch hour to buy a few things to take along.

"When we arrived in Saint Thomas, the weather was perfect. Me and my buddy stepped off the plane and into a tropical paradise. I planned on taking a few tours around the island and do a little snorkeling, and my buddy planned to sit up at the bar and catch single women. We were all smiles as we walked slowly towards the taxis that were lined up. It was going to be a good week.

"After the taxi driver drove like a bat out of hell for about thirty minutes and got my stomach all upset, we finally arrived at the house and found it to be a neat little place, painted in tropical colors, like most of the homes on the island. It had two small bedrooms upstairs with a sitting area that separated them, and each room had its own bathroom and balcony. There was a nice-sized kitchen and dining area downstairs, with a large entertainment room that was complete with a stereo, television, and fully stocked bar. My buddy looked at me and said, 'Yeah man, this is what I'm talking about. I'm already loving this.'

"I took my luggage into one of the bedrooms, and when I opened the closet, I saw all these cute little summer dresses lined up inside, and I figured she just kept extra clothes at the house to keep from having to pack so much when she came in the summer. I looked in the dresser drawers just to reassure myself that I wouldn't be having company, and I'll be damned if her things weren't in there too. I looked in the bathroom, and her makeup was lined up neatly on the counter, and a still-damp toothbrush was in a clear glass jar. That's when I got pissed.

"She had baited me into coming down there for the week under the pretense that I'd be able to get away from work and just rest, and all along she knew she'd be there too. What in the hell did she think she was doing? What if I had brought another woman with me? I looked up and said, *Dear Lord, I don't want this lady, especially if she'd do something like this. Now what am I going to do?*

"By that time she was standing in the doorway, smiling and wearing a bathing suit with a sarong wrapped around her waist. I looked at her, and my anger must have been apparent, because her whole smile just froze. She goes, 'What's wrong, don't you like the house?'

"I told her that the house was beautiful, just like she said it would be, but I couldn't believe that she'd set this up after all the talks we'd had about relationships. I reminded her that we were just friends and that I wasn't looking for a serious relationship. I wasn't saying that I didn't ever want to be committed, but when I was ready to be committed and if our relationship had progressed beyond our just being friends, we could deal with it then.

"So me and my reluctant buddy left and got a room in a hotel because I didn't even want to be bothered. There are a lot of men who would have taken advantage of her for the week, knowing they didn't plan on being in a serious relationship with her. There are some men who would have stayed with her for the week and maybe nothing would have happened, but you're not going to force me to do nothing. It just doesn't work like that.

"You would be surprised at the things women do, the way they come on to men. I went to a banquet one night, and I didn't take a date, because I didn't feel like catering to anyone that night. One of my lady friends told me there was a lady at the banquet who was trying to figure out who this tall, dark-skinned man in the blue suit with the red handkerchief was, so she told her my name. The next thing I knew, she came over and started telling me she liked what she saw and that she'd like to go out with me, and I looked at her real good and realized that she lived in my neighborhood. I let her go on with all of that talk, and when she finished I said, 'You don't even recognize me, do you? I bowl with your husband, you have two kids, and you live a block over from me in a beautiful home. I don't date married women.'

"I will not date a married woman, regardless of what she has to offer. Now, that's not to say I haven't done it before, because I did when I was much younger and I didn't understand what the repercussions could be for an entire family. But I don't do that anymore, because if I date a married woman, I'm hurting another brother and I'm hurting myself. It reminds me of when I was working on my master's degree in counseling. We talked about homicide and suicide, and we got into a discussion of why black folks commit homicide and white folks commit suicide. White folks don't have no problem with killing themselves, but most black folks would never kill self. Still, they're disgusted with their life and with self, and they see other blacks as they see themselves, so they go out and kill another person who looks just like they do."

PIERRE

"Everybody has a spirit—some people call it a guardian angel—and you have to be in tune with your spirit because it will warn you of stuff and keep you from making mistakes. Your spirit helps to guide you, if you listen. If you don't listen to it, then you're on your own. If you listen, it'll help you each and every time. It never hurts you. I can meet somebody and there will be something about that person I'm not comfortable with, and I may not be able to put my finger on it, but I'll know that something's not right, so I'll keep my distance. Then later on, I'll find out what it was that wasn't right about that person or I might hear from somebody else that this person is really crazy or something. Just like those women who aren't women, but they're drop-dead gorgeous? I'll see one of them and say, *Man, she is so beautiful, but something's not right,* and I'll find out later that it was a dude.

"I'm picky. I like women with hair but I saw a chick with this bad short cut, and I thought she was fine. I don't like women with no class, I don't like women who laugh too loud, and I don't like women who don't take care of themselves. There may be things that other men don't look at that I notice. Like if a woman talks a lot but doesn't listen, that can be a turn-off to me. I need a woman who knows how to listen and a woman who can say what she means, don't dance around looking for an answer when I ask you a question.

"I'll give you a good scenario: My girl told me one night that she was going out with her girlfriends, which isn't really like her, so that made me suspicious. I work late at my part-time job, so it's normal for me to be out until five in the morning, so when I got home at four thirty and she wasn't there, I was wondering what was up.

"Before I could call her, she called me and said she was downtown, which is about fifteen minutes from the house. I called her back about five minutes later and asked her where she was, and she was already at the gate, and that didn't add up. I asked her who she'd been with, and she was like, 'What? Why are you tripping?' so I asked her again, 'Who were you with?' but she kept on beating around the bush, and it really pissed me off. She finally told me she was with her friend Dionne at some club called Ray's or some shit like that, but see, what she was doing was stalling, and I knew it.

"I told her, 'When you do that, you're trying to take a few minutes to think about what you need to say, and I don't like that shit. When I asked you who you were with, it should have rolled right off your tongue because *you* don't stay out until four thirty in the morning. Besides that, Ray's doesn't even stay open that late; they close at two, so something's up. The next time I ask you something like that, don't hesitate.'

"Hell, I know when I'm being played. Anybody can come up with a good answer if you give them a minute—I know I can. She ought to know better than to try that shit on me anyway. I'm a hustler, so I know when somebody's trying to run game on me. I've been taken many times before, so I know the game.

"Even if a homeless person comes up to me asking for money, I would respect them more if they just tell me they need some money to get a drink. Don't come up with that bullshit about you need some money to eat—your ass is forty pounds overweight. And don't tell me you're homeless and you've got a card to prove it. Just be straight with me. Don't be giving me no long speech about how I can call the center, 'cause you know ain't nobody gonna call the center to see if you sleep there at night. That gets on my nerves. Just come up and tell me you're trying to get a drink, and I might give you a dollar, but if you come up to me with some long-ass story, I'm gonna be like, 'Can't help you man—I'm busted.'"

Pierre sighed and looked toward the ceiling when asked about how many women he's had sex with.

"I wouldn't say I can't count them—I would say that my memory tells me that I just can't remember them all. When I was younger, I was like, *If it moves, I'll hit it.* No feelings were involved. I was at a bar one time, and a woman sent me a drink over with a note that she wanted me to take her home, so I took her home and hit it. She smoked too, and I don't even like women who smoke—but what can I say, I was young. I used to think it was easier for women to get sex than it was for a man, but men can get it easy too. All you got to do is walk into a club and be dressed halfway decent, and it's on.

"Now, I ain't going to go to no white bar and do that—that's not me—but one time I did go into a biker bar with a friend of mine. It was a hole in the wall, and I was in there less than five minutes and this nasty white chick walked up to me and said, 'Redheads have more fun.' She didn't come right out and say what she wanted, but basically if someone tells you that, you don't really have to read much into it.

"I was like, 'I ain't even been in here five minutes, and you're talking about laying down and spreading your legs? Please get away from me 'cause you don't know me like that.' Damn, she could have made it a little more challenging, but if you're that willing to open your legs, there's no challenge to that. Actually, to tell you the truth, it doesn't matter how you look, 'cause I know plenty of dudes who look like shit and they don't have no problem getting women. It's just a matter of having game, knowledge, and skills. You just got to know how to talk to people.

"I saw one dude pull this bad chick at the club, and before the night was over, she was under the table sucking his dick. She sucked his dick and her girl sucked his dick, and then he fucked both of them in the bathroom—it was a trip. You can't even begin to comprehend the stuff that be going on out there. I could tell you some wild shit.

"Basically people have certain mentalities, and once you know what type of mentality they have, then you know how to go about getting into them. If you're in the club, you're gonna run across at least one person with the mentality you're looking for—be it a white girl or a black girl, it doesn't make a difference.

"I don't know how they got on the subject, but by the time he got to the table, one of them told him, 'If you pull your dick out, I'll suck it right here.' So he pulled his dick out, and she went down and sucked it.

"So then he asked her girl, 'Can you suck a dick like your girl can?' and she was like, 'Well, my mouth isn't as big as hers, but let me show you what I got.' So she went down and sucked his dick too. Then he took the first girl to the bathroom, tore her up, and then told her, 'That was good, but now I'm going to go get your girl.' Now how could a woman who respects herself do something like that?

"You got just as many women out there who don't want a relationship as those that do. You got women out there who are just off the chain—they'll run from a relationship. If you just want to hit it for one night, you can have it. And most women like that don't want a good guy, because they're trying to protect their heart. Most likely they've been hurt before, and if they don't have to put their heart into it, that works better for them. They can just get their rocks off and be done with it. I don't like to judge, and I always say to each his own, but women like that are scandalous, and I'm not into women like that. I'm a freak, but now that I'm old enough to know better, I'm not into fucking no woman I don't know nothing about.

"I say I'm a freak because I like doing different stuff, wild stuff with my girl. I'm into risqué sex, like doing it in a public place where there's a chance I might get caught, but I don't actually want to get caught, and so far, knock on wood, I never have been. I've done it on the beach in the daytime, outside leaning against the car in the street, in the park on top of a slide in the rain in the middle of the night—stuff like that. I like to watch tapes and role-play—that's cool too. I'm not saying I don't like straight sex, but sometimes that gets old. You need variety to keep things from becoming repetitious.

"Me and my girl just had this conversation yesterday because she asked me why I don't fuck her more. She asked, 'You tired of me, you ready to get somebody new to play with?'

"But I told her, 'We don't do things anymore because I let you decide when we're gonna do something. You were raised to be a good girl, so you have big issues when we do something freaky. You get quiet afterwards like we've done something wrong, and I don't like anybody to feel guilty or ashamed of something they do with me. If you feel like that, I'd rather not do it, because that doesn't make me feel good. So, until you can come to grips with what I like, I'll leave you alone.'

"She tried to say she was fine with it, but the last time we did something freaky, she acted like she was going to trip. We'd gone to this place which is an X-rated video store on the bottom floor, and you can pay to go upstairs, like sixteen bucks a couple. Upstairs there's a little lounge area and a hallway with all these doors to separate rooms, and inside the rooms there's either a leather couch, or a bed, or just a chair if that's what you want, and each room has a TV so you can rent a movie to watch while you're in there. All the way at the end of the hall, there's a large room with a big-screen TV and theater seats, and they show movies there. You can go in there and just chill out while you're waiting on your room or whatever, but all around you, people are having sex.

"Most of the couples are just involved in oral sex, but on the back wall where there are no seats, people sometimes lean against the wall and fuck. So I took her there, and we had oral sex, but I told her I wanted to actually fuck her there, and she said, 'I promise you the next time we come back, I'll let you fuck me.'

"So we went back, and when we got upstairs to the large room, we went to the back. Now most people in there look from say average to kind of tore up. When we walked in, people were looking at us like, 'Be for real,' because we looked good, way above average compared to what they usually see in there.

"We stood up on the back wall, and couples who had already been fucking were sitting in some of the seats. But there was this one couple who was watching us, and when we started fucking, they came and stood beside us. The guy's girl was giving him a blow job, but the whole time he was watching us. I tried to ignore them 'cause it was kind of dark anyway, but then I bent my girl over and started doing her from the back, so he bent his girl over and started doing her from the back. Then this crazy fool told his girl to rub on my girl's breasts, and when she reached over to rub them, I thought my girl was going to knock the shit out of her because she don't play that. I was thinking, *Oh no, oh shit*, but she didn't say anything. She was cool with it, and that was a turn-on.

"On the way home she acted like she was offended by the girl touching her, but she said she wasn't because that's how white people are. When she got her breasts done, the white girls she worked with were like, 'Oh, you got new titties—Let me see them, let me feel them, ooh they're pretty,' so that's no big deal to her. She was used to it.

"I'd like to do a threesome with her, but she won't do it. She says if we got married, she'd do it, but not until then. I'm not stupid, and that's not going to make me get married, so she can forget that if that's what she's working on. I know a lot of women wonder why men like threesomes, but I think the reason we like it, or at least the reason I do, is because I like to know I can handle two women at the same time, and it's a turn-on to see a female with another female, but even then, you've got to make sure they don't get too involved with each other, because then they'll cut you right out of the picture. I've done it before, so I know I can handle it, but with every woman it's different. A lot of women don't want to do it, because they're too jealous, and if you really care about a person a lot, it's best not to because then your feelings get involved. It's best to do it with two people who you know don't have feelings for you, because then you don't have to deal with that jealousy."

ANTONIO

"If you want to know about bad dates, let me tell you—I've had my share. One of the worst dates I've had was with a woman who talked on her cell phone throughout our entire date. We went out, her cell phone rang once, and I thought, *Okay, cool, she had a girlfriend call to make sure everything was all right—no problem.* Then the girlfriend called back, and she missed that call, so she called her back. We were in the middle of playing pool, and I was like, 'It's your turn,' and she did the hand-in-the-face thing."

Antonio held up his hand, fingers splayed.

"I said, 'Not the hand in the face—oh no.' I wanted to go home right then. Then we played skeetball and basketball, and all the while she was on her cell phone talking to her girlfriend: 'Oooh, girl, I'm having so much fun. We're playing skeetball, and we're doing this and we're doing that,' and all the while I'm thinking she don't know better because nobody ever taught her, even though this was a woman in her early thirties who should've known better.

"Later on that night, I walked her to her car and said, 'Thanks for the date,' and got the hell out of there. I don't lie to women and say, 'I'm going to call you,' if I know there's no future. I just say, 'Thanks for the date. Bye.'

"The second bad date was when the woman talked marriage on our first and only date. I had just gotten divorced, and we were driving to a concert, and she said, 'So you're divorced, huh? I know how you feel right now. You've just been divorced a short time. I'm divorced, but you can't let being divorced make you bitter towards marriage.'

"I said, 'I'm not bitter. I just don't want to talk about marriage yet, because I just got divorced. I need some time, and they say it takes three times as long to heal as it does to get hurt, so it's going to take me a while.'

"'It's just like cutting your finger. That only takes an instant, but look how long it takes for that cut to heal. Relationships are the same way. She was like, 'Well, I'm just saying—I'm divorced, and I'm not bitter on marriage. I pray every day that God will send me a good man, and that man might just be you.'"

Antonio raised both eyebrows and scowled. "I said, 'You know what, girl, I'm pretty spiritual myself, and funny you'd bring that up. I talked to God this morning, and He said that if this topic came up, to tell you I'm not the one."

Antonio laughed. "It pissed her off royally. So she was like this in the car—" Antonio crossed his legs, folded his arms, and turned his head away. "We went into the concert, and I was sitting there, and to get her attention, I had to pat her on the back because she still had her head angled away from me just like she did in the car.

"We headed back to the car after the concert, and she had not talked to me the entire time. I asked, 'Would you like to go get something to eat?'

"She goes, 'I don't eat this late.'

"So I said, 'Well, would you like to go get a drink?' and she got this nasty attitude and said, in this snotty voice, *'I don't drank.'*

"So I got nasty right back and asked her, 'Would you like me to take your ass home, then?'

"She goes, *'That would be a good idea.'* So I took her ass home and never saw her again. And some women wonder why they can't get and keep a man. I hadn't even been divorced a year, and here she was bringing up the subject of marriage.

"I like dating because it's fun. If it's not fun, why do it? When my male friends ask me, 'Are you ever going to get married again?' I say, 'Why do I need to buy the cow when they sell the milk in the grocery store and it comes in every flavor? You get variety when you're dating, and you never have to get tired of the same old person.'

"I do get lonely sometimes, like on a cold or rainy night. Sometimes I wish I had somebody in bed with me but then I think about the trade-off. I think, *Okay I can have somebody to cuddle with right now but then I couldn't go to the gym as much as I wanted, I couldn't write whenever I wanted, I couldn't watch two football games at the same time on TV because flipping back and forth between channels drives a woman crazy. I couldn't read a book and just be quiet and I couldn't listen to my music loud.* All of these are trade-offs, so I like being by myself.

"The only thing I don't like are all the games and all the baggage that people bring to a relationship. One of my favorite quotes is, 'Work like you don't need the money, love like you've never been hurt, and dance like nobody's watching.' That's it right there. Women come to a relationship with all the baggage of their previous relationships. Like, 'Oh, you can't come to my house and know where I live,' and I can respect that for a while. I'll meet you somewhere. But why do I have to pay for what your previous boyfriends or husband did to you? That's the worse part of dating: you have to go through the initial stuff. You got to unwrap it to see what's in the box, and sometimes you don't like what you find once you get it unwrapped.

"I like beautiful, smart women. A woman who can get me excited is a woman who is beautiful to look at but at the same time, keep me interested with her intelligence. She's got something to talk about, she's funny, and she understands references I make. For example, if I quote Socrates she won't go, 'Oooh, does he play football?' I like a woman on my level, somebody with the same intellect, somebody I can relate to. My goal is to find a woman who cares about me like I care about her—that's all I want. If I could find that, it would be awesome.

"I had a friend who suggested that I do what she does in regards to men. She said, 'Write down the things you want in your perfect woman. Write down twenty attributes, and whenever you meet somebody you might be interested in getting to know better, start checking that person against that list.'

"I wrote that I wanted a woman who's cute and petite, I want a woman who's intelligent, I want a woman who's stylish, I want a woman who's this and who's that, and this woman that I met last week, Rose, she has like seventeen of the twenty attributes that I'd written down. I don't know her well enough to know if she has the other three, but I'm saying all of this to say that you got to *know* what you want, to *find* what you want. When somebody asks you what kind of woman you like, you can't be saying, 'Uh, I don't know. That one over there looks all right.' That definitely decreases your chances of being successful.

"If a woman has a big belly, I can't get aroused. I like a woman with big hips, a big butt and a small waist, but I don't like a big belly. The hip-to-waist ratio, where she's got that small waist and those big hips—that gets me very excited, and most black women are shaped that way. I love that because that small waist indicates that she's in shape, but her body is naturally curvy. Most black women are thick, and thick doesn't automatically mean fat, it means fine. She's fit, she's in shape, and she can go a long time.

"The biggest turn-on to a man is for a woman to say, 'Oh, it's so big,' while you're inside her because subconsciously you always compare yourself with every other man she's had. When I was younger, that was important to me, but now that I'm older, when she can just give me a compliment like, 'Oh, it's so *hard*,' that's good 'cause that's the best I can do. If she says, 'It's really hard—you must really be aroused,' I'm like, 'Yeah, that's as hard as I can get.' Let's just keep it real. That's the ultimate compliment at my age, and I'm not ashamed to admit it.

"In my experience, it seems that white women are a different kind of freaky. You can be as nasty as you want to be, and that's fine with them. I remember driving home with Lauren in my pickup truck and she tried to have sex with me while I was driving down the interstate. She was pulling off my clothes and sucking and kissing and grabbing and trying to ride me. I was almost being raped because I was fighting it. I said, 'Girl, we're going to get killed. I'm going sixty-five miles an hour, and people are looking at you butt naked in this truck.' I had to pull over or else we were going to die.

"I could do anything I wanted with this girl. Anything, no problem.

She liked to give, receive, anything, anywhere, but she didn't tell me she wasn't monogamous. She was sleeping with at least one other guy that I knew of, and he was in a band, so I knew he was getting around. That scared the hell out of me, so I went and got tested right away and put her ass on the inactive list. She was also into things that hurt like biting your nipples or biting your balls but pain turns me off. Don't be biting me, because that hurts, and I don't like being hurt. That shit ain't erotic at all to me."

EDWIN

"My one date from hell was with this woman in Maryland. One of the guys I worked with hooked me up with this woman whose husband had left her. He was like, 'Man you need to meet her. She's nice looking, she's got this big house, she got a good job.' So I went out with her.

"We went to this expensive Italian restaurant, and we were sitting there eating, and she had spaghetti hanging all out of her mouth, and then she started sucking and slurping the noodles like a three-year-old kid. She was gorgeous, but I couldn't handle her table manners.

"As we were heading back home after the date, she said, 'A friend of mine is having a house party tonight, would you like to go?'

"I told her no, I had some stuff to do early the next morning, but I was really thinking, *If you don't mind, I'd just as soon take your ill-mannered ass home.* That was a huge turn-off. Eating with your mouth open is a turn-off no matter how you slice it, and she didn't even have a clue. But I didn't tell her, because I didn't want to hurt her feelings, and at her age, she should have known better anyway. She called me a few times after that, but I never returned her calls.

"If you were to ask me if I'd ever dated a crazy woman, I'd have to say yeah. Hell, I was married to one. The marriage isn't on record, because I got it annulled, but I was married to a real crazy sister. Even after we separated, she was pushy. She would call me two or three times a day, crying and saying how much she loved me and how she couldn't live without me, and there were even times when she would just show up on my doorstep. She lived in Vegas, and one day she called and said, 'It's cold.'

"I'd visited her in Vegas and used to get up and go jogging in the morning, so I knew how cold it could get there. I said, 'Yeah, it does get cool there this time of morning,' and she says, 'No, I'm at your front door. It is cool out here, and my key doesn't work.'

"Well, I was flabbergasted—and we'd already talked about her showing up unexpectedly like this. We were having a trial separation, but she wanted to come see me, and I'd told her no, it was best that she stay where she was and that I stay where I was because we needed to think some things over. She thought by just showing up at my doorstep, she was going to force the relationship to work, but she was also checking to see if she could bust me in the house with somebody else.

"The cab that had dropped her off had already left, so I took her to a hotel to get a room to stay in until her flight left the next day, and all the while I was explaining to her why it wasn't a good idea to just pop up like this. When I told her that, she started threatening me, and the whole time she was talking, I was thinking, *This woman could fool around and try to kill me 'cause her ass is crazy as hell.*

"She said, 'You made a promise to me, you married me, so I'm going to take you to court and sue you and make you stay with me.' That is probably the worst relationship I've had in my life so far, and that's saying something because I've had some doozies.

"Now I try to go out with women who have something going on in their lives, women who don't want any type of drama or embarrassment. I try, but every now and then I go out to the club and sometimes . . . the liquor gets to me, and the women with the drama always seem to seek me out.

"One time I picked up this woman at a club at about two in the morning when I was full of liquor. I went home with her, and the next morning I woke up, looked across the bed, and said to myself, *Oh shit.* She was fat and ugly, and I had a hangover like a motherfucker. I looked at her and thought, *Oh no, please tell me I didn't.*

"She looked at me and said, 'Good morning, handsome. Would you mind if I took my hair off?'

"I was like, 'You know what, if you don't mind, wait until I leave.'

"One of the worst mistakes a woman makes is putting pressure on a man to commit and trying to take up too much of his time. Fellas want to just hang out with the fellas sometimes—everybody needs their own space. Women have a tendency to think that if a man is not with her, then he's with another woman. When the conversation starts going in that direction, that's another sign to me that it's time to go. I'll be thinking, *I don't need this in my life,* because I could see myself being married and hearing that crap all the time.

"I like women who are independent. If a woman is independent, she doesn't have to rely on me for everything. If she needs gas for her car, she knows how to go and get it. I don't mind doing that for her if I'm home, but I don't want her to be so helpless that she has to sit around and wait for me to do it because she doesn't know how. If she wants to go to the mall, that's cool, and I'll even go with her, but I don't want her to sit and wait for me to have some free time before she's able to do something she likes, because my schedule is very un-structured. I may get home at four or I may get home at ten, so I like a woman who can carry on when I'm not around. I do want a woman who cares enough about me so that when I am there, she likes having me in her presence or she'll make me feel needed even though she knows how to do things on her own. If she's independent, she knows how to survive, but she also knows when to appreciate having that loving man in her life.

"I don't like being smothered. Me and my woman can be in the same house, but I still need my space sometimes, and it's nothing against her. If I'm just reading a book or watching a baseball game and I'm sitting here and she's over there, that's fine. I just don't want to be smothered, and I respect that a woman needs her own space as well. I want a woman who can understand that.

"A woman who doesn't present herself well turns me off. If she uses a lot of foul language or it's obvious that she's uneducated because she's speaking in Ebonics, that turns me off. I don't like a woman who can't hold a conversation. I don't like a ghetto mentality, and I don't like a woman who dresses like a slut."

WARREN

"I think most men would prefer an independent woman because he doesn't have to sit there and babysit her or worry about whether she's going to be able to handle what she needs to handle while he's gone. That's more challenging than having a woman who's got to depend on a man for each and every little thing.

"As for women who say they can't get no man, because they're too independent—naw, there's something else going on. Her independence ain't driving those men away. Every man would prefer a woman financially stable because everybody that goes up that ladder got to come down at some time, and if you got an independent woman and you get laid off today, that woman can help you carry on. That's the kind of woman you want, and most men look at that. They want somebody who can help them, not somebody all the time with their hand out. You got a lot of independent women who don't tell you the whole story. The whole story is not so much that they're independent; some of them are just real greedy. They want what they got, and they want what you got too.

"I always hear women saying they're having a hard time finding men, but it depends on where they're looking for them at. Where would you go and look for a good man? You not going to go in a bar and find him. You're not going on the corner to find him. Where are good men? Good men are in places like church, business functions and seminars, office parties—that's where you meet people that are into something. You can go out to these clubs, and by two o'clock in the morning, everybody looks good. If you don't allow yourself to get out there and see what's in the world and find other opportunities to meet men, then sure you're going to have a problem. It doesn't make sense to keep looking in the same old place. If you're not getting anywhere, look someplace new.

"Being an independent woman has nothing to do with it. It's your personality. What do you have to offer? You got to sell yourself—you can't just go out there and think, *I'm this, I'm that, I got this, I got that, I can do this, I don't need no man.* Yeah, you're going to intimidate a man with that attitude because if you don't need no man, you're going to come across that way, so don't no man need to bother with you.

"I don't think men are intimidated by independent women. I think they look for independent women because if you look at it, the women who are not independent and not working, what are they doing? They're on welfare and having babies, and they looking for somebody to take care of them. Some of them even have babies just so they can get child support, but why should a woman sit on her butt and wait for child support when she can go to work? I realize that man is just as much responsible for that child as that woman is, but she's more responsible because she had the ultimate control. It's her body. She didn't have to get no baby if she really didn't want one. I know the man plays a part, and his part is the fact that he's going to try you, but you got to think for yourself, and a real independent woman wouldn't get caught like that. She may have sex, but she's going to protect herself. She's not going to allow herself to get stuck with babies until she gets the ring. That's a decision both of you should make because you got to prepare for children."

RUBEN

"To me, a relationship is like a twig. You nurture it, you prune it, you water it, you fertilize it, and it grows. That's a relationship. If you take an old tree that's been around forever, there ain't a damn thing you can do with it. You might prune it, and it might flower, but it ain't gon' grow, just like that big old tree outside, and that's the man's job. That man had better be the keeper of his garden because if he's not, that little tree is going to be looking for somebody else to take care of it. If a man doesn't pay attention to his garden, he won't know who's going in and coming out."

LANDON

"Every man is attracted to a different type of woman. For some men, it's all about the looks. Take me, for instance: I used to take a dime piece over a woman with an intelligent mind any day. A dime piece is a woman who's got it all. She got the body and she got the looks, so you can't measure her on a scale of one to ten, because she's a twelve.

"I need a woman who can stimulate me mentally; my biggest problem is finding a woman with brains. You can find a woman who's a dime piece all day, but most of them are dumber than a box of rocks, ain't got no damn sense. She'll get pissed off at you, go off and throw a flowerpot at your head, spit at you, the whole nine. You got to find a woman you can work with. Women these days have been raised up a whole different way. There ain't too many good women out there no more.

"I dated six different women a week the first four years I was in the military, so I know there ain't that many good ones out there. The good ones are too thick for me, and I don't mean *thick* as in 'fine.' They might have a real pretty face, but they're overweight. Yeah, I know it's superficial, but it's also the truth. It's no worse than sitting in a restaurant and turning down dessert because you don't like chocolate. It's that simple: I know what I like and what I don't like.

"I don't want no size sixteen or size twenty woman. I don't like the way it feels when we make love, and yes, I have made love with big women, but I prefer a woman I can wrap up and still feel my hands on my own arms when I hug her. I like my woman little, so little I can just spin her ass around when we're fucking.

"I've tried to be with intelligent, ladylike, quiet women, but I run over women like that. I prefer a woman that will be like, 'Nigga, where you going?' or 'You better call me when you get wherever the hell it is you going.' But she got to have the look I like because if she don't have that look, I ain't going to be bothered. I need a woman I can look at 24-7, every day, and be like, *Damn, baby is fine as hell*. If she ain't got it going on like that, she can't question me about shit.

"I've gone out with strippers, but I didn't date them seriously, because I can't deal with a woman I'm with grinding on some other man. When I date a woman, I want to see her every day, every minute of the day if I can, and I don't want her seeing nobody else.

"I attract all types of women because of my looks and my laid-back personality. If I'm into a woman, I'll do whatever she wants to make her happy—that's me. Unfortunately, every woman I've been with for the last few years has been crazy, and at the rate I go through women, that's a lot of crazy-ass women.

"It's just like a woman who attracts a man that beats her ass. When she finally gets out of that relationship, she ends up in another one just like it, and it's because she attracts that type. I know for a fact that I attract crazy-ass women. I got to be careful with that now because I have a child. I got to understand up front just how crazy this woman might be because if she harms my child, I might kill her ass.

"Right now I dictate how my daughter's personal life is going to be, so if I go out there and be a player and run a bunch of women, my daughter's going to grow up and be a ho point-blank because that's all she's seen.

"Women always think that the way into a single father's heart is to act like they're crazy about his child, but that's bullshit. It ain't that I don't respect her—we'll end up being friends, and she can call me if she needs some emotional support, because I'm one of those people that everybody wants to talk to. But the woman who would catch my interest is the one who would actually think about *me*. A lot of women will buy your child something to get next to you, but that don't work with me.

"A woman who would say, 'You know what, it ain't even about your child. It's about you because I'm trying to be in it with you, so I bought you a sweater, I bought you this CD. I'm not going to try to swindle my way into your heart through your child. I'm going to come at you and buy you something because I was thinking about you.' To me that's coming real. Coming fake is, 'I'm going to buy his child something so he'll take notice of me.' But naw, come at me. If you was thinking about me, if you thought I was a nice man, whatever, get something for me because you know what, my child is going to be taken care of—you knew that when you met me. When you met me, she was dressed nice, her hair was done, she was clean, and she's going to be taken care of, so you take care of me."

4

WHY LIE?

SIMEON

"The biggest lie a woman ever told me was that I was her baby's daddy," Simeon laughed.

"My ex-girlfriend told me that big-ass lie, and I found out because I had some suspicions and asked her to get a DNA test. What happened was I was having this house built, and we were dating, but it wasn't working out. She'd gotten herself into a bad situation financially, so I said, 'Look, I'm going to be in this apartment for a couple of months, I'm already paying these bills anyway, so you're welcome to stay here, but let's be realistic: our relationship is not going in the direction it should be going, and we both know it. So when I move into my house, you're not coming with me. Save all the money you can, don't worry about the bills here, and you should have an adequate amount of money to do something when I move out,' but evidently she thought, *Uh-uh. It ain't going down like that. You buying a house, and we both going to move into it.* I know that's what she thought because she helped me move in, papered the shelves and everything, then told me she was pregnant.

"Lying about your baby's real father is what I would call 'the big one,' and I shouldn't have let it get that far. But you know what—I need to take the blame for that because I put myself out there. I could spend a lot of time blaming her and saying, 'Oh, you did this or my friends did that, and they should've told me,' because normally when you've just gotten out of a bad relationship and your friends find out that you've ended it, that's when they start telling you about things that person was doing all along. It's like if you saw your friend being cheated on. You should tell him now instead of waiting until the marriage is over ten years later.

"I don't usually lie, but my biggest flaw as a man is holding a grudge. I believe that a man of character has the ability to forgive and move on, and I don't know if it's a pride thing or what—but me? Man, I can hold on to something forever. I'm going to give it to you from a male point of view: a man can cheat on a woman and insist on her understanding. He's like, 'Look, okay I cheated. Forget about it, and let's move on.' But most men, if he finds out that his woman has cheated on him, he has a hard time forgetting that his woman has laid up with another man. He'll be thinking, *Was he better than me? Was his dick bigger than mine? Did he last longer than me? Did she do this to him?* That kind of stuff is hard for a man to deal with. That's why if a woman cheats on me, I'm through.

"Life is a whole lot easier if you don't bullshit, so I don't lie if I can help it, and I don't like women who lie. Just stay straight with it, be honest with it. If you want to do something else—sure, I'm going be hurt, but just say, 'Simeon, you aren't the man for me,' and go on. Don't string me along and have another guy over here and then have me up in a confrontation with this other man when he approaches me and says, 'Hey what you doing with my woman?' I'm going to be like, 'What is he talking about,' because I can get stupid real fast. Yeah, I work with numbers all day and I'm a nice guy, but if you step to me, if you push me, I'm going to push back."

QUINCY

"One time I met a woman who said she only had one child, and then I found out she had four. I've met some who said they didn't have any kids, and then when I got to know them, they casually mentioned that their mama or grandmama was raising their kid in another state. That happens a lot. As a matter of fact, one woman I met even told me that women hide their kids—especially if they feel like they can't get a man because they have kids. They'll get to know you, and then you find out the truth. I'm thinking, *If a woman lies about her own kids, I got to wonder what else she's lying about or hiding,* so when I find that out, the relationship is over as far as I'm concerned because I can't trust her.

"Men lie too, but I try not to do that. I might lie to get out of a situation, but even then I won't really lie. I might just tell a half-truth like, 'I thought I was ready to be in a relationship, but I've been single so long that I just don't think I'm ready.' I'd rather do that to save a woman's feelings because I don't want to be cold or mean. Other than that, I wouldn't lie about nothing, because I don't have to.

"Let me give you some more examples of the lies women tell. My buddy set me up with his girlfriend's homegirl, and when we talked on the phone, she described herself as being a Hispanic woman about five-four, with a cute face, a pretty smile, and shoulder-length hair. We set it up, and when I got to her house and she opened the door, all I could see was this woman who looked like a Shetland pony. I wanted to *run* back to my car. She had actually lied about how she looked— like I wouldn't find out she had a long torso and really short legs. To make matters worse, she was watching me like a hawk and I was her last meal, and the whole time I was trying to think of a reason to leave. Finally, she asked me if I had any good CDs in my car, which I did, and when I went out to get them, I got in the car, started the engine, and took off.

"Another time I was working, and a woman called for one of the guys who worked with me, and I told her he wasn't in. Then she asked me if I knew this guy's wife, and I said, 'No, I don't know his wife. Would you mind telling me what's going on?'

"She said she just had to tell somebody what she'd overheard because she didn't like to see people being tricked. She said, 'I heard his wife talking, and she said she put something in his food.' Then she completely changed the conversation and said, 'You sound nice, are you married?' We had a brief conversation, and then she started calling every night because I wouldn't give her my home phone number.

"Don't ask me why, but after about two weeks I gave in and agreed to meet her, but I got there early and parked so I could check her out first. She pulled up in a '72 Chrysler that was longer than three cars put together, but I played it cool and just sat there and waited for her to get out of the car and go into the bar. Man, when she finally rolled up out of that car, I saw that she was no more than five feet tall and weighed about two thirty. I waited until she got inside the bar then drove off so fast, I shot gravel all over the parking lot because I was not in the mood to lie my way out of another bad date.

"Then my mom set me up with a young woman she knew. The woman was half-Hispanic and half-black, and her ex-husband was Hispanic and had been a jerk, so she'd decided that she wasn't going to date any more Hispanic men. Judging from our phone conversations, she seemed to be pretty nice, and she was trying to get her life together, so I was looking forward to meeting her. When she drove up to meet me she was in a '64 Chevy, and it was a wreck. I thought, *Damn, here I go again.* She got out of the car, and I could see that she was gorgeous, but tall and thin, which is not usually my type, but I figured I'd give it a chance anyway, so I headed for the door.

"By the time I got close enough to really see her, I noticed that she had hickeys on both sides of her neck, and when she smiled she had some kind of green shit around her gum line that looked like algae, but it was too late to back out of the date. We went inside and ordered an appetizer, but when she started eating and talking at the same time and food started dropping out of her mouth, I lost my appetite. I just couldn't believe a pretty, halfway intelligent woman wasn't taking better care of her teeth and that she would even show up for a date with hickeys all over her neck in the first place. What the hell was she thinking?"

GREG

"Hell yeah, I've lied to my lady. I might lie when she asks me where I've been or who I've been with because I may not want her to know. I've been with some women who lie a lot, and they mostly lie about the same things I lie about: finances, affairs, and stuff like that. It's difficult for me to verbalize my true feelings with a woman, and I think it goes back to me opening myself up because I don't want to be hurt again. It's not hard for me to say 'I love you,' because I can say it and not even mean it. The lady I'm with now, when I say that I really mean it, but anybody else, I can say it and not mean it because I know that's what they want to hear. I learned from my male relatives to just tell women what they want to hear. They always said, 'If you tell them what they want to hear, you can get anything you want,' and that's the truth."

XAVIER

"I lie to my girl about things that I think are kind of dumb, but the reason I do it is to avoid arguments or unnecessary questions. The reason I say unnecessary questions is because no matter what she asks, I can tell her whatever I want to, and it's up to her whether she believes it or not. A woman can wear you down with all that fussing and stuff, and sometimes it gets to the point where it's easier to lie than it is to tell the truth, because she really doesn't want to hear the truth. They ask, and ask, until you tell them a lie. Then they say, 'You're just telling a damn lie to get me to shut up,' and my response to that is, 'Well, why the hell did you ask me, then?' I think women lie just as much or more than men do."

PIERRE

"I don't lie to women—like I said earlier, I'm pretty up front, so I'd prefer the women I date to be honest with me. I can respect someone's honesty regardless of the issue. I know a lot of women who have fucked a lot of guys. I've met women who said they used to be prostitutes or did all kinds of crazy stuff, but it doesn't faze me, and I'm not going to judge them. The thing most women lie about is whether or not they're seeing another guy. Women are out there trying to be players like men, but most of them aren't really good at it. There are some who are, but I'd just prefer a woman be straight with me. I can respect her more that way."

COLLIER

"If I've ever lied to my lady, it's for her benefit. I don't just lie to lie. But I have found that a woman is quicker to believe a lie than she is to believe the truth. Now, you want to know what would hurt me? If I tell you something from my heart and you don't believe me, that hurts. It's the little bitty things like that that hurt me, not something big. I'm a very sensitive person, maybe more sensitive than a lot of women. I feel things in my heart. I feel deeply for the people I care about, and sometimes that ain't good. That can be a hurting thing, because if they hurt, I hurt worse than they do.

Your soul can go all the way down to the bone. That's why love can be a hurting thing. If you love someone with everything you got and that person mistreats you, lies to you, or cheats on you, that can hurt you to the bone, and some people never get over a hurt like that."

ANTONIO

"Honesty is important in a relationship. You got to be able to live with yourself, so you need to be honest from the get-go. Always be honest—that's my thing. I never lie. I never lie to a woman or just tell her what she wants to hear. If she asks me if I think she's fat, I won't say, 'Naw, girl, you're not fat!' I'll say, 'You're a big-boned girl, and I like it. Only a dog wants a bone.'

"It's so easy to be honest and be yourself, and most guys don't realize that. Just be yourself, be natural, be friendly. Don't be threatening, and don't be too aggressive. Relationships seem to work better when you let a person know how you really feel. Just like the saying goes, 'To thine own self be true,' more so than being true to somebody else, I'm being true to myself. I'm not trying to get over, I'm not trying to get anything from her, I'm not going to get anywhere by lying. I always try to be honest, that way six months down the line when she asks me, 'What do you mean you don't want to get married?' I can honestly say, 'Girl, I told you the first time I met you that I'm enjoying living by myself. I finally got my child out of my house, and living alone is nice.'"

EDWIN

"I don't lie to the women I date." Edwin grinned.

"I just stretch the truth a little. I may say something like, 'I'm just going to stay home tonight and rest,' when in reality, I may be going out to the club.

"I don't lie about involvement. I'll tell a woman when I'm in a serious relationship with another woman. I only date the one woman I'm in the serious relationship with, but I do hang out or go to the movies or to dinner with my other lady friends, and I'm pretty much up front with them. I don't even use the term *dating* with them—some I've never even kissed. We're just hanging out.

"Now, there is a chance that I might be kissing the one I'm in the relationship with and a few of the ones I'm just hanging out with, but they don't need to know all that. They never ask, and if they were to ask, I don't know what I would say. I'd probably stretch the truth. I'd definitely stretch the truth with the one I care more about because we've been dating for a while now and I owe her that respect. I wouldn't want to hurt her.

"Women lie too. Just like the times when we're supposed to get together for a movie or something and she calls the next day and says, 'You know what, the battery ran down on my car and my cell phone went out, so I couldn't call you.'

"When I hear an excuse like that, I'm like, *Yeah right, that sounds like some shit a guy would say.* The first thing you think about when she starts doing stuff like that is she could be married, so you wonder if she's being honest about anything.

"I was dating a woman for an extended period of time and found out later she was married, and when I asked her why she didn't tell me, she said, 'You didn't ask.' She was separated, but still, I don't date women who are married, and I don't date women with obligations. That's just something I don't do. No matter how good they look, I don't do that.

"When I use the word *obligation*, I mean she's either engaged or she's in a serious relationship with another man. I don't want to get involved with her, because it's not right, and I don't want a woman coming back to me and saying, 'Well, I left my husband or I left my boyfriend for you, and you aren't doing me right.' I don't want to hear it.

"Like I told this one lady when I found out she was married, 'If you decide you want to divorce him, then give me a call afterwards, but until then there is no use in me seeing you.'

"My fourth wife was married the entire time we were dating and didn't get divorced until about a month before we got married. As soon as I found out about that small oversight, I had the marriage annulled. She'd had a child in her previous marriage, and I was trying to help her get custody of the child, and the lawyer said, 'About your divorce—' Well, I jumped in and said, 'Oh yeah, she was divorced eight or ten years ago,' because that was the shit she'd told me. But when the lawyer started pulling out paperwork, I saw that she'd gotten divorced only a few weeks before we got married, and I was like, *What the hell is this?*

"She told me that she'd been separated for six years, and I asked, 'So why didn't you get your divorce?' She said he wouldn't sign the papers, so I was like, 'You know what, something is very wrong here, and we need to step back.' That was the biggest lie a woman ever told me, and if she hadn't needed to see that lawyer about getting custody of her child, I never would've known."

WARREN

"I would lie to keep the peace, just to keep her from being angry or upset or worried about something that really doesn't matter. I was talking to a friend of mine the other day who has a motorcycle, and he'd recently gone to the casino. This girl he'd had a previous relationship with asked for a ride home. Well, just as she got on the motorcycle and they were leaving, his wife pulls up and sees them, so she starts chasing him. He finally shakes her, drops the woman off, then goes to his brother's house to lay low until his wife can calm down, but when he gets to his brother's house, his son is there and says, 'You might as well go home Pops, she's waiting for you.'

"As soon as he pulled up in the carport, his wife came out the door asking, 'Who was that with you on that motorcycle, and why didn't you stop?'

"He told her, 'I didn't stop, because I knew you wouldn't listen. You were going to get out of your car and want to fight the lady, and you were going to make a scene that wasn't necessary.' So you see, she forced him to lie. He felt that if he'd told her this was a girl he used to date, she never would've believed it was all innocent, but that's what happens when you don't take the time to be with your spouse, when you don't really know the person you're married to.

"If he comes in and says, 'We're invited to a party tonight, and I want you to go,' the first thing you want to know is, 'Who's giving it?

Where is it at?' What difference does that make? Your man asked you to go to a party with him, and that should be your focus and your concern. It don't matter what kind of party it is—they can be running around jumping off the ceiling, it shouldn't matter. What matters is he invited you; he wanted you there with him.

"That is one of the big problems with relationships: women force men to lie, men force women to lie, and the only way you can solve that is be with your mate, spend time with them. This is not a sixty-forty deal; this is a fifty-fifty deal. When you take those vows, you take those vows seriously, and if you don't want your man out there in the street with somebody else, then you go out there with him. If you spent more time going with him, you wouldn't even think about it when he's out there by himself. If you're doing the things you're supposed to do, it's gonna work. Trust me."

5
MARRIAGE

TERRENCE

"Marriage . . . All I can say about marriage is that I love it. I've never been happier than I am now. Even though I had a good family and my parents loved me, I never felt like I was complete. I dated a lot of girls before I met my wife, and I didn't ever think that I would meet a woman who would make me feel like the perfect man, the perfect lover, or the perfect friend, but then when I met Sienna, it was like I'd known her all my life. There was nothing I couldn't share with her. I feel like I've married my best friend, and I feel very blessed, to say the least.

"I know some guys who don't like being married, and I often ask them why they stay married if they feel that way. Why would you spend your days and nights with a person you have to bitch and moan and complain about all the time? They always tell me, 'Man, you don't know nothing about life, 'cause you're too young. You've only been married a year, and right now everything is wonderful. She looks good, she feels good, she still wants to have sex three times a day, and all that—but just wait until you get a few years under your belt. Then you'll be singing a different tune,' but I don't believe that. My wife and I went to premarital counseling at our church for a year before we got married, and one of the things I learned is that before you marry someone, you need to know who you are as a man. I had to find out what happiness means for me because it's not her responsibility to *make* me happy, and I had to learn about compromise because I never had to compromise before. If a woman did something I didn't like, I just dumped her."

KEN

"The thing that makes a woman marriage material is knowing that I can trust her absolutely, that we can communicate, and that we have a love that transcends everything the world will throw at us. I wanted a woman who would always be able to make me laugh and I would be able to look at her every single night and still want to make love to her like it's our first time. I wanted a woman who would love our children as much as we love each other, a woman who understood what the vow 'till death do us part' meant, a woman who would be my best friend. I got all of these things in Zonora."

QUINCY

"The experience I had with my ex-wife was the worst relationship I've ever had. I met her when I was twenty-five years old, out there living the single life. I was tired of playing that old game, and at first she played the role of wife and mother so well that she appeared to be everything I thought I wanted. You know they say the way to a man's heart is through his stomach, and the girl threw down in the kitchen like my mom could, not to mention that she could throw down in the bedroom like a pro too.

"She had two beautiful children, and I think I clicked with them more than I did with her. We dated for about four months before we started living together, which was too soon, and about six months later we got married. Once we said, 'I do,' that's when I found out what she was really about, but I thought if I did everything I could, or gave her everything she wanted, things would get better. But in reality I knew three months into the marriage, maybe sooner, that she wasn't all she pretended to be. It was just a big mistake all around. It finally got to the point where we'd be in bed and it seemed like there was a big partition between us. I'd just lay there and think, *What in the hell am I doing here? I've got to go; this shit ain't gonna' work.*

"Three years and two babies later, when things still weren't better after trying to hang in there for my kids, I decided it wasn't worth it for any of us, because that house was like a war zone, and I just couldn't stay. Even her oldest daughter, who was only seven years old, would say things like, 'You do more than she does. You're here more than she is, and when she is here, she don't do nothing and you do everything,' which was sad. We were pretty much just married on paper anyway because she was doing her own thing, even though she said she wanted to be married.

"When we finally divorced, it got ugly because she used the kids against me, knowing that would hurt me. She'd do things like crack the door open and say they weren't there when I'd go to pick them up, or say they weren't feeling well or something like that because she knew how bad I wanted to see them. I don't know why women do that, especially when so many men don't even want to be bothered with their own children. Sure, it hurt me, but it was also hurting my boys because they need a father in their life, and her girls were hurt too because their dad never came around. I was the only father figure they had.

"I wish I could say I loved her so much that I was heartbroken, but after all the shit she put me through, how could I be? Once you start feeling that way about a woman, your heart closes down. You say to yourself, *Okay, I'm getting tired of this shit, so I'll be glad when it's over.*

"I used to get lonely when I first got divorced. If my phone didn't ring, I'd feel kind of bad, but lately, I'm glad when nobody calls me, because I can come home and do just what I want to do. I mean, it's nice to have somebody here when I want company and sex, but then I want her to go home so I can have my space and do things my way without having to answer to anybody. I don't have a problem with being alone; I never have. I actually enjoy doing the things I want to do without having to worry about considering what someone else might like to do. Don't get me wrong, I enjoy women, but I don't have to have a woman around to be happy, because I'm comfortable with myself."

GREG

"I'm not married now, but I was married before, for about a year. It didn't work out, because we just didn't see eye to eye. She was not family oriented, and I couldn't get along with my in-laws, because they were too involved in our marriage. I was about twenty-eight at the time, and she was a year younger than me, so you would think that at that age we both knew what we wanted. We'd dated for a long time, and things were fine, but once you get married, things seem to change.

"One of the things that really messed our marriage up was that she was listening to her friends who had been married for a while and were more established. We were newlyweds, and she didn't understand that we couldn't have the same things her friends had, because we were just starting out. She wanted everything to happen too fast, and I couldn't give her everything when she wanted it. I kept telling her, 'Hey, we just got married, and it takes time to accumulate things,' but she just couldn't or didn't want to understand where I was coming from, so we decided to go our separate ways. There was no love lost, because for me, when it's over, it's over. If I walk away from a relationship, that means my feelings were already gone anyway."

DANTE

"Being married doesn't stop you from being attracted to other women, not even women you're related to, so for men there's always a fine line to walk. Men have to be careful because it's easy to lust after another woman, real easy. Being with a woman sexually is on a man's mind ninety percent of the time. I fight against it every day, and I do mean *every day!*

"That's why I say I'm not sure it was such a good idea to stay a virgin for so long, because I didn't get that lust out of my system. All of what I could have had is still in the back of my mind, even after being married ten years, and that's a threat to my wife. She's always worried that I'll have an affair because she knows she's the only woman I've ever been with, and she knows there's temptation out there for me. I pray that I don't ever get involved with another woman, but man, it ain't easy.

"Marriage is the greatest institution in the world, but it's hard work. It's work every day, but I'd do it all over again. I like the stability, I have a friend, and I can have sex any time I want to—well, just about any time I want to. You got to have somebody to share your life with, so I'm glad I've got her.

"There's nothing really bad about marriage, but sometimes you stop and think about what you might be missing out on, and your mind starts to wander. Really, the feeling of a good sexual partner is based on tenderness; it's what you feel with that person. Yeah, I have plenty of opportunities to get with other women, and it would probably feel like the best sex I've ever had because it happened in the heat of the moment, but when it's all said and done, shit, the love ain't there—it's back at the house.

"You start thinking, *Damn. I'm laying up here with this woman and I shouldn't even be here. With my luck, the damn car probably won't even crank when I get outside. Then I got to get a tow truck and explain all of that when I get home. Or, I'll probably have a wreck, and this other woman is sitting up here in the car with me, and she'll try to sue or some crazy shit like that.* That's the kind of luck I have.

"But on the serious tip, what makes my marriage work is that we have God in our lives. That's the only reason we're still together.

Every night we say a little prayer together and we read the Bible together, and that's what keeps it going. Of course, I could make more money so we could pay off the bills and have less stress, and that would make it better, but that's everybody's story. That's life. The hardest thing is staying faithful, 'cause I could be locked up between another woman's legs in a heartbeat, just like flipping a light switch."

G.G.

"I got really close with one of the married guys I dated. I met him at the pool hall and then started going over to his house to watch football with him while his wife went out shopping with her girlfriends, and she never had a clue about us. He told me that he was bored with his marriage and said that since his wife had the baby, she never wanted to have sex anymore, and when she did, he'd have to initiate it and it only lasted about ten minutes.

"I used to think it was funny when he'd say, 'Man, I don't know what happened to that little freak I married. Homegirl used to give the best blow jobs I'd ever had and could work that ass until I was worn out. Now I can't even get her to touch my dick, let alone suck it. She won't even put her mouth in the general vicinity. If I place my hand behind her neck and even apply a little bit of pressure to it like I'm leading her head in that direction, her whole neck will stiffen up like it's in the last stages of rigor mortis. I can't ever get my freak on no more, and the shit is beginning to piss me off. I'm not asking her to be nasty all the time, just every now and then. Just lick my balls or something, damn!'

"One Saturday afternoon she went shopping and left us at the house to babysit and watch football. He must've known that I was attracted to him because after he put the baby down for her nap, one thing led to another, and we had our first brief encounter. After that, whenever his wife would leave the house, usually leaving the two of us sitting on the couch staring at some game on TV, we would end up having sex, or there were times when he would tell her that we were going to go and drink beer and shoot pool, but instead we'd get a room for the evening.

"One time we played this game. We went to a straight club and made a bet on who could get phone numbers from the baddest ladies there, and the loser was supposed to pay for the room the next time we got together. It was a lot of fun, especially when we ended up with some of the same numbers. We called it even and went home to our women. In the end, we had to break up because once again, this was a brother who could not admit to being bisexual. He told me that he just happened to be a man who liked to get his freak on, and just because he was getting his freak on with another man, that didn't make him gay or bi."

MALIK

"It wasn't until this past year that I even learned a lot about marriage. I ran across a Bible thing on the Internet that talks about the institution of marriage, and learned a lot of things I never knew before I got married. Not ever being taught, not having a good role model, not knowing what you're supposed to know about marriage makes it hard. All I knew was what I saw on TV or what I heard. You get married, you have kids, you try to get along, and if you don't, you get divorced, you know? I began to understand why it's important for couples to go to church. That's a good place to learn *how* to be married, because I didn't have a clue. I didn't know what it took for a man to please his wife in any area except sexually, and I didn't know what it meant for you to get along in a godly or spiritual way.

"It's the same way with Christian marriage counseling. You go to the counselor before getting married to learn what marriage is all about. You don't just get married and expect things to work out because you exist in a household together, and I have to admit that a lot of the problems in our relationship on my end was that I never had a role model to pattern myself after.

"I've been married fourteen years, and if I had it to do all over again, I still think I would do it. We've had a lot of good years together, and she has the same life goals that I do, but if I knew early on in our marriage what I know now, things would be a lot better. When we're getting along, I really enjoy having her as a partner. I have somebody I can talk to, somebody to comfort me, and somebody to celebrate with when we achieve things, and that's nice.

"But I hate all the bitching that you've got to listen to, all the times when we're not getting along, and all the arguments we have. I'm married to one of these women who wants everything done today. Not tomorrow—today—and I'm a procrastinator, so I don't always agree that what she asks me to do needs to be done right then and there. If she wants a picture hung and it's sitting over there by the wall not hurting anybody, then I don't see why I can't wait until the weekend to hang it. What's the urgency in getting a picture hung? I've talked to my therapist about it, and he says that a man can do ninety-nine things right and then do one thing wrong, and it knocks the ninety-nine things down to nothing, and you've got to build them all up again.

"On the other hand, a woman can do ten things right and do one thing wrong, and it takes a man less time to forgive her and let her back into his good graces. I think men are just more forgiving than women when it comes to small things. Now if it's something like an affair, then that's different because in a situation like that, either party can lose it and never want to forgive, and they may be justified.

"I think a lot of the time I'm the one who makes the marriage work. I give in a lot and give up a lot. I love golf and I love basketball, and she feels that with our kids being the age they are, they need more of my attention. So me sacrificing a lot of the stuff that I like doing is probably what makes it work. I know I give in a lot more than she does, and that makes her happy, but then I'm not happy. A lot of my friends tell me they wouldn't go through the things I'm going through, but I have my two kids and my niece to think about, so maybe I have to put up with more than what someone else would put up with, and that causes a lot of arguments.

"My daughter always tells me she hates it when me and her mom fuss, but I try to explain to her that people have different opinions, so that's automatically going to happen. I tell her, 'Just like you fuss with your brother and your cousin because you all don't agree on everything, it's the same way with me and your mom. I'm sorry that we do it in front of you.' There are times when I try to hold back so that we don't fuss in front of the kids, but sometimes I just can't. I wouldn't be myself if I did that. I find myself backing off because I realize that if I just say exactly what I want to say, it's going to make things worse. Not saying what I'm feeling doesn't hurt me in the long run, but at that moment it doesn't make me totally happy either.

"If she would just meet me halfway and be more understanding, things would be so much better, but I think she's worried that I won't do enough for our kids because my niece is here now. She has a hard time disciplining her or saying anything negative to her because she says that's my job. She said she prayed to the Lord about it and has decided to stay out of it, but I told her, 'This is your house too, so it's all right for you to get on her ass if she messes up.'

"But no, she says, 'That's your place because she's your niece. She's had discipline from a woman all her life because all she had was her mom. Now she needs to get it from a man.'

"But you can't just say that the man is the only one in the house who should discipline the kids. If a kid is living in your house, you need to discipline them whether they're yours or not.

"A month ago, I talked to my wife and told her that I really would like to sit down and reevaluate our marriage. Now that I'm reading more and understanding the commitment that marriage requires, I would like to discuss renewing our vows. That's not something she's too keen on. She says she's not sure. If we get to the point where we can renew our vows, I feel that our marriage would be somewhat stronger, but we've got to get some kind of handle on where we are with each other. I'm trying to do what I've learned that a man should do, but it's almost like if I don't do anything, she won't either, so I guess it's all on me."

NEAL

"Listen at me good—I was married in 1973, and we stayed married until 1989. During that marriage, I would say that I really only had a marital relationship from '73 until '83, because during that time I felt we were one. After that, we weren't married. We were just living together.

"It's a tremendous experience to go through a divorce, but after my divorce, plenty brothers came to me to comfort me. I'm talking about guys I knew who were doctors, lawyers, professors, preachers—all kinds of guys. They came to express their sympathy for me concerning my divorce, but in turn they needed to talk themselves. My divorce presented them with an opportunity to come and vent. They felt they could talk to me about what was going on in their homes once they knew I'd gone through some of the same things.

"I think as black males we need to push that old macho mentality aside and start sharing our concerns with each other. I like to use the word *concerns* rather than *problems* because men usually won't share their problems with each other, but they will share their concerns. Women think differently—they're much more open. But it's not manly to tell another man that I have not had sex with my wife, or my wife is sleeping in a different bedroom, or we have separate bank accounts. I tell guys every day, 'You think you have a personal problem, until you start discussing it with another man and find that it's a universal problem.'

"There were a number of things that caused my marriage to fail. First it started with her accusing me of having affairs, and once she accused me of that, it changed things because you always feel the way you think, and you're gonna act the way you feel. So for a number of years, I was accused of having affairs with women I worked with, female friends, and church members, and it wasn't true. Then this guy who lived across the street called my wife and told her that I was sleeping with his wife. He showed my wife a picture of a guy he thought was me, but it was a guy who looked like me. It was his wife's boss, and they were having an affair.

"I've always been the type of person who will tell you one time that what you're accusing me of is wrong, and if you still want to believe I'm lying, there's nothing more I can do because I'm not going to keep repeating myself over and over to make you believe me. You're going to believe what you want anyway, but if you're not a real strong person, things like that can overwhelm you, and before you know it, you've allowed someone else to ruin your marriage. I felt the change in our marriage, and I went to her and said, 'Hey, things are different. What's going on?' All she would say was, 'You'll find out,' so it progressively got worse because the weak link was already there.

"Soon after, I found out she was having an affair herself simply because she thought that was what I was doing, and once I found that out, my focus changed from keeping the marriage intact to focusing on raising our kids and making sure I was always in their life. From that point on, I knew divorce was inevitable because I've always had the mentality that if we were mature enough to come together in a relationship when the fire was burning and the flame was hot, we should be mature enough to move on if that flame went out, because life goes on. We don't have to be enemies and be in and out of court because we can't come to an agreement. All we need to do is sit down and divide our community property, have it notarized, go to an attorney and pay two hundred and fifty dollars, then you go your way and I'll go mine—because life is too short for either of us to be unhappy. I'll be damned if I'm going to be in a situation where I'm not happy, and I'll be damned if my children are going to be raised up in a negative environment.

"I didn't know for a fact that she was having an affair until after the divorce, but I wouldn't be truthful if I said I didn't have some idea that she was. I knew that something was going on and that somebody else was in her life.

"It wasn't until she told me that she wanted the divorce and actually moved out and got her own place that I even considered dating another female, because I didn't want to put my children in a situation like that. I could have been the one to file for the divorce once things got bad, but I was raised in a family where both parents were present, and I was not going to be the one to create a situation where my children would have to be raised any differently. I could have put up with her for as long as necessary, but the Lord works in mysterious ways, and when she filed, I didn't try to change her mind.

"I was never bitter or angry about it, and I never sat back and wondered, *Why me?* I don't believe in looking back and wondering what could have been or what should have been; I just looked at it as another learning experience in my life, because everything happens for a reason. All I wanted was my children and my health and strength, and I still tell guys I counsel with today, 'Do everything in your power to make your marriage work, and if you do all of that and still reach the point where it's unbearable and you can't stay, then do everything in your power to get your kids. Get your kids and raise your kids, because if you're a man, you can do a better job of nurturing your kids alone than a female can. Even if it's a girl. Kids these days need their fathers. They need a father, not a baby's daddy.'

"Once we got the house and the money issues settled, I took her to court because I wanted my kids. I'd already seen that she wasn't strong enough to raise them alone so I told her, 'Each time I have to take you to court, I'm gonna kick your ass until you just get tired of me, because I don't think I can lose,' and that's what I did until I got custody of them. I didn't care what I had to do—I wanted my kids, I didn't want anyone else to raise them.

"To make a marriage work, you've got to be on one accord. I believe that both individuals must have faith and trust that there is a God.

Two individuals are just like magnets: if there is no togetherness, they will repel. You've got to have common goals. You've both got to want to have something and be something, and you have to want to come together to accomplish those things because if not, it becomes *mine* and *yours* when it should be *ours*. If there's something positive, it's ours, and if there's something negative, it's ours. We face the good and bad times together. Regardless of when it happens and where it happens, don't focus on the negative side of any situation. Immediately start thinking about how you can correct it.

"If I have a wife whose knowledge and experience is greater than mine regarding finances, then I'd be a fool not to realize that she's probably going to come up with a better financial plan than I would. Just because I'm a man and the head of the house doesn't always mean that I'm right, and it takes a *real* man to realize that. The vows that you take in marriage that say 'In good times and in bad, in sickness and in health, for better or for worse,' all of those vows still stand when things get bad. It's a *we* problem, not *your* problem or *my* problem.

"Another thing you must realize in keeping it together is that you cannot allow things to become routine. Every year a husband and wife need to have something special for just the two of you. State it, name it, date it, plan it; then you'll have something you're looking forward to every year. These are the type things that keep that positive energy going in a marriage. Your marriage will just blossom. Just like your wedding. If you remember when you planned your wedding, you were excited about it, you planned every detail together, and you both looked forward to it. Keep the marriage that way, do impromptu things, don't let your life be so regimented or stiff that it becomes boring and unhappy."

JARED

"I've never been married, but I would like to get married someday. Right now I don't have time for a serious relationship, because I'm so focused on my career. I date, but the long hours I work and all the traveling I do doesn't really leave time for a relationship.

"I was serious about this one woman a few years ago, but that ended because she was never a challenge. She caught my eye and my attention because she was beautiful, intelligent, extremely opinionated and forceful when it came to her career—she was a lawyer—but in our relationship, she was the exact opposite.

"If I said, 'Look, the sky is red,' she'd agree. If I asked her a question, I knew how she'd respond before she even opened her mouth. I would even pick fights with her just to get her to argue back, but she wouldn't. She'd simply bend over backwards to make things right. I know you might think I'm crazy—after all, what man wouldn't want a woman that agreeable—but I want a woman with some spirit and backbone. One of my main weaknesses is that I get bored real easy, so I need a woman who's going to offer me a challenge. Now, that don't mean I want a woman who always wants to argue all the time either.

"If a woman can't keep my interest, if she can't hold an intelligent conversation with me, if she wants to be up under me all the time and she's all like, 'I want to just breathe in the very same air you're breathing,' and all that shit, I start to get bored, and once I get bored, that's it. I'm out of there. I need a woman who will keep my interest, 24-7.

"I don't want to get married only to turn around and get a divorce, because to me marriage is a serious thing. You can't take that kind of commitment lightly, and I'm afraid that if I got married and then divorced, I'd never try it again. That's why I'm going to be very careful and make sure I ask the right woman to marry me because I only want to do it once. I've had too many friends go through painful divorces, and that's not something I want to experience. I have one good friend who was two hundred pounds when he first got married and this dude loved to eat. He knew how to throw down in the kitchen—he makes the best sausage I've ever eaten. Man, by the time his divorce rolled around, he was down to around one hundred and seventy pounds, and it wasn't because he was trying to diet either. He had just gotten so miserable throughout the separation and divorce that he lost his appetite.

"I realize that marriage is a lot of work. My own parents have been married for some forty years, and I've heard them have their disagreements and such, but they've still managed to stick together and see things through, and that's the kind of marriage I want. I want someone I can make a life with. I want a woman who will always have my back. Sometimes people will get divorced for the smallest things. Just like my friend I was just talking about—his wife divorced him because he preferred staying at home, cooking and entertaining friends, instead of going out every weekend. I told him when he met her in the club, and she was *always* in the club, that her wanting to go out all the time might end up being a problem.

"I think couples who pull together have a lot more to show for it in the long run. Take my parents, for instance: not only do they have the material things like the nice vacation homes or the luxury cars, but most importantly they were able to give us a stable family life while we were growing up. They taught us the difference between right and wrong, so me and my brother are extremely well-grounded individuals. Even if I didn't set foot in another church from this day forward, it still won't change the fact that I believe in God, I believe in the Ten Commandments, I believe that Jesus died for our sins. I know how to treat a lady, and I know how a man should raise his children. Me and my brother have seen firsthand what it takes for a man to be a good husband and father.

"My mom was a stay-at-home mom, and that's all well and good, but I want the woman I marry to have her own thing going on. She needs to be successful in her career, she needs to want things out of life and not just be satisfied with simply making ends meet. I'm accustomed to a certain standard of living, and I believe I've earned the right to have certain things because I've worked hard for it, and I want a woman who has some of those same beliefs. Now, I wouldn't have a problem with my wife wanting to be a stay-at-home mom as long as I can support all of us comfortably, but until she becomes a mother, she needs to work and pull right along with me."

PIERRE

"I've been married twice, and both times it was when I was in the military. The first time, I was around nineteen or twenty, which was too young, and I just did it 'cause I was in a situation where I would've had to move back home, and I didn't want to move back home. We stayed together for about two years, but it didn't work, because she was crazy. She was extremely jealous, and I don't know why. It's not because she found out I'd messed around on her, because I only did that when I was out of town."

Pierre laughed.

"Our problems started when I was on a temporary duty assignment, and I was in California at Edwards Air Force Base away from my wife for six weeks. I took leave and went to Chicago to see my childhood sweetheart because she needed some money. I didn't tell my wife I was going, but I figured I'd kill two birds with one stone because I wanted to see my childhood sweetheart anyway, and taking her the money gave me an excuse. Even though I wanted to, we didn't have sex, because she didn't initiate it, so I just left it alone. We slept in the same bed, but nothing happened. Anyway, when I was at the airport on the way home, I got paged for a phone call, and it was my boy from back at the base in California trying to call and tell me that the phone in my room had been blowing up. It turned out that my wife had been calling like crazy, and I think he fucked up and told her I'd gone out of town, but since I hadn't mentioned it to her, she was furious. When I did tell her I'd gone to Chicago to see an old friend, of course she didn't believe me, because she knew I didn't really have any old friends.

"The second time I got married, I was twenty-five, but that one didn't last either. The way it happened was I had lost contact with my childhood sweetheart after my divorce from my first wife because I went overseas. When I came back from overseas, I was stationed in Louisiana, and one day I remembered her mom's phone number off the top of my head and I called it. The phone rang and I got the answering machine and her voice was on it, so I left a message. She called me back a few days later, we started talking regularly again, and then we would take turns flying out to see each other every other month. We got engaged over the phone and were engaged for about a year.

"I met Gina while I was engaged to my childhood sweetheart, but I'm pretty much up front, so I told her everything about my being engaged, and we decided to just be friends. But then it developed into more just friendship, so I was in turmoil. I was like, *Oh God, please do something, give me a sign 'cause I don't know what do to.* I loved the girl I was engaged to, but I was starting to feel like we really didn't know each other that well, because our relationship had been long distance for such a long time. Even prior to us getting engaged, we really hadn't spent that much time together since we'd grown up. A weekend here and a weekend there is not substantial enough to build a relationship on, especially if you're going to get married.

"I asked her to move to Louisiana with me so we could work on our relationship a little more before we actually got married, and she said, 'I'm not going to move in with you without your marrying me first. You know my parents aren't going to go for that.' So I felt like I was stuck. We weren't really compatible anymore, because since I'd graduated high school, I'd done a lot of traveling, and she'd been at home the whole time, so she was more sheltered.

"She was also used to getting anything she wanted, and I felt like that could be a problem because I couldn't afford to cater to her every need financially. When she started college, her dad went to the car dealership and wrote a check for a brand-new car. After her first semester, she decided she didn't want to stay on campus, so her parents got her an apartment and furnished it. She definitely had a silver spoon in her mouth, and my life was totally different, so that was beginning to bother me.

"Typically I've always dated older women because they're more mature, and Gina was older and still hanging in there, and she wasn't saying anything about me getting married or putting any pressure on me about anything. Since the girl I was engaged to wasn't around, Gina and I were spending a lot of time together—a whole lot of time together—and it was cool. It was nice. We had a really good relationship with very little arguing—everything was just cool. I guess I was kind of going through a metamorphosis, so to speak. At that time, I was starting to develop into the man I am now. We'd sit down and talk for hours about different stuff, and I guess the way I was raised and the fact that my parents were so spiritual kept coming up. They always had certain expectations of me, and I felt like I had to live up to those expectations, so I was kind of struggling with that.

"Gina told me one day, 'You know, you don't always have to do what they want you to do just because they're your parents. You don't always have to try to live up to their expectations. You're your own person, and you're free to live your own life. You don't have to do everything as if they're watching you—you're a grown man.'

"During that time, we'd been having sex for a while. I mean, we were having an obscene amount of sex. We couldn't even leave the house sometimes when we were supposed to go somewhere, because we'd end up fucking instead. Sometimes we'd stay in the bed and fuck for so long, we'd get hungry, and then the only reason we'd get up was because we needed something to eat.

"But anyway, this whole time I was still engaged to this other girl, and I was just praying for God to give me a sign, to show me what I should do. Well Gina and I had kind of discussed what we would do if she got pregnant. We'd talked about it, and both of us decided that if that ever happened, she'd get an abortion. And then it happened. We went up to the abortion clinic and we were sitting outside because they made us wait for a long time. It seemed like forever. I had written a check, and we'd gone outside to sit in the car and wait. Then it hit me. I thought to myself, *You wanted a sign so you'd know what to do. Damn, what bigger sign can you get? She's pregnant, stupid.*

"So I told her, 'Go get the check, and let's go,' but when she walked inside, they called her name. She thought I was getting tired of waiting because I'd been complaining about how long it was taking, so she went on in. She didn't understand that I'd changed my mind and didn't want her to have the abortion. So when she didn't come back out after about ten minutes, I went inside to look for her, and the lady at the desk told me she'd gone in already. I was like, 'No, no, I need to talk to her,' but it was too late. They wouldn't let me go in.

"She went through with the abortion, and on the way back home, I was trying to explain to her why I wanted her to go get the check, and she was like, 'Well, it's done now.' That was one of the biggest mistakes of my life. Then to make matters worse, I went ahead and got married to the other girl anyway, and Gina was heartbroken.

"I won't try to make excuses, but that was unfamiliar territory for me. It's really hard to think straight when you're in a situation like that. I loved the girl I married, but not like I loved Gina. I wore a white tux with tails for the wedding, had the top hat, cane, white gloves. I'm looking tight, but I was numb. My body was there, but my mind and my heart were a hundred miles away.

"After the wedding, when we finally got a chance to be alone, my wife told me, 'I really didn't expect you to follow through with it. I was thinking that you were gonna cancel the wedding, and I was prepared for it,' and I'm thinking, *I'll be damned. I wish she'd told me that before the wedding 'cause I damn sure would have canceled.* Like I said, my parents have these expectations of me, and the way I was raised was that you should always keep your word because that's all you have. Do what you say you're going to do, and then you don't have to make promises to people, because they know you'll keep your word. People respect that.

"After I got married, I had to move my wife to Louisiana where

I was stationed. I was working in Shreveport and had gotten an apartment in a little town about twenty minutes away because I didn't want to be in the same city as Gina. I'd left my car at the airport in Shreveport, flew to Chicago and got married, got a U-Haul, put all of her stuff in there and put her car on a trailer behind the U-Haul, and drove back to Louisiana. I figured I'd be happy with everything now that we were finally married, but Gina was still in Shreveport, and that's where I worked, and I knew in the back of my mind that inevitably that could be a problem for me.

"The first time I saw her was the week after I got married. I drove past her, and then backed up, and we started talking. Then we both pulled over to the side of the road, and the whole time my heart was about to jump out of my chest because I was sad, and happy, and everything else. I was an emotional wreck over this whole thing. Two days later, we were back in bed again, and it got to the point where I couldn't even go straight home after work. I'd go to Gina's house, and we'd make love and cry and all that, and then I'd get my shit together and go home, and my wife never knew. She never knew a thing, but I got tired of it because Gina was becoming more and more demanding now that I was married, and it was really wearing on me, so I decided to tell my wife. I told her, 'I made a mistake. I shouldn't have gotten married, and it's still early enough where we can get it annulled because I'm in love with somebody else.'

"Of course, she didn't do what I expected her to do, which was to say, 'Okay, since you're cheating on me, I'll just move my ass back to Chicago, and you can do what you want to do. Fuck you.' No, that would have been too easy. If any woman, any black woman, any normal black woman finds out her husband is having an affair, she's gonna be like, 'I can't believe you're messing around on me and we just got married. You must have been sleeping with that bitch the entire time we were engaged.'

"But no, she says, 'I'm not going anywhere. I love you, you married me and brought me down here, and I'm not leaving.'

"She called home and told her parents what had happened; then she called my parents and told them, and of course they were disappointed. They weren't going to ostracize me or anything like that, but I hated to let them down, and I really didn't want to hear what they had to say. I had Gina pressuring me, my wife was pissed, and my parents were on my ass, and it was just too much. I was the bad guy, I admitted that I was the bad guy and that I'd messed up, but you don't get no kudos for being honest when you're in a situation like that. I probably would have been better off if I'd kept it to myself.

"So I took a trip to New York to go talk to my father because I had no idea what I was going to do. I was like, 'Dad, I want to be with someone I'm in love with, like you're in love with Mom.'

"But he shattered my world when he told me, 'Son, at this point in our marriage, me and your mom just put up with each other. If you stay with your wife, you'll grow to love her,' but I could not grasp that concept since I was so in love with Gina. That would have been good advice for someone who had never experienced love before, but not for me. Old-school people did things that way: they got with somebody, and they stayed with them even if there was no love there. They stayed for the sake of the children and the family. Well, that's cool if you've never experienced love. If you don't know in your heart what it is, then you can do that. But if you've experienced it, that's like owning a Mercedes and then going back to a Pinto. You might drive it because you have to, but as soon as you can get on your feet, you're going to get yourself another Mercedes or something comparable to it.

"I listened to my dad and I went back and tried to stay and work it out. Then I got a transfer from Louisiana to Texas, and that's when my wife got pregnant. I was saying, 'She got pregnant,' and other people would say, 'No, you got her pregnant,' but in a situation like that, where she knew I was in love with someone else, she could have avoided that if she wanted to. Why bring a baby into a situation that's already bad?

"We ended up getting divorced anyway because we had a horrible communication problem because of the differences in how we were raised. She always wanted to tell her parents everything that was going on, and then they'd start asking questions about what, when, where, and how we were doing stuff.

"I told her, 'If your parents have any questions about my household, you need to send them to me, and I'll talk to them. You don't need to tell them anything. Just have them talk to me.' But she would always get them involved in our business anyway, and that used to piss me off. We were having enough problems that we needed to work out without the added pressure we were getting from them, but I felt as though she was inviting them to give their opinion because she kept telling them everything.

"After we moved to Texas, her dad planned on retiring, so he was going to move to the same area. Her parents came down and bought a house that cost about four hundred and fifty thousand dollars in this bad-ass neighborhood, and it was gorgeous. It was like five thousand square feet with five bedrooms and four full bathrooms. It had solid wood floors, granite countertops, and a huge game room with an indoor pool—the shit was tight. They wanted us to move into it because they wouldn't be moving down for at least a year, so we did, and that ended up being a problem too. They would come down about once every other month, and her father would want to dictate stuff about how the yard was to be kept and all that, and it was getting on my nerves.

"Anyway, the marriage lasted three or four years, and then the communication broke down so bad that it was unbearable. She was so immature and had such a terrible understanding of things that she always felt like I was trying to belittle her. I couldn't tell her she felt that way because she was immature, so how was I supposed to explain other than telling her, 'You'll understand in time—don't worry about it.'

"Every time I said that, she'd come back with, 'What the fuck is that supposed to mean?' but I'd already explained it to her in every way I could. I'd break things down as simple as I could, and she still wouldn't understand, so there was nothing else I could do.

"She's remarried now, even though she was always telling me she'd never get married again, but it doesn't bother me, because I have no feelings for her anymore. She's history, but she can never be totally out of my life because she's the mother of my child. I don't even think it would bother me if Gina got married as long as she was happy. I mean, I love her and everything, but the way things are between us geographically, I probably couldn't make her happy, so I'd rather see her happy with someone else."

COLLIER

"Me and Anne have been together for twelve years now, but we just got married a year ago, and most people don't know that. There are a lot of people who see things, but very few who know. It's kind of like when you walk into somebody's kitchen and you smell something cooking. You may say, 'Ummm, I smell some greens,' but when you get to the stove and look in the pot, it may be something else.

"There are some situations where you won't know what you think you know, until you take the lid off, and when you take that lid off, you still might not know. A lot of people see us together and think one thing, but they really don't know, and I keep things to myself because it's really nobody else's business. We have so much in common that we should've been married a long time ago, but I couldn't marry her, because I was still married to my first wife. I can't say it's nobody's fault, 'cause it's like this, at least from a man's point of view: when you marry a woman, she may feel like, *Oh I got him now*, and then she changes, and I didn't want that to happen, so that's probably why it took me so long to marry her.

"I think marriage is beautiful if the two of you are compatible, but sometimes you have to grow to love the way a woman is. Marriage and love is a growing thing. You may think you're in love at first, but then you find out that love is more than just holding hands and talking sweet. I'll tell you what love is: love is action shown. That's the bottom line. It's not just words. You can love a dog, and a dog knows that you love him by how you treat him. But now, if you don't feed your dog, guess what? He ain't gonna hang around you too long before he'll be gone. He'll get tired of starving and just skip the premises because love is action shown.

"There is a girl I used to date way back in the day, and listen now—I'm talking about action shown. Her name was Raquel, and she was a very smart girl. Her parents sent her away to college, but I really loved her and had planned to marry her after she graduated, but while she was away at school, I got another girl pregnant, and that hurt her so, she never got over it. She did finally marry someone else, but she divorced him because she said every time she looked at him, she thought about me, and she felt like that was wrong. When she found out me and my wife had broken up, which was about fifteen years later, she called me and we had a long talk. She told me that she never stopped loving me, and would never love anyone else the way she loved me, and that's the reason she never got married again. That's what I call action shown.

"You see, somebody can say, 'I don't know if you love me,' but if you're showing it, they can't ask for nothing else, because that's the bottom line. You can say you love anything, but show me. With Anne, I've shown her love. We're close, like sister and brother. We're tight, and she knows me.

"Now, love can be a hurting thing, but I ain't never had my heart broken. I was touched a long time ago by a lady I was seeing named Dorian who was older than me. She had long, pretty black hair and a real young face. She was beautiful. We used to do a lot of things together, but then she moved out of the country. I talk to her every now and then, and she's still in love with me too.

"You see, love is everlasting. You can love somebody and leave love within them. If you part with that person and go your own way, if it was really love, it stays within them. So even though I'm not with those two women who touched my life, I know they still love me and they always will. It don't give me no big ego to know that, but as long as I know and they know, the love will always be there. It's in my heart to be worthy of them loving me.

"Agreements make a marriage work. Agreeing will make anything work. Marriage is beautiful, as long as you can agree. What good is it if you're always arguing and fussing and fighting and disagreeing on things? That ain't no good. Even when two people are discussing marriage, they should be asking one another, 'Can you agree that it would be possible for you to make me happy for the rest of your life, and hold yourself to your word?' And you got to have a word. That means a lot because in the beginning was the word, and the word was God. In the beginning of a relationship, in the beginning of a marriage, in the beginning of anything, is a word. If you got a word and I can believe you, can't nobody tell me nothing to make me change my mind about you. Nothing in the world could ever change the love I have for you.

"I was married to my first wife about fourteen years, and we broke up because we didn't agree on a whole lot of things. People wanted to think it was my fault, that there was something I was doing, but I wasn't doing anything. I'd heard that she was out there messing around, but I loved her so much that I was blind to it; I thought I was too smart to be dumb. But my mama saw it coming a long time ago, and she tried to warn me. She told me that I loved my wife more than I loved myself, and that she would end up breaking my heart because she knew it. I never understood that when Mama said it, but I finally saw it with my own eyes one day, and that was all it took, because what your eyes see, you let your heart believe. You don't have to be going on no 'he say, she say.' Wait until you see things clearly for yourself.

"After I actually caught my wife out there doing her thing, I went back home to stay with my mom. Later me and my wife talked about getting back together, and my mama seen me getting my things together and asked me, 'Where you going?' I told her me and my wife were going to the movies, and she looked at me and smiled and said, 'Colli, let me tell you something. Either you're gonna be with your wife or you're gonna be without her. You can't court your wife and you can't sweetheart with her, and if y'all are apart, you're courting her.'

"After she told me that, I left anyway because I didn't want to hear it, but I got to my wife's place too early and there she was standing in the yard, leaning all on some dude's car talking and laughing up in his face, so I just kept right on driving, thinking about what my mama had said. After that I never tried to court her or get back with her. She ended up marrying that guy, and they only stayed married about a year.

"I finally let it go. You got to let it go—I don't care how much you think you love someone, let it go if that person isn't loving you the same way you love them. What happens is that after you leave something alone for a while, it gets rusty. Time brings about a change, understand what I'm saying. Just like if a woman is in love with her husband, don't you know if they part for a while, there will be other sisters watching, hoping that they never get back together, actually praying that they never get back together? You got more working against you than for you in a situation like that, and if you ain't crazy and you're both healthy and normal, you know that at some point he's going to be courting somebody else.

"Now, this is where the word *fool* comes in. A fool is someone who can wait a long, long time on something they know will never be. They know it's never gonna happen, but they still want to make it happen, even if it's not good for them. That makes about as much sense as some white folks who hate you because you're black and they don't think you're as good as they are, but yet and still they kiss their dogs in the mouth, and here I am a human just like they are, and they want to hate me. Does that make sense? Well, waiting around for someone when all the signs show that it will never be doesn't make sense either.

"Me and my first wife hardly ever talk, but she came up on my job about a year ago and asked for me. I went out to meet her, and she said she was hurting so bad, because I'd forgotten our anniversary, even though we've been divorced about twenty-something years. She says to me, 'The kids usually tell me when you said happy anniversary, but they didn't tell me this year.'

"I told her, 'Well, damn, Tammy, we been divorced over twenty years. How long you think I'm gonna keep on saying that?' But see, sometimes you don't find out you really loved until you have to go through a change. She took it for granted, and you shouldn't take nothing for granted. If you ever do that and it comes back on you, don't be like her. Be woman enough to handle it."

ANTONIO

"I think marriage is beautiful, but the problem is most people rush into it. I know I rushed into it—I was too young. With most women I know, the problem is that by the time they hit thirty, the biological clock has started ticking. It's what I call the thirty-year-old insanity defense. A lot of women get married because of their biological clock. They're like, 'Man I'm thirty, and if I don't have a baby soon, I won't be able to have no baby.' So when she meets a guy who is halfway decent, she doesn't wait to find out enough about him before she says, 'Yeah he's good enough, I'll take him. He can take care of me; he can give me a baby.' That's a major mistake women make.

"People get married for the wrong reason. The institution of marriage is great if you take your time to find the right person and get married for the right reasons. You should get married because you're compatible and because you love him. Not because you *can't* live without him, but because you don't *want* to live without him. That bullshit about "You complete me" ain't how it works. You're two separate entities, and together you make a team. You don't make one whole person. You don't give up your individuality.

"I was married fifteen years, and my wife was crazy and she just kept getting crazier and crazier even though she was seeing a therapist. At first we went to couples therapy, but when the therapist determined that my wife was the one with the problem, she stopped going. She was like, 'I ain't going no more because everything is *my* fault. I'm going to therapy on my own.' She went to her own therapist, and one day she came home after a session and announced to me and my daughter, 'My therapist has given me permission to be happy, and she says I'm not happy being a wife, I don't do it right, and I'm not happy being a mother. She says I need to be happy doing whatever I want to do, so I want to leave, go start a new life, go do something on my own, and try some different things, so I'm leaving.'

"I told her, 'Look, we can work on this. We can get back into couples therapy, we can do anything to save this, but if you don't want to work on this and you leave, don't come back. My daughter isn't going to have no boomerang mama.' She left in March, and by July we were divorced.

"I got screwed in the divorce—it was terrible. She got everything except our daughter, the house, and the bills. She even got half of my retirement and half of my savings. I just took it up the ass to give her a desirable deal, and I'm still paying for it. I used the other half of my savings to pay for the divorce, so it cleaned me out. To this day, I am still recovering from that financial hit. I'd worked hard so she could be a stay-at-home mother, and she took my retirement money and blew it.

"The only thing I liked about marriage was finding out that I'm a good daddy, but you don't have to get married for that. Other than that, I can't think of a single thing in that marriage that was good. The only positive side of marriage is the regular sex. I remember when my wife got all geeked up about wanting to have kids. She was like, 'Come on and jump on top of me every night, please.' She was begging me for it. So sure, I was ready to go along with that.

"But our marriage was never any good. She was a weak person, and she was never there for me. I was the caregiver. I took care of her, I did for her, and after she took all she could take, she left. She never gave nothing. Maybe that's why I don't want to get married again. You know, I hadn't really thought about it, but I can't think of a single good thing to say about marriage. It would have to be the right person for me to get married again—that's all I can say. With the right person, marriage could've been wonderful. With the wrong person, hell—pure hell."

EDWIN

"I think marriage is the cornerstone of America. It's very important, even when you're older and no kids are involved because it's good to have that friend you can do things with. I have a cruise booked for next year, and I'm going to take my lady friend with me, and we're going to have a great time because we enjoy each other's company. That's the way marriage should be: you should enjoy spending time together.

"When I'm looking for a woman to marry, I'm looking for a woman who has good moral values, good family values, she's only drinks socially, she doesn't do drugs, she doesn't smoke, she's a one-man woman, and she knows how to carry herself in public. You've got to look at the overall picture. I attend a lot of business functions, and most of the time the wives attend also, and it's important in that environment to have a woman who is presentable and knows how to handle herself.

"I want a woman I have things in common with, whether it's traveling or going out to dinner or just hanging out. I don't want a woman who's a clubber, because I know for a fact if you meet a woman in a club, you need to leave her in the club. I met every last one of my exes in the club, and they wanted to keep partying after we got married. If you meet a woman at a club, that's probably where she likes to be, and if you don't understand that, you're going to have problems.

"The women I date have to be forty and above. I've dated younger women. Just recently I had a twenty-two-year-old woman tell me, 'You sure look good,' and I said to myself, *No, I don't need to mess with that,* and same thing for thirty-year-olds. You might find some women in their twenties and thirties who are mature, but as a whole I'm more comfortable with women forty and above. That's the age where they really start thinking about family values and settling down and they've got all that running around out of their system.

"Now, don't get me wrong—I like looking at young women. I enjoy looking and thinking, *Ooooh weee, what I could do with that*, but you won't see me taking her home, because that's nothing but trouble. I was at the basketball game last night, and there was a fine little twenty-one- or twenty-two-year-old. She was a law student at UNC, and I went, *Damn, uh uh uh*, but then my sanity kicked in and I started thinking, *She don't need to get a hold of my retirement money*. I want a woman I can lay back and grow old with. She might be a little younger than me, but at least she's going to be mature.

"I've gone through some serious relationship issues because some of the women I married were immature, but now that I know what I'm looking for, I refuse to settle for less. Before it was just, *You need to go ahead and get married*, but now I know what I want, and I'm okay being by myself. I prefer to be married, but I'm not going to settle.

"I've been married three times—well, really four, but I don't count the last one. It was annulled. The first time I was married six years, the second time a year and a half, and that was a year and a half too long. This woman was wild, and she still is. She came by my house recently, and I complimented her on how good she was looking, and she asked me, 'Do you want to take me back down the aisle again?' and I said, 'Shit, you must be crazy. I don't even want to get close to you, 'cause you might get pregnant again.' Ain't no way in hell I'd marry her ass a second time after what we'd gone through.

"She still looks good, but that relationship had too much drama. Every third day, it was some kind of hell. She just liked to raise hell. If I didn't tell her how beautiful she was or if I didn't give her as much attention as she thought she deserved, it was hell. When the baby came along, she started to complain that I was giving the baby all the attention. I said, 'Girl, you ought to appreciate that,' but she didn't, so it was a constant mess. She was pregnant when we got married, and the divorce was a pretty rough one because I didn't want to leave my child.

"The worst period in our marriage was the adultery. That's why we broke up. And I wasn't the one involved in the affair; it was her. I was at a pool hall with my brother's buddy, and we were having a few beers, and he says, 'I don't know how to tell you this, but I was at a bar the other day, and these two soldiers came in, and one of them was talking about a girl he was dating over in Galveston named Monique. There's only one Monique I know, and that's your wife, so I asked the guy to describe her, and I'll be damned if his description didn't fit your wife.'

"I asked my wife about it, and she was honest. She admitted to having an affair. So I said to her, 'I'm not an angel myself. I haven't been the perfect husband either, so maybe we can push this aside and move on,' but she told me, 'I can't stop seeing my friend,' so there was nothing else I could do, and that was that.

"She is the reason that the relationship between me and my daughter is strained right now. My daughter lived with me while she was in high school, and I contacted the child support people to let them know, and they said, 'You don't have to pay child support since she's living with you,' so I'm thinking everything is fine. When she was a senior in high school, I bought her a car, and then she decided to move back in with her mother. A couple of months later, I got a letter from the child support office saying I was behind fifteen thousand in child support payments. I called the office and told them that my daughter had been living with me, so I didn't have to worry about payments.

"They said, 'Well, the mother says you haven't been paying.'

"I said, 'Well, I'll get my daughter down there, and she can explain that she's been staying with me,' and they said, 'No, your daughter came in with her,' and I was shocked.

"I contacted an attorney, and it was going to cost about five thousand just to get the paperwork started, so I said to myself, *You know what, I'm going to pay these people their money,* but I was also paying three hundred a month for my daughter's car note and almost two hundred per month on her insurance, so I stopped. I paid that fifteen thousand, but I haven't given them an extra penny since—maybe a few dollars here or there, but nothing like I used to.

"My ex-wife got the money she wanted, spent it all in no time, and now she's struggling again. I told my daughter that if she wanted to go to college, my company would pay for her tuition and books, but she wasn't willing to do that, and I wasn't willing to offer her anything else. The car I'd bought her was in my name, and I was obligated to pay for it, so I got rid of it. Yesterday she called me and asked me if I would be wiling to co-sign because she was getting another car, and I told her I wasn't going to do it, because I would be the one stuck if she couldn't pay her car note. Then she asked me if I could just put the car on my insurance, and I asked, 'What's wrong with your mother? You're living with her—have her put your car on her insurance because my insurance is set up where the car has to be here or you got to be in school. As a matter of fact, tell her I said if she had some of that fifteen thousand she lied to get, she could pay cash for a car and a year's worth of insurance up front.' Twenty years was enough—I'm not doing another thing.

"I got married again six months after my second divorce was final, and I'd only known this woman for a short time. I met her right after I got divorced, and we stayed married ten years. I've always been married to women who have issues—hell if I know why. My second wife was known to go apeshit without drinking or doing drugs. She didn't need a reason to act crazy, but my third wife was even worse.

"I'd get up and go to work at six a.m., and she'd already be on her second beer. She was also smoking weed, and it wasn't that bad when we were younger, because she could handle it better. But as she got older, she just could not hold her liquor. She'd drink a few beers and then she'd want to fuss, fight, and run the streets, but I wouldn't divorce her, because I wanted to make it work. On Father's Day she said to me, 'I know you'll never divorce me, but I'm going to make you a happy man. I'm going to file for divorce tomorrow,' and I said to myself, *Yes, Lord. Hallelujah, there is a God.*

"We didn't have a child together, but I had helped raise her daughter, so we were real close. It was just like she was mine. To this day, I still send her money to help her with college and take care of bills and stuff. They say opposites attract, and the two of us were as opposite as day and night. I don't know how we ever got together in the first place.

"If I were to marry again, I would make sure that person was my best friend in the sense that I know that this is a real commitment and not a fly-by-night or hormones-kicking-in type thing. And hell yeah, hormones still kick in at age fifty-four, and I don't need no Viagra either."

WARREN

"Me and my wife have gone through a lot of changes during our thirty-year marriage. When you get married young, you still got a lot of growing up to do, and sometimes you get sidetracked and lose focus. The experience has made me a stronger person and has made me realize that you should never take your woman for granted. When you got a good woman, you got to do what it takes to keep her.

"Marriage is not going to be what you want it to be all the time. It ain't no fairy tale. It's a two-way street, so you learn to deal with the good and the bad. I heard a guy say the other day, 'The longer you've been married, the longer you learn how to go without sex,' and that's true for a lot of men.

"We've had our problems in this marriage—I've done my thing, and she's done hers. When she got her first job after finishing school, she got a little too close to one of the lawyers at work, and I didn't like it. She'd always talk about this particular lawyer: then she started staying after work later and later, sometimes she wouldn't even make it home in time for dinner. At first I was only suspicious—then I found out that she was having an affair with this man. Here I was, always working and always doing stuff with the kids, so I never expected that she would have an affair. I mean, you see it happen to other people all the time, but you never expect it to happen to you, and once you find out about something like that, your whole relationship changes.

"I have to honestly say that's the reason I cheated. After I found out she was having an affair, things weren't the same—even after we had counseling and decided to stay together. She became negative about a lot of things, and I could never seem to do anything right, probably because she was comparing me to her lover, or ex-lover, I guess. I swear, I think she went to Wal-Mart and bought all the long, flannel gowns they had because that's all she wore to bed. For about a year, we probably had sex about once every other month, and even then she really didn't seem to enjoy it.

"Then one day her mother came over to the house and sat us both down. She said, 'Both of y'all listen at me real good 'cause I'm only going to say this once. You both walking around looking all long-faced, like the world done come to an end, and you got children to raise. The way I see it, both of you messed up, but that's life. This ain't nothing new. Y'all need to remember that old song about what it took to get your baby hooked because Warren, there's always gonna be another man out there who will send flowers and cards if you won't, and Sheila, there will always be another woman out there who will have sex when you won't, so both of you need to learn to appreciate each other. There's nothing out there in those streets that you don't already have at home, so you might as well go back to doing what makes the other one happy or get a divorce and move on.' That was twenty years ago, and things are better now than they ever were."

RUBEN

"My parents will have been married forty-nine years this year. I'm sure they've had their moments, but in them I've seen an example of what the verse in Genesis means where it says 'A man shall leave home and take a wife and the two will become one.'"

LANDON

"You got your thugs, ghetto hos, and chicken heads, and then you got black men and black women who want to prosper. The problem is that sometimes a black man who is trying to prosper meets a ghetto ho, and because he has this mentality that he's invincible, he thinks he can change this woman into what he wants her to be, so he'll hook up with a woman like that already knowing she ain't about shit, and sure enough, he'll get burnt. That's what I did, and I got burnt. I thought I could change my wife, but she ended up being more like a second child than a wife.

"I would have to explain situations to her like, this is what you did, this is what they said, and this is why it didn't work, and this is what you should've done. She was older than me by three years, but she was raised in a single parent home, and a woman who is raised in a single-parent home has no idea what marriage really consists of. Her mama is on her fifth or sixth husband, so my wife was led to believe that if a man didn't work out, you just replaced him with another one.

"She got tired of the marriage and just quit, but I was raised to never quit. I didn't quit until she left. She was unhappy being married, and she said she needed some time and space for herself, so I let her have it. It wasn't like I really had much of a choice anyway.

"Even though things went bad, I'm not afraid to be committed again. The only thing I would be afraid of would be that the woman I'm serious about is not fully ready to commit to me. I stepped into marriage blindly and realized in hindsight what marriage was really about. When you get married, you come to a real quick understanding of what commitment means.

"I've always thought marriage was a beautiful thing, and I still do, but for it to work, you got to have two compatible people with a spiritual background that coincides. I don't believe a marriage will work without God. I honestly don't. I've read the Bible twice, and I understand that marriage is *for* God. And if a marriage is supposed to be for

God, it's not going to work without Him, so a couple needs to see things eye to eye spiritually and have the same views. When you meet a person who has different views from yours and the two of you still get together, you're going to have problems. You'll have children and she'll want to raise them one way and you'll want to raise them another, and that alone can cause the marriage to fail.

"My wife always felt that I was too hard as a man, and she doesn't know any better because, as I said, she wasn't raised with a man in her house. As a man, I always felt she was being too easy on our daughter, so we started arguing and became distant from each other. Then I started noticing little things that irritated me about her, and she started noticing little things about me that irritated her. Then we weren't having sex or we were making agreements or basically pacts on when to have sex. I'd give her so much money to go shop, and she'd give me sex for a certain amount of time. We were making pacts, and that shit got old. That's not a marriage.

"I was married for two very long years, and she was like my child from the time we started dating until we separated. My uncles had always taught me that a woman is a beautiful thing, but your wife was different. Your wife didn't have to be beautiful; your wife could be average. A dime piece is not wife material; a seven on a one-to-ten scale is wife material because she doesn't have her head blown up by a man, even though she still looks good. She doesn't have to wear makeup to look good. When you wake up in the morning and roll over and she smiles at you and tells you good morning and she got that morning breath, she still looks pretty —That's a wife. And to me, she was that woman.

"When I met her, there were some things I didn't understand about her, but people are raised differently. I felt her hands, and her hands felt rough like my grandmother's, so I thought, *She's a woman who works*. Her nails were neat—they were filed, and they were nice. She had a pretty smile, she had a nice personality, and she could deal with me. She had a perfect body, and she was willing to give me whatever I wanted, and I felt the way about her that she felt about me, so I fell in love with her, but I fell too fast because there were things under the surface that I couldn't see, and I jumped in too fast to give myself time to see them.

"Even at my age, knowing as much as I know and seeing myself as peers with people older than me, I would still listen and take advice from my uncles because they are they ones who gave me the knowledge. She was the same way, but her aunts, her mom, and the other females in her ear weren't giving her good advice.

"She came to me and said, 'We're having problems, we're fighting and this and that, so this marriage must be a mistake.' Now, this was during our first year of marriage, and everybody knows that your first year is your hardest year, but she had never been told that. One of her aunts actually told her, 'Well, if you don't like being married, just stop doing everything.' So she stopped cooking, she stopped cleaning, she stopped taking care of our daughter, she stopped helping, she stopped making love, she shut everything down, and I was like, *What the fuck is going on here?*

"At this time I was working twelve hours a day, and she wasn't working at all. She didn't tell me nothing—she just stopped doing anything because she wasn't happy. So I said, *Okay, I'm going to do everything.* That's how I was raised. *I'm going to do everything to make her happy, so now I'm giving one hundred and fifty percent.* I would go to work. I had to be to work at six, by eight we'd have a break, and I would take a break from eight to eight thirty because I would go home. Our daughter would already be up, and my wife would be sitting there watching TV or she would be asleep. I would change my daughter because she hadn't changed her; I would give her some breakfast, clean her up, and go back to work.

"Lunchtime came around, I'd go home and change my daughter again because my wife ain't doing a damn thing but sitting in front of the TV. I'd cook something for my daughter to eat, clean her up again, and go back to work. Two o'clock, I come home and change my daughter again because she'd been sitting in a wet diaper, got diaper rash and stuff out the ass, and her mama is just sitting there like she don't give a damn. I'd give her something to eat, clean her up again, and go back to work. I get off work and get back home, once again the same routine, change the diaper, cook, clean, play with the baby a little, and finally put her to bed.

"After a few weeks of that shit, I'm just sitting there thinking, *Damn, I'm doing one hundred and fifty percent, and this woman won't hug me, won't kiss me, won't even ask me, 'How was your day?'* I would come home and I would try, because I didn't know anything else to do. I'd be like, 'Hi, how was your day? How you doing?' And in order for me to even think about having sex with her, I would have to do something for her like give her a hundred dollars so she could get a babysitter and go shopping for shoes the next day.

"This all started because she felt like I spoke too harshly to her. I wasn't having an affair, I'd never cussed at her—it was just something in her head she couldn't deal with, and I still don't understand what I did to her to make her feel that way. I think in a lot of ways she felt inferior to me because she didn't have much education. She would always say, 'You talk to me like you're above me.' But I was raising her. I didn't talk down to her intentionally, but damn, I had no idea that she didn't even understand how to balance a fucking checkbook, and she never did catch on. Just wore me out, and I went through this phase with her for about a year and a half before we finally broke up.

"We had only dated six months before we decided to get married. The day before we got married, I went to get her purse to get the cell phone, but she snatched the purse from me so automatically, I'm thinking that she's trying to hide something. Why else would the woman I'm getting ready to marry snatch her purse from me?

"We fought about it for an hour, and she finally gave me the purse, and I looked inside and she's got her ex-boyfriend's picture in there, the guy she'd dated for three years before she met me. She had his cell phone number, work number, pager number, mama number, grandmama number—she had like eight numbers on the back of this picture and was carrying it around in her purse, so I was pissed. I told her to kick rocks. She had already been kind of staying with me off and on and had a few things at my place, so I took all her clothes, folded them military style in little squares, and put them out in the middle of the floor.

"She called me and said she was coming to get her clothes, and I was like, 'Whatever.' She came by the house, and when she saw her clothes all folded and stacked in the middle of the floor, she started crying. We ended up making up, but I didn't give her back the engagement ring for like two weeks, and yeah, I fell back into it. What the hell, I was young. I loved her, so I gave in.

"After we got engaged that second time, her mama called me from New Jersey and told me that all I had to do was buy myself a plane ticket to get there because they had already spent like eight thousand dollars on the wedding, which I found out was another lie, and this is two days after we'd gotten engaged again, so now my morals kick in. I was like, *Damn, they done spent all this money, so I got to do it.*

"My mom didn't care about them spending all that money. She was like, 'If you don't want to get married, don't.' But I couldn't see not doing it. I thought, *I'm twenty—I can make it work.* I'm thinking I'm invincible.

"So we got married in New Jersey, but I had to report back to work the next week because I didn't have that much leave, and her mom got sick, so she had to stay there with her for an extra couple of weeks. I got back to the base, met an ex-girlfriend at the club, and she invited me over to her house, and for some reason I went. She undressed and took a bath in front of me. She was all in my face, and you know what I did? I walked away, straight-turned and walked away, because I was in love. I walked away and got in my car and drove home.

"During the first six months, me and my wife lived together, I went through a lot of torment because I'd finally realized from living with her these few months and getting to know her better that she was not the woman I really wanted to be with. I loved her, but I was having issues because I still wasn't through playing the field. Other women were constantly throwing stuff in my face, and I was feeling trapped, so in order for me to untrap myself, I felt like I had to cheat. This was within the first six months of our marriage, where she could've had the marriage annulled. So I went on a temporary assignment for two weeks, and I cheated, and then I felt real bad because I was like, *I'm going to hell*.

"I always believed that if you cheated, you would go to hell. I was like, *This is fucked up*. And it was weird because the woman was coaxing me to do it. It wasn't even like I really wanted to do it, but I was talking trash and it just happened. She had already taken off her clothes, so I felt like I had to follow through. I fucked her, but it was hard for me to come because I felt so guilty. As soon as I came, I got up, washed off, and left.

"The guilt was eating me up, and when I got back home from my assignment, everything felt different. I felt like my wife could tell that I had cheated. We were going to church, and I was praying every night, and I said, *Lord, I don't know how to tell her, but I need to get this off my chest*. We went to visit a new church, and after about two or three weeks, the pastor pulled me out of the crowd, looked at my wife, and said, 'He's got something to tell you tonight.'

"So that night when we got home, I told her. I told her straight up that I'd had a one-night stand. She left, but a month later, she came back, and dealt with it, but she held it over my head, and she put it in my face every chance she got. Then a few months later I found out she had dirt too.

"Remember the man we had argued about and broken up over before we got married? Well, she had given me a gold chain before we got married, the first thing any woman had ever bought for me, and I was so happy I got a gold chain. It was something nice. I wore it for almost two years, and one day after I had confessed to my infidelity, she came up to me and said, 'You know that was his chain, right?' I had been wearing some other nigga's chain for two years, and that pissed me off, so I pawned that shit. I got fifty dollars for it and spent it on my daughter.

"The only reason she even told me about it at all was because we were having a heart-to-heart confession-type thing. I was talking about, 'Oh baby, I'm sorry. I didn't mean to yell at you last night. I was just frustrated because of this test coming up,' and she was like, 'Oh, well, you know that was his chain you got on.' I was like, 'What in the hell did you just say?' I was proud of that chain; I had shown it to everybody: 'Look at what my baby got me.' And now I find out that I got some other nigga's chain on my neck, the same nigga that we done had fights over? That hurt me for real. She had bought the chain for him, and when they broke up, he gave it back, and she gave the shit to me like it was okay. That's what got me. She thought it was cool, acted like it was nothing, but that's the mentality she had. I was hurt, but she thought it was cool.

"So I asked her, 'What's up with our marriage?'

"She said, 'The marriage is okay, but it's not gold or nothing.'

"I was like, *What?* I had done everything I could do, and she acted like she could take it or leave it.

"I thought about that for three days, and during those three days, I kept hearing that in my head. I was reliving it every thirty seconds for three days. I woke up Sunday morning, and I said to her, 'You know what—I think it would be better if you just go.'

"And she said, 'Okay,' and called her mom. Four hours later, her mom was at the airport with a ticket for her and my daughter, and they took off. Just like that, they were gone."

6
FATHERHOOD

MALIK

"I have two children of my own, and my niece who lives with us. I've always been fond of kids, even though I grew up with a lot of brothers and sisters. I could always go anywhere and play with anybody's kid, and they'd make my heart melt, so I knew that I wanted two or three of my own. After I got married and we had two children, people would say, 'Oh, don't you want to have another one? Don't you want to try for another boy?' But we got one of each, and they were healthy, so we decided to leave well enough alone.

"My niece is eleven and had a problem with me showing her any affection at first because the men who'd been in her life were abusive, but she's finally gotten to where she'll hug me around the neck and ask, 'Hey, Uncle, how's it going?' and that makes me feel good. When I think about it, it almost makes me cry to know these kids really need me because I didn't have that kind of relationship with anybody when I was growing up. I never knew what it was like to get affection from a man, because my mother's husband was too busy drinking and being mean as hell. I even questioned whether I'd be able to give affection to my children when my wife was pregnant.

"Growing up, I always thought that mom was the only one who

needed to be there to raise us because she was the only one we could depend on. But once I became a father myself, I found out that I was wrong to think that. Both parents are needed to keep the right balance when raising children.

"My greatest hope for my kids is that they all grow up and finish high school, then go on to college and get their degrees because I'm a living example of stuff they don't want to have to go through as adults. I'm working on my bachelor's degree right now, and I tell them all the time, 'When I'm in here doing my homework, y'all can't come and ask me to help you with yours because I won't always have time, and that hurts me. I don't want you to have to worry about that with your kids, so you need to go ahead and get your degree before you get married or anything else. You want to already have your education out of the way before you start a family because you won't have to worry about neglecting your children. You can already be into your career, and that way you can devote more time to your children when they need it.' Sometimes I get frustrated and start fussing because they're asking me questions when I'm trying to do my homework, and then I have to go back and apologize. I tell them constantly to finish high school and that me and their mom will help them in any way we can while they're in college. We'll do whatever it takes.

"They're going to college no matter what we have to do, and there's no *if*; there's only *when* concerning college. That is not an option in my house, and my kids know it."

NEAL

"I never gave any thought to having kids, because I have a lot of nieces and nephews that I helped to nurture, but I did end up with two daughters and one son, and they will always be my babies.

"Even with my parents, once I became an adult, there were things I could have purchased on my own, but I'd go and borrow it from my parents in order to keep that relationship going. I feel there should always be a need that only a parent can meet for their child, no matter what age they are. As long as that need exists, that relationship exists, communication exists, the visits exist, and that keeps the relationship intact.

"I've learned that parenting is a continuous thing. There should always be love and respect between a father and his children, and you should always be truthful to your kids and expect them to be truthful to you. *Don't lie to your kids.* I cannot stress that enough. Always be willing to help them, but don't be eager to give them financial help, because things that come easy are not appreciated all the time. Stress to your kids that they should have respect, faith, and trust in God and that they should respect themselves, their elders, and their country. It's really important that they love themselves because if you can't love yourself, you're not capable of loving anyone else.

"Being a parent, you have to do some things that may be difficult in order to keep that line of communication open. And sometimes that may entail listening to that rap music so you know where your kid is coming from. If you have kids who are under twenty and still in your household and they listen to rap music, then you need to take some time and listen to that music too because if you remember, back in the days of slavery, music was our method of communicating, and that still exists today.

"We are so quick to tell our kids, 'You don't know what hard times are,' but the times that our kids are living in today are much more difficult than the times we came up in. Look at all the violence, gangsta rap, drive-by shootings, drugs, prostitution, AIDS, and things of this nature that they have to deal with. When you look at rap music, you can see that these kids are trying to get our attention. They're trying to tell us, 'We're scared. Our friends are being killed every day, my brothers and sisters are using and selling drugs, life doesn't mean anything, I will never own a home or a car or have a good job, and I'll probably die before I reach nineteen.' That's what they're saying, and when someone says something like that to you, they want a response or an answer. In fact, they need an answer."

PIERRE

"I feel like a mother who remarries when her child is very young should not change her last name, because she's alienating her child when she does that. That child grows up and doesn't understand why everybody in the house has the same last name except him. If the kid is a teenager and she remarries, then he has a better understanding that they have different names because that's his stepfather, but if a kid is like five years old, he don't understand that. I don't think my ex even thought about what she was doing when she got married again. She did it just to spite me, but she's not hurting me—she's hurting our son. I would like to get custody of him so I can move him out of that environment, but I can't afford to take her back to court, because the lawyer wants like twenty or thirty thousand dollars. I call it irony—that's life. It's like there are mothers who wish their kids' fathers would come around more often but they don't. I'm one of those fathers who wants to be with his son, and his mother does everything she can to keep me away from him. I sometimes wonder why I couldn't have married one of those women who would want to give their kid up. Why did I get the one who's so bitter and angry, even though she put me out? She's the one who filed for divorce, and I didn't fight her on it, so I don't understand what her problem is."

COLLIER

"I once read a book called *The Prophet*. The story is about a prophet leaving a town, and before he leaves, he shares some of his knowledge with the people in the town. There is a portion of the book where someone says to him, 'Tell me about children.' He said, 'Your children are not your children. They are the sons and daughters of life, longing for themselves. They came through you, but they are not from you, they are from the heavenly wings of God. You can house their bodies, but you can't house their souls, because their souls dwell in the house of tomorrow, which you cannot even visit within your dreams.' Can you feel that?

"I have four children: two girls from my first marriage, and two boys from my current marriage. A lot of men I know have babies all over the place, but it just wasn't in me to do that. I give my heart to my children, and there's no way I could have done that if I had too many. It's not that I always used protection, but the women that I've had were right with me. Even the no-good ones had good in them at one time till somebody made them no good.

"I have to have deep feelings for a woman to have sex with her; I don't just lay down with anybody. That's not natural for all men, but then some just don't care, and they can do that very easily, but all men are not dogs.

"I love being a father because I love giving, and I give so much sometimes, I think it's wrong. That doesn't mean that things are always perfect in a father–child relationship, but even when they aren't, you have to keep on being a good father. I don't think I could be a better father than what I am—ask any of my kids.

"Let me tell you—Leslie, one of my daughters, always wanted to be a lawyer, and she wanted to go to law school. Tuition was high every semester, and she got some grants but she didn't get the rest of it from nobody but me. In her last year, she worked part-time to help pay for some of it herself, but she didn't even know how to ask me for the rest, and when she came to me, she started crying. She said, 'Daddy, I'm a senior, and I've saved some of my money, but I still need some help because I didn't have enough.'

"I was so mad at her, I told her, 'Now, if you want to piss me off, keep crying. I done brought you this far.'

"But what really bothered me was when she was real young, her mother told her that she had to get the white folks to make me take care of them, and that made me feel so bad. When we went to court, she brought my children in there wearing sweaters with big holes in them like she got them from the trash at the Salvation Army, and I got so mad, I wanted to tear the court up.

"After she stopped crying and I wrote out the check for her, I said to her, 'Leslie, let me ask you something. Remember when your mama told you she had to get the white folks to make me take care of y'all? Well, now you're over eighteen, so who you think making me do this now? I've given you over twenty thousand dollars, so I know you don't still believe that.'

"She dropped her head and said, 'Daddy, Mama just wanted us to be angry with you. I know the white folks didn't have to make you take care of us. Mama thought we believed that, but I knew that wasn't true, because you never told us no when we asked for something. The only reason I feel bad for asking you to help me with school is because you've already done so much.'

"About a year ago, she was trying to buy one of those trucks, but I can't recall the name of that thing. I think it's an SUC or SUD or something like that. All I know is it's the latest model. She got a good job coming out of school, but she hadn't been on her job long enough to buy a car. Well, anyway, wouldn't nobody sign for her to get it, and her mama . . . Anyway, who she had to call? Me, her daddy. What you think her mama told her when she needed help? 'Call your daddy,' just like she always did."

ANTONIO

"You've got to be prepared to be a father. All of the things that I learned in my life about responsibility, about taking care of people, about loving people—everything in my life prepared me to be a father. You have to have that maturity, you have to have that knowledge, you have to have that love to be a father. I mentor a child, and he lives with his mother and father, but his father is a drunk. His mother, his grandmother, and his aunts are basically raising him, but they baby him too much, so I started taking him on outings and spending time with him. I took him to a football game, and just listening to him talk, I could tell he was being raised by women because he's got that 'hug him to the bosom it's okay baby don't worry about it' attitude.

"I love being a father because it's very fulfilling to know that you can have such a positive effect on a child's life. There are so many studies and statistics that show when fathers are active in their daughter's lives how much better they come out. They are more motivated, more educated, and less likely to get pregnant as teenagers when a father has an influence in their lives. I'm a role model for my daughter; hopefully she'll look for a man like me because I raised her from age twelve on my own.

"I told her when she started going out with her friends, 'I don't want no drinking and no unprotected sex. If you drink and get drunk, don't come home driving drunk. Stay where you're at, stay at your little girlfriend's house, or call me to come get you. Don't try to come home and get killed in the process because you were driving drunk. And I'd prefer you don't have sex, because you're too young, but if you're going to have sex, don't have unprotected sex. Don't get pregnant.'

"To this day I don't know if she is a virgin or not and don't want to know. I do know she drinks every now and then because a few times she'd call and say, 'Daddy, I'm staying at Sue's tonight,' which was fine with me because I knew where she was.

"One of my issues as a child was being moved around and not having a home of my own. My daughter can always come home, and she's done it a couple of times. But she's in college, she's single, and she works, so that's okay with me. One of the reasons I don't sell my house is because I still have this image of my daughter crying. It makes an imprint on your heart, and it never leaves you. I remember one year I was working in Los Angeles on a temporary assignment, and we'd rented our house out because we were planning on moving back. We eventually did come back, but it was during the Christmas holidays. I was tucking my daughter in bed, and she started crying because somebody else was spending Christmas in our house while we were in a hotel.

I felt like such a failure. I felt like I let her down. So I made a promise to her that I'd never let her down again and that she'd always have a place she could call home.

"Once we did get moved back into the house, the divorce was still hard on her because she was so young. I came home from work one day, and she was on the couch crying. She had her head buried under a pillow, she said, 'I just can't believe she left us like that. She just left us.' That was hard on me, and I'll never forget it. That sorry-ass woman left her daughter and hurt her like that, and it scarred her badly. I don't know what the effect is going to be. I don't have a clue, but my ex-wife is out there in the world not even knowing and not caring, and I just despise her. I can't even date a woman who has the same name—black, white, or whatever, I can't date her. I can't even call her name because I just hate what she did to our child.

"Even though my daughter's been through a lot, I hope I've instilled good values in her. I hope she's motivated. All the things my grandfather told me, I told her. I'd tell her stories about what I did and where I came from, how I lived in a little ramshackle house with rats the size of cats making noise under my bed at night and how I used to cry myself to sleep hoping those rats didn't get in my bed. I'd lay in my bed and look out the window, because I'd rather look outside at the world than look inside at my house, and I'd just dream about what was out there. Every night I'd hear the train whistle and just close my eyes and wonder where that train was going, wishing it would take me away. I'd say, 'I got to get out of here—I got to do better than this for myself,' and I came further than I ever dreamed."

EDWIN

"I have one child that I know of." Edwin winked.

"Seriously, I never planned on being a father so early in life. It more or less just happened. I've learned how enjoyable and important it is to be with your child and how difficult it is when they're taken away from you. You love them, they're snatched away, and there's nothing you can do about it. It's a horrible feeling.

"My daughter came along nine months after my second wife and I first slept together. We broke up right after my daughter's first birthday, and I didn't see her again until she was five or six years old. My ex-wife moved to Austin, and I didn't know how to get in touch with her, so all I could do was to keep paying child support. I couldn't get the courts to tell me where the checks were going or anything. Then my daughter's grandmother brought her by to see me when my ex was back home visiting, and that's how I got back in touch with her.

"I thought about my daughter a bunch when they first left me. I had wet eyes and everything else, but then you get to a place where you have to block it out. It's all about survival. It would still surface over and over again, but that's normal because my dad died over ten years ago, and that still surfaces. I still think about him, but you got to put up a mental block. You got to keep going.

"Once I knew where she was, I got to see her more frequently, and then I would get her during the summer and every Christmas. Then, after my ex remarried and had a baby with her new husband, she wanted to combine the family, so once again I didn't see my daughter very often.

"I had a scholarship set up for her at UCLA. I know a guy who works there, and she went to visit and said she liked it, but then she said, 'My mom needs some help, I need to stay close so I can help her.' So she's stuck in a rut. She's working in a little home-care business that her mother has, and her mother is paying her a couple of hundred dollars a week and putting pressure on her so that she doesn't leave and go away to college, and that's a damn shame. My ex-wife has lawsuit after lawsuit from supposedly being hurt here and there; somebody bumped into the back of her car, she slipped and fell, always something. So of course my daughter feels like she needs to stay there and help, but I'm telling her, 'You need to go to college and stay on campus and get out of that environment.'

"My stepdaughter isn't quite as bad. Unfortunately, she wanted to get married, so now she has three kids and a husband who won't work and ain't acting right. I'm just trying to help her get through college and become independent so she can get out from under that. I let her keep my other car so she can have transportation, and she won't have to depend on him to take her places and do things. She'll graduate this spring and hopefully she can become independent and realize that she doesn't need that life."

WARREN

"I've learned that your kids can be so much more if you're there for them. When my kids were growing up, me and my wife always had a house full of other folks' kids hanging around. I coached baseball, I was all over the state of Louisiana with other people's kids but most of the parents weren't there. Me and a couple of other parents had to put the money up to pay for their hotel rooms and feed these other kids, and they were starved for that attention. When it was all said and done and my oldest son went on to college, some of those same kids that I had to pay for and do for ended up going to jail. They dropped out of school, they got into drugs, and they got into everything else because their parents weren't there for them, but those were good kids, and they had potential. They just needed guidance but instead they went down the toilet because of the lack of attention from their parents.

"I've got a good friend whose mother is just run-down; I bet she's got twelve grandchildren living in her house. Her daughters go out there and make babies and come back home and drop them off on her and just go on back out in the streets, but I don't fault her daughters. I fault her, because she should have never taken on that responsibility. When those girls went out there and had those first babies, she should've made them take responsibility. They might have thought twice before having another one, but she made it too easy for them. I told my boys, just like my mama told me, 'You can go out there and get a baby if you want to, but I'm not raising it for you. If you're man enough to get a baby, you're man enough to raise it. If you get one, that's your business. I'm not raising no child. I'm not going to miss going out with the fellas because I got to babysit my grandchildren. I've done what I was supposed to do. You need to do the same thing. Now, occasionally if I ain't doing nothing, I'm at home, and y'all need a babysitter—fine. But don't make it a habit. I'm not going to cancel my plans for you.'

"People will dump their kids off on someone else in a heartbeat. I look at the Michael Jackson situation, and I could shoot those parents because if anything happened to that child, it's just as much their fault. The court should just tell them people, 'Get on out of here—we ain't giving you nothing.' I think they're just trying to get money from that man because if they were afraid of him doing something to their child, they wouldn't have taken him there in the first place."

RUBEN

"I'm raising my fifteen-year-old son because his mother is trifling. She's in her late thirties, and she's still out there. She gets a new boyfriend every six months, and she doesn't see anything wrong with bringing them home to live with her. What kind of example is that to set for a teenage boy? A boy doesn't want to see his mother sleeping around like that, and as soon as one of those boyfriends does something to hurt her, he's going to try to protect her. I know how I am, and I know I'd have to kill one of those bastards if they were to lay a finger on my son.

"When I found out that my son, who was fourteen at the time, was seeing a girl who was eighteen, I went ballistic. I put my foot down and told his mom that he needed to come live with me. I would usually get him in the summer and on different holidays, but he'd never lived with me full-time. Hell, I think she was glad when I took him; it made life easier for her because she couldn't do anything with him anyway.

"When I travel, my mom comes to stay with him. I don't believe that a fifteen-year-old boy should go unsupervised, because there are too many distractions out there. I remember how I was when I was fifteen— no telling what I would've done if my parents had left me with the house to myself. I can't depend on his mother to supervise him, because it's always been easier for her let him do whatever he wanted. He's lived with me for the past year now, and it's a full-time job trying to instill discipline. When he lived with his mother and said he was going to the movies with friends, she wouldn't even ask who he was going with, how he was going to get there, and what time he'd be back home, and that was because she was too busy doing her own thing.

"I date a lot of women myself, but I don't bring any of them home, because I don't think that's the proper thing to do when you have a child at home. How am I going to tell my son that he shouldn't do certain things if he sees me doing them? I'm not a fan of the 'Do as I say, not as I do' mentality. I believe you teach your children by example.

"I let him know that every time he disobeys my rules, something's going to be taken away from him—either his TV, his cell phone, his music, whatever. Whatever it takes to get his attention is what I do.

"There are some women at work, single parents just like me, and I'm able to go to them and get their input on things that have to do with raising a kid. I'm astute enough to understand that men and women are different. I would ask them, 'How would a woman handle this?'

"My son twisted an ankle and was on crutches when I picked him up from school. I said, 'Why didn't you call me?' and he said, 'What for? You would've just told me to put ice on it and put it on a pillow and elevate it.'

"My friends at work said a mother would be more nurturing: 'Oh sweetie, what happened? Blah, blah, blah,' and I understand that I am not conditioned to think like that, and besides, he's a boy. Biologically I was not made that way, but it doesn't mean that I can't learn how to be more understanding, so those women, along with my mom, are key in helping me raise my son alone."

LANDON

"I've always wanted children, and I believe in predestination. The Bible says, 'You raise a child in the way he should go and in his later years he won't stray from those ways.' In his later years, when he's gone through all this stuff and he realizes what mom and dad said was right, he'll get back on track. What I'm saying is, I've screwed up and made some bad decisions, but it's all part of the plan for the man I will become. I'm a great father and going through what I've been through has only helped to strengthen me.

"The biggest thing I've learned as a father is how important it is to interact with your child. A lot of the black men don't interact with their children, because of the baby-mama drama. When they try to interact, it's almost like a hassle, and they don't feel like dealing with the hassle, so they say, 'Fuck it. I ain't got time for this,' and just give up.

"I don't believe that black men are raised up mentally ready to be good fathers and to take care of a household the way they should, and that's where the problems lie. They're not being raised right, plain and simple.

"You got people who are consumed with being the greatest, and they raise their kids to be the greatest. Their kids will be overachievers or turn away from that because their parents are always pushing them, and they're pushing them too hard. The Bible says, 'Fathers, do not provoke your children to wrath.' Fathers have that strong voice. They have that forcefulness. When my dad told me to do something, he was like, 'Get it done,' and *boom*, I'm doing it. But if the father were to overbearingly do that, it would cause the child to lash out in whatever way he saw possible. He'd provoke that child to wrath.

"One thing always leads to another, and the biggest thing I've learned so far about raising a child is that I have to be there for my daughter, because I can already see that she's the emotional type. She always wants hugs, she always wants kisses, and if I don't give that to her now, when she gets old enough to understand, she's going to get it from somewhere else, and it's not going to be from the right source. Then she's going to become a ho or she's going to be getting pimped out.

"I love being a father. It's a joy to have a child look up to you and make you feel like you're the superhero. There's nothing you can do wrong in her eyes. The only thing I don't like about being a father is the fear. The fear of knowing that you have in your hands the ability to steer a child in the wrong way. You are their only channel to the outside world until they get old enough to get out there, and by the time they get to be teenagers and get out there, you done already showed them everything. Now they're going to do their own thing, and they're going to make their mistakes, but if you didn't teach them right when they were kids, if you didn't properly raise that child, the streets or the jail's gon' raise them."

2
SEX

PECAN PIE

1 ½ cups all-purpose flour

½ teaspoon salt

2 tablespoons granulated sugar

½ cup (1 stick) butter, chilled

¼ cup ice water

3 eggs, beaten

¾ cup light corn syrup

2 tablespoons dark corn syrup

¼ cup packed light brown sugar

3 tablespoons butter, melted

1 pinch of salt

½ cup finely crushed pecans

1 cup quartered pecans

1 cup pecan halves

Preheat the oven to 350 degrees F.

CRUST: In a medium bowl, combine flour, salt, and granulated sugar. Cut the butter into the flour mixture until it resembles coarse crumbs. Gradually sprinkle the water over the flour mixture, stirring until the dough comes together enough to form a ball.

On a floured surface, flatten the dough ball with a rolling pin. Roll the dough out in a circle that is 1 inch larger than the 9-inch pie dish. Place the pie shell into the dish, and refrigerate until needed.

(continued)

(continued)

PIE FILLING: In a medium bowl, mix together the eggs, light and dark corn syrups, brown sugar, butter, salt, and finely crushed pecans. Spread the quartered pecans over the bottom of refrigerated piecrust. Pour the syrup mixture over the pecans; then arrange pecan halves on top of the pie.

Bake for 1 hour, or until firm. Let the pie cool for 1 hour before serving.

7

SEX IN GENERAL

QUINCY

"I'll admit that when I was younger I didn't have to care about a woman to have sex with her, but now I do. I have to really care, and I'm talking about care about her enough to date her. Ain't none of that booty-call stuff with me—uh-uh—because there's too much shit out there that you can catch, and like I said, you've got to worry about women going off on you if you make them think there's more to the relationship than there really is. You can't be out there playing with a woman's feelings, because you don't know what she might do.

"You can't be switching partners and having sex with every new woman you meet, because it's not safe. People always say sex gets boring with the same person after a while but it doesn't get boring with a woman if you really care about her and both of you do things to keep it interesting. It's all what you make it anyway, so if you're bored, you need to do something different, and men shouldn't put all the blame on the woman. Sometimes we're the ones who are boring. Men need to do things to keep the woman interested, and we usually have to work at that.

"It's not fair for us to think we can let our stomachs get all big or come home from work and sit around scratching all evening while she's up cooking dinner and taking care of the kids after she's worked all day long too. And then we have the nerve to expect her to have all this energy and desire for sex when we get to the bedroom. I don't want to walk out of the bathroom and see my woman laying on the bed looking like a damn beached whale—that shit turns me off—so I think it's only fair that I keep myself up too so she will like what she sees.

"If you're in a relationship, sex is maybe twenty percent of what makes that relationship. As the relationship gets older, it's even less than twenty percent, so that's why you need to be friends and understand each other, because if your relationship revolves around sex, what do you have when that's gone? Sex can't possibly be the foundation of any relationship unless the two people involved are sixteen or seventeen years old."

GREG

"It is not true that everything revolves around sex for men. I don't think about sex all day long, so I don't know where the statistics came from that say men think about sex every few minutes. I'm usually thinking about trying to make me some money so I don't have time to think about sex all day. I usually don't even get into that mode until I get home from a hard day of work and settle down and maybe drink a little wine and turn the TV on. As far as men saying they have to have sex every day, I don't think the majority of men feel that way, because I'm a strong, healthy man, and I couldn't have sex every day. I wouldn't even want to, because then it's not even special anymore, and you'd get tired of that person. You have to be really creative to keep it exciting with the same person if you're doing it every day."

DANTE

"My parents didn't talk to me about sex; they didn't tell me anything. Nothing. I learned about sex through a man I knew when I was about thirteen years old. He was in his fifties, and I used to call him Pops. I used to go over to his house and talk to him while he sat there and drank beer under a tree, and he used to tell me about life, sex, what I needed to do and what I shouldn't do. He would tell me all this stuff, and I would listen, and that's how I learned. The people I hung around always thought I knew a lot about sex because I was mature for my age. Although I never told them I was a virgin, I never told them I wasn't one either. I just let them assume that I was really out there because being a virgin isn't something you brag about, especially if you're a man.

"I was twenty-four and married the first time I actually had intercourse. I did jack off a lot before that, and I had a lot of women who gave me blow jobs and stuff like that, so I knew what it felt like to ejaculate, but I just didn't know how it felt to be inside a woman. The reason I say I have skills is because during the time I was single and jacking off, I learned how to prolong my ejaculation. Some women like to go for fifteen minutes, some like to go for half an hour, and some like to go at it hard, all night or as long as you can hang, and if I wanted to do that, I could hang with the best because I'm skilled in that area. I could do porn films and get paid if I wanted to, but I don't want to live like that.

"The first time I actually had sexual intercourse it was all right, but it was excellent the second time because I felt more comfortable. I hadn't told my wife I was a virgin, because I was afraid she wouldn't marry me, and besides, I wanted to see if she could tell. I wanted to know if I was up to par and if I was as good as the guys she'd been with before.

"Don't think it was easy for me to wait, because I like titties and thighs, just like any other man. It was problematic, and I'm not so sure I want to tell my kids to wait, because I think it messed up my mind. Not having sex when everyone else around you is doing it goes against your nature, and it's a hard thing to do even though it's the right thing to do. To this day, women proposition me with money, sex, gifts—all kinds of material things that I'd like to take—but I'm stronger than that. One of my coworkers, an older lady, asked me the other day if I wanted a sugar mama. She said I could have whatever I wanted if I'd just spend a few hours a week with her, and this lady is beautiful, but sex isn't everything, and I play life on a higher level than that.

"This physical life is serious, but it's only temporary, so you have to think about your future. I drink and curse and stuff like that, which I know is dead wrong, and I'm not trying to validate it, but that's about the most I'll do. I'll drink a little, get to talking shit and flirting, but I know where I'm going every night; I'm going home to my wife, and I ain't making no stops along the way."

MALIK

"Of course, you always had your sex education class at school, and then there was *I Escaped From Devil's Island,* or *Nigga Charlie,* or whatever slut movie your daddy took you to. There was a movie theater downtown that my mother's husband took me to when I was in the seventh grade, and these were Jim Brown and Fred Williamson movies, the first movies I remember seeing at a theater. They were rated R, and one of the ladies who was selling tickets didn't want to let me in, but my mother's husband said, 'Well, he's my son, and I want him to go in and see this movie,' so they let me in. That's how I was introduced to sex. He didn't discuss it with me afterwards or say anything about it at a later time. We just watched the movie and left. Of course, it looked interesting, and I'd heard other kids talking about sex, but I'd never experienced it, so I was glad I'd got to see it for myself. Hell, I may as well tell the truth—my dick got hard, and I couldn't wait to get my first piece, but of course I couldn't tell my mother's husband that.

"I was a junior in high school when I had my first sexual experience, and it wasn't all that to me, because I really didn't know what I was doing and neither did she. We talked about it a lot at first, then we started kissing, and I started feeling on her and worked my way to getting my hand inside her panties. I got my finger just inside her vagina, and she started squirming and got real wet, but she only touched me through my jeans. That's how I learned what blue balls were. I went to school the next day with my balls all sore, and I was miserable. I finally had sex for the first time later on that year with the same girl, and the first time we tried, she kept saying, 'I'm not going to just lay here and let you do it. You gonna have to fight me if you want to get it in.'

"The whole time I was trying to hold her down and get in, she was moving around, and I thought, *There's something wrong with this picture.* What was really happening was she was trying to keep me from getting in because she was scared to do it, and so was I, and we didn't really know what was going to happen, so she made it difficult. By the time I did finally get in, her brother came walking through the door, so we got busted.

"We were lying on the living room couch with the lights out, and he came in, took one look, and asked, 'What the hell do y'all think you're doing? Get your asses up and get the hell out of here right now!' He and I knew each other—we'd played baseball together a few times before—so he didn't tell on us or anything, but needless to say, my first experience wasn't all that good.

"We were curious after that, so five days later we tried it again, and we got it right that time. This time we did it in her room. I had snuck in through her bedroom window, and it was kind of funny afterwards because a few days later her mom told her, 'You're going to have to be careful, baby. We saw some footprints out by your bedroom window. Make sure to keep your windows locked because you just never know.'

"That first time we had sex it was nice, but it didn't make me feel like a man or anything. Of course, after that first time, I became preoccupied with sex just like any other young boy, and I wanted to do it all the time, but not with every girl I saw. That was one of the things all my friends teased me about, because in school I was always on the B honor roll and always had girls who liked me and wanted to get close to me, but I wasn't interested in a lot of those girls. After my mother's husband left home, I was always working, playing sports, or doing my schoolwork, and I didn't have time to be bothered, so I didn't pay attention to their advances.

"My friends would say, 'Damn, man, you just don't know how much pussy you're turning down. You're turning it down left and right, and we ain't even getting it offered to us like you are.'

"I didn't know what they were talking about, so I'd tell them, 'Man, that girl ain't even thinking about me. She's like a sister to me.' I always called everybody my sister; I wasn't interested in everybody who wanted to give me the panties. I wasn't a dog, but now that I look back on it, it could have been real easy for me to be one. Fortunately for me, I'd made the right choice because almost all of my high school buddies who were screwing every chance they got now have kids who are grown, babies they had when we were in school while I was turning down the coochie, and some of them got babies with girls they didn't even like that much. Some of them even have grandchildren already, so I guess there was a blessing in my being the way I was."

PIERRE

"I was about seventeen when I experienced sex for the first time, and it was not a good experience. It was with this older chick who was in ROTC with me in high school. We used to play and flirt with each other all the time, and I was good at flirting, but that was all I'd planned on doing. I was at work one day, and she called me and said she needed to talk to me, but I had worked a double shift, so I told her I'd have to talk to her another time.

"She insisted, so I swung by her house, and she came outside and said, 'Let's go park somewhere so we can talk,' and we did. I found out right away that talking was the last thing on her mind 'cause she pulled out this pack of condoms and hopped in the backseat of my Bonneville.

"In my mind I was thinking, *Damn*, because I didn't really want to have sex with her, but I couldn't be no punk, so I got in the backseat with her and we started kissing and messing around for a minute, and the next minute my dick was out. She put the condom on me, got on top of me and tried to put me inside her, but I wasn't really feeling her, because I didn't want my first time to be like that, and I really didn't want it to be with her. I mean, she was a lot of fun, and I liked flirting with her 'cause she had big titties, but I didn't want to have sex with her.

"She was all over me, trying to put it in, but it just wasn't working. My shit kept folding up. Then she got frustrated and took the condom off and started blowing me, and I was like, *Oh, damn! Is this what a blow job is about?* but I still couldn't get into it, 'cause I just didn't want to do it with her. So she finally stopped, and we rearranged our clothes, and I took her home. On the way back, everything was kind of quiet, and all I could think of was, *Damn, she's going to go to school tomorrow and tell everybody I was a lousy lay.*

"But the next day at school, before I even got to ROTC, I was in history class with some of her girlfriends, and they came in and gave me a note. I was like, *Oh no, here it comes,* but the note said, 'We heard that you're big. Are you this big, this big, or in between?' and there were lines on the paper that I was supposed to fill in to show them how big I was.

"I was like, *Whew. I'm sure glad she didn't tell nobody what really happened, 'cause I would have been so embarrassed.* I think after that, I stopped flirting with her or anybody else.

"When I was in high school, most of the girls were more experienced than the guys anyway, because living so close to a military base, they were dating GIs. These guys would graduate from high school and join the military the next day, so they were only eighteen or nineteen years old, and they'd come up to the school all the time. They had cars, they had money, and a guy in high school couldn't compete with that, so most of us wasn't getting no play. I remember one guy who used to come get his girl at lunchtime, and they'd go out to the parking lot. He had shades on his windows, and he'd pull them down, and they'd fuck right there, in the school parking lot—no lie. See, parents think their kids are safe at school, but nowadays ain't no telling what these kids will do *at school*.

"I believe you have to love a person to make love to them, but you can have sex with someone whether you love them or not. I don't do anything different with a woman I love, but I think that's part of where I make my mistake. I can be dating somebody, but I can be in a lovemaking mood, and after that, she either starts to think I'm crazy about her, or she falls in love with me. I can be really affection-ate, and you don't need to be like that with someone you're just kick-ing it with. When it's rainy outside or cold or something like that, it can put you in that mood. You roll up in there and make it real good by doing all the kissing and cuddling, and talking, then you sex her real good and kiss some more afterwards, and when you're finished, she's all messed up. She starts stalking you and calling you with that, 'I want to be with you,' and all that kind of shit, and that's when you realize you've made a mistake."

COLLIER

"Like I said before, I have to have feelings for someone to have sex with them. That's why I don't have no more than four children. That old 'wham, bam, thank you, ma'am,' that's not in my blood. I wouldn't even allow a relationship to go that far. I was at a bar one time, and a beautiful young lady was sitting there at the table by herself. I love music, so I went to the jukebox to play some music, and she came over, and we started talking. We had a nice little conversation, and she told me she hadn't been out in a while. Finally she asked me to take her home, and I did.

"It was cold, and she stayed in an apartment, and when we got there, I found out that her utilities had been turned off. Two little boys was laying on the couch, and when she went to put them in their beds, I went over and opened the refrigerator and didn't see nothing but a jar of water, some milk, and a lettuce—that was all she had in there. I noticed that when I looked in the box, the light didn't come on, so I say, 'Your light burned out?'

"She looked at me and said, 'No, my electricity is off.'

"I thought she was running a game, so I went to the circuit breaker, right? I wanted to make sure she wasn't running no line on me, but all the breakers was turned on.

"That next morning, I went to the bank, got eight hundred dollars, had her utilities turned on, gave her four hundred for Christmas for her kids, and then took her shopping for some food. She was down, she needed help real bad, and I felt sorry for her. When I took her shopping, I asked her what she was doing in that club, and she said she felt so bad, she just had to get out of that house, but I told her, 'Don't you never leave your kids alone like that no more. That's too dangerous. And don't think I do this for any and everybody. I ain't no fool.'

"But anyway, she thought she had to give me her body after that, and I told her, 'I'm not like other men. I did that out of the goodness of my heart.' I know that women do things like that for men too, so I'm not trying to brag on myself, but I've had a lot of women tell me they do nice things for men, and they don't seem to appreciate it, but it's not that they don't appreciate it—it's just that they have never had anybody be nice to them, so they don't know how to act. They ain't used to nothing.

"That reminds me of a friend of mine who was dating a real nice lady, and one morning after he'd spent the night at her place, she fixed him breakfast in bed. Know what that fool said? He was talking about, 'Man, guess what that bitch did? She come bringing my food to the bed. I told her ain't nothing wrong with my feet, take that back in there and put it on the table, and I'll be in there to get it.' But see now, that's a fool. He ain't used to nothing, just ignorant. You can't change people like that. Matter of fact, they don't want to be changed. They been like that so long, they don't know no better."

ANTONIO

"The sex rule is you can date as many people as you want, but you're only having sex with one person at a time. The obvious reason for this has to do with your health, but the main reason has to do with emotions, not just her emotions but yours as well. You get more attached to the woman you're having sex with. The woman I'm having sex with would be the favorite—she's the queen.

"I've dated Nikki off and on for the past four years. We'd date for a while, and then we would start having sex, so she'd be my sex partner again. Unfortunately, every time we get back together, the question of having a long-term relationship will inevitably come up. We'll be lying in bed, and she'll ask, 'So where is this going?'

"And I'm like, 'Girl, I done told you before. This relationship ain't going nowhere.' Then she'll say, *'Well, kiss my ass, then, motherfucker!'* and then just get up and leave. So I call her the 'kiss my ass' girl.

"I saw her a few months ago. We went out and had dinner and talked about old times, and she said if I wanted to get with her again I could, but I was like, let's not go there right now. If we do get back together and fall back into that situation, like around the holidays, go to a few Christmas parties and maybe start dating again and sleeping with each other, that old 'Am I your girl?' will come back up, and I'll have to say, 'Girl, I done told you no.' Then she'll yell, *Kiss my ass, motherfucker. I'm gone, then.'* She'll get up in the middle of the night, get dressed and leave, and I'll go to sleep. Nikki is on the inactive list, but she keeps popping up every now and again.

"I never sleep with more than one person at a time. I tell the women that I sleep with, 'You're the only one that I'm sleeping with. I'm not sleeping with anybody else, and I hope it's the same with you,' and I get that commitment so we're exclusive sexual partners.

"Sex is a release. It's going through the motions of love, but it ain't love. I've learned that. I've learned that when you really love somebody, just being with them, just the excitement of looking forward to seeing them is something amazing. You're like, *Man I'm going to go pick her up. We're going to have fun. I can't wait to see her. I can't wait to hold her and smell her, to be close to her.* That's as good as sex if you really care about somebody, so I'm able to deal with that. Some guys would say, 'Man, that's gay as shit. What the hell is that?' So I would never tell that to a man, because with men, it's all about the booty.

"The most common mistake a woman can make is to put so little value on her body, and then after she gives it to you and finds out you're not interested in having a committed relationship, she comes back and says, 'Wait a minute—you slept with me.' It's like having sex on the first or second date. Some women make it too easy, and then when you say, 'You're not my girlfriend. We're not exclusive,' she'll ask, 'Then why did you sleep with me?' Well, I slept with you because you gave it to me like it was nothing, so even when a woman just throws it at you, you can't always take it. You got to hold out, you got to say, 'No, baby.' If she appears to be a quality person and you want to get into a relationship with her, you need to wait until you really know each other. Having sex is like breaking the seal. As soon as we have sex, everything is going to change, so we need to wait.

"Unfortunately when you tell some women you want to wait, they'll look at you like, 'Are you crazy? Are you gay?' Then again, there are situations where you're just going to hit it and get the hell out because you know you ain't ever going to see her again.

"Women need to understand that when they have sex with a guy too quickly, he doesn't value it, because she gave it up too fast. She's thinking, *I gave him the biggest gift I could give him, and he's acting like that ain't nothing.* He's acting like that because you did it on the first or second date. You acted like it didn't have any value.

"The first time I saw a live naked woman up close was on Halloween, and it's a great memory. I was about ten, and I was out trick-or-treating with some friends of mine. We were too old to be with adults, so we were by ourselves. What we'd do is leave our neighborhood and go into the white neighborhood to get some better candy. We'd go as far as we could walk and start knocking on doors. We walked up to this porch, and there was a white couple with their window open and they were in the living room having sex. They had the blinds closed, but we could hear them moaning and groaning, so we're standing on the porch listening, and one of the guys is wondering if we should say trick or treat, but the rest of us were like, 'Naw, shut up, shut up. We're listening,' but finally my Jamaican friend, Baptiste, hollered 'Trick or treat!' and messed it up for the rest of us.

"The woman looked out the window and said, 'Honey there's some trick-or-treaters at the door,' and the guy said, 'I ain't giving them niggers no candy,' so we figured we'd better go. There was a jack-o'-lantern on the porch, and Baptiste grabbed that pumpkin and reared back and smashed it against the guy's front door and said, 'Yeah, I got your nigga right here.' The guy jumped up, pulled on his pants, opened the door, and started chasing us down the street, but at the same time his girlfriend or wife or whatever she was didn't bother to put her clothes on at all. She opened the front door and just stood there naked, saying, 'Baby, come back here.' So we were running from him and staring at her. We'd run two steps and walk back one. We were circling the yard, coming back, trying to see this naked woman. That was a Halloween night to remember.

"The first time I had sex, it was surreal. I was eighteen years old, my mother had just died, and I was dating this white girl. It was springtime, and there was this big festival in our community that we had every year called the Spring Festival. She was a debutante, but her father wouldn't hear of me taking her to this dance, because I wasn't in her class socially and basically because I wasn't white, but she had to go to this dance because she was a debutante. We were all staying at my mother's house, and my sister and her husband were in the front bedroom asleep.

"I heard this knock on the back door around midnight, and I answered it, and there my girlfriend was in her debutante gown. She said she wanted to see me, so we just walked into my bedroom, started kissing, and eventually had sex and probably didn't say one word to one another. That was my first time. I think it was an act of rebellion on her part because her daddy didn't think I was good enough to take her to the ball, so she'd snuck off to see me anyway and had sex with me to get back at him. If he'd found out, he would've killed both of us.

"Sex is important under the right circumstances, but it's also dangerous in a lot of other situations. You have to deal with feelings, emotions, and diseases, and that's scary. I'm very level-headed, and this is real hard to say, but I have a hard time even getting an erection unless I'm very comfortable with somebody. The equipment ain't going to work unless I'm really confident that it's okay to do this. It's like there's some type of mechanism in my body that shuts down and says, *Uh-uh, we ain't ready. We ain't doing it with her.*

"I haven't had sex with a lot of women, because I'm sensible about it. Being a mature man with a little bit of sense, I know the damage it can cause emotionally. The investment that women put into the act of sex means a lot to them. Even when they make the mistake of giving it up too early, it still means a lot to them, and unless you're ready to make some kind of commitment, don't do it, because it's just going to cause grief.

"With a man, the act of sex is so easy—all you have to do is get an erection and stick it in—while women have to do so much more. If you're a level-headed man, you got to realize what she's investing in it, and you'd better think long and hard about it.

"There is a difference between having sex and making love, and the difference is when you have a connection with somebody. When you care about her, when you want to please her, when you're being pleased by her, when you just feel that bliss of, *God, I want her so much.* She's wonderful, and you love everything about her, but to tell you the truth, that really hasn't happened for me.

"I guess it's due to my Catholic upbringing because a lot of times after having sex, I have this terrible guilt. I feel like, *I shouldn't have done that, that wasn't right. It wasn't right for her and it wasn't right for me.*"

EDWIN

"My parents never talked to me about sex. That was taboo when I was growing up. I learned about sex from listening to the fellows talk. You start hanging out with the guys, and—monkey see, monkey do—you usually get with some little fast-tail girl who's already been around the block a time or two, and she can't wait to teach you.

"I was kind of old when I first had sex, at least by today's standards, because I was about nineteen. Hell, the only things around to have sex with in the country were cows and pigs, so I wasn't getting no action. I wasn't dating any of the girls at home, so there wasn't anything going on for me in the sex department. I usually stayed at home and studied. I was more into school than anything else, and I didn't want to do anything to hurt my mother. I was being considerate in one aspect, but sex didn't faze me. I didn't find anyone attractive enough that I wanted to date, so I wasn't bothered. Our town was pretty small, and it seemed like by the time I got to be a senior, all of the black girls had gotten pregnant or had moved on to someone else.

"One time, some girls came over to the house. There was a carnival being held in town, and they asked my mother, 'Can Edwin come out and go to the carnival?' And she said, 'No, he's too busy in there doing his homework. He ain't got time for you pissy-tail little girls. Y'all better leave my son alone—he's trying to get his education.' She'd run them off, and in hindsight, I have to say thank goodness, because I might have become a father even earlier than I did.

"The first time I had sex, it wasn't that big a deal. Shit, we did it standing up. I had gone back home for a visit. I was this big-time college boy, and it was between semesters, and I thought, *What the hell, no time like the present*. A group of us had gone out, and later on that night we'd parked, and two of the couples were in the car necking, and me and this girl were standing outside by the trunk talking. Then we started to kiss, and before I knew it, she had unzipped my pants, sat back on the trunk of the car, and guided me into her, but it didn't last more than a minute or two.

"There was one other time I came home to visit from college, and me and a friend of mine went over to another small country town because we knew of some girls who all the guys could go to for their first experience. If they wanted sex, they knew that they could always hit these sisters up. There were about three or four of them. So my friend and me went over to visit these girls, and he was a bit more experienced than me. He carried this quilt in his trunk for just such occasions. We didn't have any money to get a motel room, so he took this quilt out of his trunk and spread it on the ground for him and his girl. I had the backseat of the car, and I'm in there just going after it like I know what the hell I'm doing, and the girl asks, 'What are you doing?'

"And being modest I said, 'I'm making love to you.'

"She said, 'No, you're not,' and she reached up and turned on the dome light.

"This was a big girl, and I looked down and saw that I was in one of those wrinkles, just working it like there was no tomorrow. Of course, when I saw that, my interest level went to zero, and I never could get hard again. She sat there and played and rubbed on my dick, and I was thinking to myself, *Boy, that's just dead. There is no way in the world it's going to get hard again*. I'll never forget that—I thought I was tearing it up, and I was in a wrinkle.

"Sex is important to men. Even for me, a guy in his fifties, sex is still very important. It's not number one on my priority list, but for a man, sex is something that takes away the tension and relaxes him. It's a way of bonding, and showing affection and taking care of his woman.

"Personally, it depends upon the situation regarding how long I can go without sex. I might be able to go one day; then, again it might be three weeks. It's easy to say, 'To hell with it—I don't want to be bothered,' but I used to want it every day.

"I've had sex with quite a few women, but when I was married, I was devoted in those relationships. Since my last divorce, I can think of about eight women I've been with, and that's over a period of three years. When I was younger and I was single, I was pretty busy. Sometimes there were two or three women a night. Not at the same time, but one time I did have a mother and a daughter after me. The daughter asked me if I'd ever been with two women, and I told her no, so she says, 'What do you think about getting with me and my mother?'

"I said, 'You and your mother?' and she said, 'Well, actually, she's my stepmother' and I was like *Damn, that's just not right, stepmother or not,* so I couldn't do it.

"When I was younger, I would go and knock off a woman, and then I would go somewhere else and see another woman who was tempting, and she'd want to have sex with me, so I'd do it. I was in my twenties, I didn't get tired, and it wasn't like it is now. These days you got to worry about AIDS. These days when I have sex, I want to lie there and cuddle and hug that woman. Back then, it was strictly a booty call.

"I don't think it's acceptable for either men or women to have a lot of partners, but that doesn't mean I haven't. I have a serious partner now, but every now and then I might go see another woman. Sometimes you just feel like *What the hell? I'm not obligated. I might want to go and see what this other woman is like,* but actually, it's been a while since I've ventured out. There is another woman I've been talking to lately, and I'm starting to think that maybe I ought to take her up on her offer to get together, but then again I'm the kind of guy who will sit there and bullshit a woman and get her all worked up and say, 'Baby, I understand your condition, but I got to go home,' and get up and walk away. As long as I'm in control, everything is fine.

"Having sex is just that—you hit it and move on, and that was what I did in my twenties and early thirties. I think that when you make love, you go into it being more concerned about your partner's needs. When you get into the passionate lovemaking, you're not just trying to hit it. You want to satisfy her first, and you know that if you satisfy her, you in turn will be satisfied beyond your wildest dreams."

WARREN

"It's not difficult to remain true to one woman. If the woman is doing her best to please her man, then it's easy for him not to cheat. Just pick up any book or magazine about sex, and you'll find two hundred billion ways to have sex, so there ain't no reason to be bored with each other. You have to be able to look at your relationship and say, 'This is getting dull. We need to do something different.' But it takes two. The problem is when one is ready to try something different and the other doesn't want to get involved. That causes the other one to look elsewhere. I work with a lot of women, and I found out that the difference between a white woman and a black woman is that a white woman will do just about anything to please her man. Black women got this, 'I ain't doing no freaky shit like that,' mentality, and it makes the man feel like he'll never be able to explore or try different things. He feels that if you're not willing to do something different with him sexually, what are you willing to do? And once again, that's another reason men go out there looking, because their needs aren't being met at home.

"Even if he wants to do something freaky and you don't, there are alternatives. Hey, I don't believe a woman is going to want to do everything that you want to do, but she can say, 'Well, no, I don't want to do that, but let's do this.' Don't say, 'Aw, hell no,' and that's the end of it, because you totally destroy your man then. That's like saying, 'Hey, this is all you gon' get, and you ain't getting no mo,' but when he walks out the house and goes to the bar that evening and has a few drinks, he's thinking about you saying no. Then he comes across old Susie Q sitting at the other end of the bar, and she starts talking to him and finds out what's going on in his life and says, 'She won't do what? Come on here. Come on, let me show you something, baby. You ain't got to take that.' And you know what? Susie Q ain't worried about him being married as long as she gets fifty dollars to pay her telephone bill or get her nails fixed. She's cool with that, but your wife is getting the whole check, and she ain't doing nothing but the missionary position, if that, and even then she's only giving it to you every other weekend. She thinks you're supposed to be happy, but it don't work like that. You should always be willing to try something different, no matter how long you've been married.

"It's not so much that it has to be something really different, but what you put into it is what you get out of it, so show some interest. Show some motivation. A man doesn't always want to be the one having to ask for sex. The woman should initiate it sometimes. 'Hey, baby, look here. Go get your bath and let me wash your back and let me give you a massage. We'll eat after while.' This is something a man wants to hear from his woman. He wants to know she wants him because it makes him feel good.

"Let me give you a good example of how a woman can get everything she wants from her man. I was watching this talk show, and this lady was saying she and her husband had a baby girl. By the time that baby girl was three years old, she was getting all her daddy's attention, and the mother couldn't figure out how. She said her daughter could just sit at the table, and she didn't even have to ask for bread. She'd just look at her daddy, and he'd know she wanted the bread. The mother started to notice that when her husband was out there pushing the lawn mower, the daughter was right along beside him, talking to him. When he was working on the lawn mower or working on the car, where was the daughter? She was sitting there on the side of the car, talking to him. The woman said she got wise. She said, 'I started going out there, walking with him while he was cutting the grass, and I started sitting under the carport with him while he worked on the car, and things changed. It's little things, simple things that you can do to show a man that you care. He wants to know you want him, that you're excited about him, and you need to make sure that the love doesn't die.'

"If I'm outside cutting the grass or whatever, come bring me a glass of ice water. That only takes a minute, but I'll bet you I'm going to make a beeline in there to you when I finish even if it ain't for nothing but to get a kiss on the jaw. That's an easy thing to do, but so many times we take it for granted. A lot of women will say, 'Eeeewww, go take a shower. You all dirty and stuff,' but before we got married, it didn't matter if I was sweating.

"I tell my wife this all the time when she says to me, 'You smell like smoke.' Hell, I been smoking for thirty-four years. How come all of a sudden now you can't stand to smell my smoke? See, women want to change a man. They want to mold him to be what they want him to be, but it don't work. If you want to change him, what you wanted him for in the first place? You should've went and got you somebody else that was already fitting your bill. Don't try to change a man once you got him, 'cause you can't.

"Sex plays a big part in a relationship, but the relationship shouldn't revolve around sex. I think just the fact that a man knows his woman is going to submit to him means a whole lot to him. That's why when a woman does that, she can get just about anything she wants. A lot of time a man isn't looking for the sex. He's just looking to know that he can have it. That's where that smile, that kiss, and that hug comes in. When he comes in the house, and after he gets through eating, if he's laying on the couch, go lay on the couch by him. If he's watching the ball game, then go crawl up on that couch, and let's watch this ball game together instead of you doing something here and him doing something there. And if you're going to do something in the house, then plan it. If you say, 'We're going to paint this room today,' well, then, that's fine—but we should do it together. I don't even mind if I'm doing all the work. It's just nice to be able to look over my shoulder and see my woman there."

RUBEN

"This one woman told me something was wrong with me because she wanted to have sex and I told her I wasn't ready yet. My friend laughed when I told him about it. He said, 'You faggot. I would've knocked that shit out the box.' She didn't know how to take me saying no. I was physically attracted to her, but I know that you got to manage those feelings and emotions. You've heard it all along: men think with the little head instead of the big head. Some men think that hole in their penis is for their brain to get air. Sure I wanted to make love to her, I wanted her bad, but once again, I wanted to be able to control those physical emotions because I wanted more out of that relationship than just going to bed.

"When I have sex with a woman and she says, 'I've never had it this good,' either she's lying or she ain't been with no real man, because the women I date are thirty-five and up so I *know* they've had at least one good lover. I take pride in ensuring that my woman gets hers, and when we're done, I want her to be totally content. When a man allows his emotions to take over, he doesn't give that woman what she needs. I've had some platonic relationships for over twenty years, and the biggest complaint I hear from these women about men is a man's inability to be sensitive to her needs and not caring about whether she's being satisfied sexually. Imagine a man going twenty years without an orgasm. Well, a lot of women do, and men don't think anything of it, but what would that do to a man? If you're in a committed relationship, sex is part of it, and you should be committed to pleasing each other.

"One of the things I don't like is being with a woman and she's experiencing multiple orgasms and then all of a sudden she stops and just lays there, and I can't finish. Awwww . . . uh-uh, we got to get done. You can make a game of counting how many orgasms you have, which is fine, but don't forget about me. I want mine too.

"A lot of times marriages fail because of boredom and the lack of caring and nurturing one another in the bedroom. If a woman is sick and she says no, I can understand that, but if everything is there, the word no should never be uttered, because there are many ways to satisfy each other. Some people like to do certain things, and that's part of getting to know your mate. If your man likes doing certain things, either you're going to like it or you're not. Saying 'I don't feel like it' isn't an excuse. It's a problem. Seriously, if you don't feel like it, why don't you feel like it? And if you can't answer that, you're going to have him thinking one of two things: I'm not turning her on, or I need to get it somewhere else.

"Even with my son, if I tell him no, I always give him a reason, and it should be the same way between a man and a woman. If she doesn't feel like making love, what's wrong with telling the man why? If the reason is you're not interested, you got to tell him, because if you don't tell him, nothing will change. How are you going to grow as a couple? Just like when I told that lady I wasn't ready to have sex yet. I said, 'I'm not ready, because emotionally I want to make sure that both of us, not just you or not just me, wants this.'

"When you start kissing and caressing, you're going to get turned on sexually, but if the emotions aren't there, you got to wait until they catch up for the sex to be good. I've learned that that's what makes it better. At least for me it does.

"I don't play games at my age. I did when I was younger, but games get you nowhere. If you want to know who I am as a person, I ain't holding back, but I'm always careful with the delivery. In other words, I could tell you that I don't want to do this, because our emotions are not where they need to be, or I could just tell you I don't want to do this, because I don't want to be with you right now—but the second delivery is wrong. I'm getting the same message across, but it's negative.

"A man has to be sensitive to a woman's emotional needs if he cares about her. How can you say you love this person yet you treat her like dirt? How can you say you care about this woman but don't take care of her needs? Why are you jealous if she's talking to some other man now that you're divorced because maybe he's tending the needs you didn't tend to? Check yourself as a man. Look in that mirror and ask yourself, *Am I doing everything that I need to do to be a godly man?* That doesn't mean you got to be celibate. That's hard because we're not designed that way. But you can be promiscuous in a lot of ways, and what does it get you? As a man, I want somebody I can hold and talk to when I'm done, but I had to grow into that over a period of time."

LANDON

"I'm what you would call a sex fiend. I'm the male version of a nympho. I'm into the whole nine—that's me, straight up. Sex has always been a big thing to me, and sex is probably my biggest weakness, especially with me trying to walk the spiritual life, because I've always had this infatuation with it. I honestly believe it's due to the emotional contact I missed while growing up. I feel more connected with a woman when I'm having sex with her than if we're just talking or just hugging and kissing. Sex holds a greater degree of intimacy for me.

"The act itself might be fleeting, but when you've longed for something for so long, one second, one minute, an hour is better than nothing. However you can get it, it serves its purpose for that moment.

"I had my first sexual encounter when I was in kindergarten. We were at this playground, and you know those big cement pillars that hold up the freeways, one of those was laying down, and I remember I was in this cement tunnel, minding my own business—I didn't know nothing. So a girl came in the tunnel with me, and she was like, 'Put your fingers down here,' and I put my fingers there, and somebody saw us and told, and we took off running. I didn't get caught, and I don't think anything happened again until I was maybe eight or nine, but I think that initial, inappropriate act somehow set the stage for me sexually.

"My mom had a friend who lived next door to us, and she had two daughters close to my age. That was when I really started learning that this was for this and that was for that 'cause we were latchkey kids. I was in maybe the fourth grade, and they were in the fifth and sixth. We would come home from school together, and that's what they wanted to do, so I'd do it. I wasn't thinking about sex, but girls are so much further advanced.

"I've had sex with too many women to count; all I can say is that I've been with more women than the average man. I was in Korea for a year, and after I left there, I went down to two women a day, but when

I was in Korea, it was four to six a day, so that's a lot of women.

"I wouldn't want a woman who was as promiscuous as me because as a female, your body is being entered, unlike a man, who's just popping in and popping out. It's different. When a man has sex, it's not an emotional tie. For a woman, it is. That's why men have no problem sleeping with hookers, because it's not emotional. It's just sex. It's, *I paid for it, I got it, and I don't have to think twice about her afterwards.* A woman is going to think about him again. She going to be wondering when he's going to call her again, all that. There's a big difference. A man is like, *I'm just trying to get mine*, and he's going to keep on going.

"There is a difference between making love and having sex, but I don't think women recognize that difference. To me, sex is sex—just getting buck wild. It doesn't have anything to do with whether or not you care about that person. You can just have sex with your wife, but to me, making love is when you take the time, when you're all about making her feel good and she's all about making you feel good. You're going from head to toe, you're licking the sensitive spots, you're actually working to please the other person. Making love is not abut you, making love is about the other person. Sex is about you and *maybe* about the other person.

"I've made love numerous times. There isn't a certain kind of woman I make love to and a certain kind of woman I just have sex with, but I learned something through trial and error. If I'm dating a woman and I make love to her that first time, she'll always come back, no matter what I do after that, so when I first meet a woman, I'll make love to her. I'll make her have anywhere from four to eleven orgasms, I'm serious, and after that, she'll never get more than one, if she even gets that, but you know what, she'll always remember the first time and keep coming back looking for what she got the first time. That's how I keep her. I make love to her that first time, and she keeps coming back. It's like a drug."

SIMEON

"The average man thinks about sex numerous times a day, and it's completely physical. If a man's testosterone level drops, his need for sex and thoughts of sex drops. If his testosterone level is normal or high, his sex drive is high. That's science. That indicates to me that it's more biological than just thinking a man is a nasty person. I *always* think about sex. The need to procreate is something that is in a man's genes.

"As human beings, we have something called self-control and self-restraint. A male dog can walk up in the front yard and jump on a female dog in heat, and I don't care if the building is burning, he's not going to stop. We as human beings know that there's a time and place for everything, but believe me, most men think about sex all the time. Just look at the advertisements. Just about everything out there is about sex. It can be very extreme or very minimal, but it's there. Sex sells."

8

WHAT IS SEXY?

JOE

"I love a woman with a big old ghetto ass—I ain't gonna lie. Breasts are nice and all, and I do like a woman with nice legs and a nice shape, but she definitely got to have a nice big ass. That shit just gets me excited, especially when she's wearing something that shows it off. I'm talking about a big firm ass now, not one of those big jelly asses that looks like it would never stop shaking if you slapped it. When a woman has a big round ass and she wears clothes that shows it off, that turns me on."

KEN

"I like a woman who's naturally pretty, a woman who doesn't have to wear any makeup at all. I don't like women with all that thick foundation and eyeliner, fake eyelashes, and weave. I like the fact that I don't have to worry about having to send my clothes to the cleaners after snuggling up with my woman just because she's left a ton of makeup smeared across my shirt.

"I like the way my woman looks and smells when she wakes up in the morning. And I love the fact that Zonora isn't afraid to eat more than half a salad and drink a Diet Coke for dinner. I've always loved women who weren't afraid to eat—as long as you work out and keep that body tight, it shouldn't be a problem. After all, food is sensual, especially here in the South.

"I love to watch Zonora shower, especially when she arches her back and pulls her hair back to wet it. I like a woman with passionate eyes, confidence, intelligence, wit, and sarcasm, and I love a woman with a great laugh, and my wife has all of those characteristics. She's never been afraid to let go of a serious gut-busting laugh. I like a woman with a nice walk too. Zonora has a way of subtly swaying her ass when she walks that just makes me hard as hell, and she knows it too."

QUINCY

"Women can be naturally sexy, and if a woman is flirty, that's very sexy to me. She can call me throughout the day and just check on me or tell me she called to hear my voice, and that's sexy. Not being the same all the time is also a turn-on. Some women are like, "I wouldn't wear *that* kind of lingerie, and I ain't wearing no thong," and that's the reason some black men will date a white woman because she'll do *anything* if she knows it turns you on, seriously. Sisters need to mix it up, and I'm not talking about being freaky or nasty, because some women can take that way too far and start being nasty but think they're being sexy. Sometimes they get so stupid, you want to tell them to just shut up. Everybody is not sexy, and if a woman isn't naturally sexy, she shouldn't try to be sexy, because it seems forced. Sexy is an attitude. It's in the way a woman carries herself. You don't have to wear everything all tight and cut low, because the clothes aren't what make a woman sexy.

"Some men like legs, some men like butts, and some men like breasts, but I like everything. I like everything in moderation. I don't like nothing fake, and I don't like a woman who's too skinny, even if she's beautiful. A thick sister is fine with me as long as she's well proportioned."

GREG

"My definition of a sexy woman is a woman with a big ass wearing a thong. That's sexy. My definition of a lady is a female who carries herself as a lady, but just because she's a lady doesn't mean she can't be aggressive. What she does behind closed doors is nobody's business, but as long as she's ladylike in public, it's all good with me. As a matter of fact, I want her to be whorish in the bedroom, definitely. You can't be acting like a lady all in the bedroom too—that would be boring.

"What really turns me off about a woman is if she's a dead lay, just laying there without moving or moaning or anything, just there. I'll be like, *Uh, okay, what's up with you, what's your problem?* That turns me off because I can't do anything with a woman like that. A woman can't be too aggressive with me—she can go all out, and I have no limitations. We can do whatever she wants to do, and she'll get no complaints from me."

G.G.

"A clean-cut, sexy man with a muscular chest, bountiful beauty, overflowing intelligence, charm, and style turns me on, but a gorgeous, independent, witty, petite, trendy woman can turn me on as well. Both types are very sexy to me. I enjoy the sex act with either sex, but I still get more pleasure out of it when I'm with a man."

DANTE

"Hell, everything turns me on. It could be the way a woman moves or how pretty and soft her hands are. It could be her posture, the shape of her eyes, or the way she enters a room. It could be the perfume she wears, the way she puckers her lips, or the way she says my name. Lots of things turn me on, so I can't break it down and put it into a category and say, 'Well, I want a woman with a big butt and big titties.' For me, it's the little, intimate things that a woman does—certain shoes she wears, the way she crosses her legs, the way she looks in a certain light—those may all be turn-ons. Those things are beautiful to me.

"What turns me off is a woman with whorish ways. Don't get me wrong, you can be a wife in public and be a whore in the bedroom, but I don't want other men to know that. You should carry yourself as a lady in public, but when you get behind those doors at home, you can let go and scream and everything else—it's cool then. But a woman who's a whore 24-7 and you can look at her and tell she's a whore—there ain't no romance in that for me. She's a skank, and I've never been attracted to women like that."

XAVIER

"A woman's sexiness is determined by her persona, the way she carries herself. I look at how she walks, how she holds her head, stuff like that. I know a lot of women who aren't very attractive and may not be as shapely as other women, but the way they carry themselves makes up for all of that. A well-dressed woman is sexy to me, even if she isn't drop-dead gorgeous.

"Sex is important to men, and yes, we think about it a lot because we're visual. Looking at a sexy woman automatically causes you to think about sex, because your mind just goes there. Women are naturally sexy creatures, and God created them to be that way so that we would be attracted to them."

NEAL

"A sexy woman is all about the appearance. She can be dark skinned or light skinned, her hair can be long or short, but it's that little special walk that she has or a certain presence that says, 'That is who I am, and I know I look good.'

"Maybe she has this sexy little swing in her walk or a certain hairstyle;

maybe there's something stylish about the way she dresses. There's not one general thing that makes a woman sexy. It's just what you see when you look at her. You may see something that others don't, and that's okay. She has her own special chemistry that attracts you, so to you, she's sexy."

PIERRE

"A natural sexiness turns me on, and to me there are three aspects that draw my attention to a woman: sexiness, beauty, and a banging body. You can have one without having the other two and still interest me. Say if she comes through that door right there and she's a little over-weight, if she's got it all together, then I'm still attracted to her. There's a woman I know who comes to the club I go to all the time, and she's a little heavier than what I'd usually like, but she is bad. She always has her nails together, she dresses nice, she has a pretty face, her hair is always tight, and the way she carries herself just makes her sexy as hell to me. I'd jump on that ass in a minute if she just said the word.

"Then there are women who may not be all that gorgeous and may not have that banging body, but they have that sex appeal in the way they move and carry themselves, and that's also sexy as hell. Some women don't even realize how sexy they are, and that's a turn-on to me because then I know she's not all into herself. I'll be like, *Damn, she's sexy as hell! She ain't got no ass, but she's still sexy as a motherfucker to me.* I've even seen women who are as skinny as a rail, but they can be sexy too, depending on the way they carry themselves. So I guess I could say I would like any one of those things even though it would be real nice if I could find a woman who has all three going for her. I'd love that.

"I can see a woman in the club whose face looks like hell, but when she walks past me and I look at that ass, I'm like, *Ooh, look at that ass,* and I start imagining what she looks like naked. Damn."

COLLIER

"It's definitely not her face. I think maybe it's the way she walks. Basically with me, it's more than one thing, but a sexy walk is number one on my list. She don't have to be wearing no high heels, but there's just something about the way she places one foot in front of the other. She's holding her head up high, and she walks with a little strut."

EDWIN

"A person has to have something to grab your interest, whether it's physical or mental. I like the combination of an attractive lady who has a good head on her shoulders. I like her to be independent and have her act together. I like a woman who carries herself well and demands respect. Physical characteristics are nice, but she has to have the respect there as well because then it's like she has this aura around her that says, 'I'm something special.'

"The first thing I look at in a woman is the way she dresses. I look at the way her clothes fit. I'll check out her shoes. I'll check out everything. I'm looking at her hair, her makeup, her hands, her neck, and her eyes. Some women have those nice bedroom eyes; I take in the whole thing.

"I do a lot of shopping, so sometimes when I'm at the mall, I check women out. I check out their clothes, I'll say, "Let me see what women are wearing these days. Let me see what's in here," and I'll go up to a woman and ask her, 'Hey, what size do you wear' or 'What kind of perfume are you wearing?' I'll buy my woman an outfit in a minute and say, 'Wear this.' I'll walk through Victoria's Secret and see some panties I like, and I'll buy them for my lady.

"A woman who has it together, has nice features, and carries herself well in the sense that she's representing herself as somebody with pride and class means something to me. That excites me."

WARREN

"My definition of a sexy woman is one who always has a smile on her face. I think a woman's personality makes her sexy. It's not her body. See, you can be fine as wine, but when you open your mouth and nothing good comes out of it, you ain't sexy at all. Some women you see are always frowning like they mad at the world. She could be a beautiful woman, could have a beautiful personality, but if she's driving down the road looking all bitter, don't nobody want to talk to her, and she's definitely not sexy."

RUBEN

"There is a glow in certain women that makes them sexy. She doesn't necessarily have to be a brick house; a woman who has the aura that shows that she's content with who she is is sexy to me.

"A woman in clothes in sexier to me than a woman with everything showing, because those clothes are like wrapping paper. You're going to unwrap that present, and you're going to enjoy that present, but it's something personal and private. It's my gift, and she's not willing to share that gift with nobody but me.

"Some women like beards, and some women like men who are clean-shaven. Well, men have their likes and dislikes too. He might not like a woman with small breasts—he might prefer a woman with large breasts. It's all in the individual, and once again it goes back to that spiritual foundation. If you walk the walk, He will grant you the desires of your heart, and your cup will overflow. A lot of times I hear men say, 'I don't know why in the hell I got to buy lingerie for my wife. It's gonna come off anyway.' Well, it ain't about the bam bam bam. What's wrong with pouring the bathwater for her and placing a few candles at the end of the tub, bringing her a glass of wine, and turning on some soothing music? There's not a thing wrong with a man doing those types of things, but some men won't, because they doesn't want their woman to think they're sensitive or weak.

"It's like I told my son, 'If you get a woman who does those nice things for you, keep it to yourself, because if you tell your friends everything she does for you, they're going to be thinking, *Shit I don't get that, I want some of that*, and in today's world, it might not be just a man.' It might be a woman that wants some of that. I told him that whatever goes on behind his doors stays behind his doors. When you smile, let them wonder what it is that makes you smile.

"I've taught my son a lot of things because I want him to know how to treat a woman. It's taboo for Latino men to tell their sons, 'It's okay to pamper a woman.' I'm so thankful that I have the mother and father that I have because while I have that machismo in me, I also got that sensitive side. They taught us that it's okay to have feelings."

LANDON

"I'm attracted to a woman who is fine, a muscular woman who really takes care of her body. I like black women with long hair, but ninety percent of black women with long hair have long hair because they put weave in it. For me, it's a spiritual thing: the Bible says a woman's hair is her glory, and I love a woman with naturally long hair.

"I like light-and dark-skinned black women, but most light-skinned black women seem to be spoiled because they've been pampered too much, so most of the women I've dated in the past few years have been dark-skinned, and the sexiest thing to me is a woman who can understand what I like. I want her to have her nails done, her hair done; I want her to look her best for me 24-7.

"To me, the dream woman is one who will ask me what I want for my birthday, and when I tell her that I want to walk in the room and see her standing there butt naked with a bow tie on, she actually does it. I'm a simple man. Women think, *Aw, you don't really want that*, but I'm serious. I'm dead serious. Get butt naked, put a tie on, wrap the tie around your waist—I don't give a damn how you hang it, put it on your head. If you do that, I'd be like, 'Whatever you want.'

"I've learned that a woman who don't take care of her nails and her feet won't take care of that coochie either. I like a high-maintenance woman, the kind of woman who will be happy with a five-hundred-dollar gift certificate to a spa because she'll use it.

"I like a woman who will appreciate what I do, and that's hard for me to find because it seems like young women aren't used to a man being good to them. I'm talking about the one where it's her birthday, and I say, 'Babe, why don't you come over here at about six o'clock.' She comes over, and I done ran rose petals from where she parks all the way into the house and to the bed and the bathtub, got a hot bubble bath going on, the lights are off, candles are lit in the bathroom and all around the bed, the whole nine. I got all her birthday presents lined up. I done spent sixty dollars alone in one of those vending machines outside the supermarket to get those little troll dolls she likes, and I put them inside gift bags, I put teddy bears in gift bags, and put ten bags of candy in there on top of the dolls and bears, and I put tissue on top of it all. I want a girl who's going to appreciate stuff like that. A girl who wants a guy who's going to bathe her and give her a massage, be proud to rub her feet. I need a girl that's going to appreciate everything that I can think of to do romantically."

SIMEON

"When a woman shows that she's independent, that turns me on. A sexy skirt and all that is attractive, but I love independence in a woman. For instance, when I sit in on a meeting and see a woman take charge—man, that is so intriguing to me because she's got her shit together. That's not to say I don't get turned on when I see Jennifer Lopez, Janet Jackson, or Halle Berry on TV and they working this outfit to death—yeah, I'm turned on, but you know what, I can't get with them.

"The sexiest part of woman to me physically is a nice ass. I love a nice, fine ass. Ooooohh . . . the rhythm. A fine ass is rhythm in motion—you can quote me on that one. You see a woman dance or just walk that walk. . . . You can take women of all shapes and sizes, and if they got a nice ass, that does it for me.

"Not all men like asses, but Simeon does. You can do what they call cut shots where you show waist and a little bit of leg and some ass, and you have the woman walk, and I think that most men would probably pick the woman with the best-shaped ass. If you took a cut shot and showed a woman from here to here—"

He motions from the waist to the top of the thighs. "Damn!"

9

MOST EROTIC

MALIK

"The most erotic experience I had was probably the year right before I got married. There was a woman who I'd been friends with for a long time, and her goal was to make me come in her mouth. She took me to a park in the middle of the day and gave me a blow job that I'll never forget, and that's the first and last time I ever came that way.

"I'd had blow jobs before, but I couldn't come like that. I could get hard, but I've always loved being inside of a woman. I love feeling that warmth and being able to give back. So I really didn't think I could go there with her if that was all she wanted, but once I told her what made me feel more like I was getting ready to come, she was right on target. Rather than sticking my entire penis in her mouth, she just licked around the head and sucked very lightly. That gave me more sensation so I was able to come, and once I started to come, she began to suck rather than lick, and it was one of the best orgasms I ever had. I just about drowned that woman when I came."

RUBEN

"One time this woman I had broken up with went crazy on me. Her name was Andrea, and I'd stopped dating her because first of all she didn't want anyone to know we were dating because she was black and I was Latino, and second because I found out that she'd screwed around on me. The guy she had screwed came and told me about it because he had no idea we were even seeing each other, and once a woman screws around on me, the relationship is over. I'm through. When I refused to return her phone calls, she started stalking me, and she followed me to this other girl's apartment one night. This was a blond chick that had been after me for some time, so I was looking forward to getting some action because she'd already described in detail all the stuff she wanted to do to me.

"I was over at her apartment, and I was getting ready to make my move when I heard all of this yelling and screaming and pounding on the door, and I was like *What the fuck?* I opened the door, my shirt is off, and there stood Andrea, and she lost it when she saw me standing there with my shirt off with this half-dressed woman behind me. She started cussing me out, she lunged for the woman, and the woman started screaming because she's more scared than anything else. I told her to chill and that I'd take care of things because the last thing I needed was somebody calling the cops, so I grabbed my shirt, practically had to drag Andrea out behind me because she was still trying to get at this other woman, who slammed the door behind me.

"I heard her turn the dead bolt, and I was pissed because Andrea had just interrupted my flow, but the whole time she was cussing me out as I walked her back downstairs and towards her car, and then she stopped cussing long enough to start crying, talking about how much she misses me and that she's sorry she fucked up and she was going to move back home since she couldn't be with me. Then we started kissing, and before long her skirt was hiked up around her waist, I touched her between her legs, and she was wet, and we started fucking right there, standing up against the wall of the complex with her legs wrapped around my hips, and the shit was better than I remembered it being, probably because we were both so fired up. I came in less than two minutes if that long, but that was one erotic experience especially since we were taking the chance of somebody walking up and catching us in the act.

"I got in my car and followed Andrea home afterwards, and we took things a little slower for the rest of the night, but we still didn't get back together after that, because I didn't trust her, and I never did get back to that other girl's apartment."

LANDON

"I can't really say off of the top of my head what my most erotic experience has been, because I've had lots of them. I've been waken up out of my sleep at three in the morning with some woman climbing in through my window telling me she needs to fuck me, all kinds of shit like that.

"I think coming in a woman's mouth is erotic. It's one thing if she's giving you head and she's using her hand, and it's another if she doesn't use her hands at all. I was with one girl, and she believed that if a woman had to use her hand to get a man off, she was cheating. I was like, *Fine, I'm with you*. I've taught women how I liked them to do it. If you a man, you know what you want, and you're going to tell her.

"I guess my most erotic experience was my first threesome. I was at a low point in my life, and I had women I could call, but I didn't want to call them. I could be sitting at a table in the club with a drink, and if a girl was sitting there talking to me, all I had to do is hold up my glass or beer bottle, and she'd buy me another one.

"There was this one woman I met at a club in Atlanta. She was thirty-three, and I was twenty-two. She saw me, and I saw her. We made eye contact across the club, and I was like *What's up* and she was like *Come here*. So I went over and talked to her, and we hit it off real good, but she would never let me get in her pants, because she knew how I was. She could tell by the way I talked. I was too smooth; I was too pretty, so she knew. We ended up becoming friends, and one day she called me and asked me if I wanted to go out, and I said yeah, so we met at this jazz club. It was a club older people went to, and those were the kinds of places I liked to go to.

"We get there, and I'm trying to be a gentleman. I ordered a beer and asked her what she wanted to drink, and she said, 'No, I got it.' I was like, 'Well, um . . . I can get it . . . ' We're on the first date, and she was like, 'Naw, baby, it ain't like that.' She pulled out a roll of damn hundreds, and I'm just looking at this roll of money when she says, 'That ain't nothing. Let's go dance.'

"We got up to go dance, and she said, 'I told you that ain't nothing, right?'

"I said, 'Yeah.'

"She says, 'Feel this.' She grabbed my hand and put it in her crotch, and I thought she had a sanitary napkin between her legs.

"I said, 'So what, you're on your period . . . . What?'

"She reached down and pulled out twenty Gs. She was wearing the money like a pad. She owned two beauty salons, rented office space to three doctors, was a clinical psychologist, and moved drugs on the side—so she had cash, plenty of it.

"One time I went down to Atlanta to see her because we hadn't seen each other in a while. I asked her, 'If I come down there this Friday, am I going to have you the whole weekend?' and she said yes, so I drove down, and we met at a pool hall and she told me her ex-boyfriend was there, so I hooked up with her sister instead.

"I was mad as hell because I'd driven a few hours to come see this broad, and she ain't even trying to hear me, she ain't even coming home with me. I'm at her sister's house. So because I was so pissed, I slept with her sister that night, and her sister was so into me that she agreed with me when I told her not to tell her sister about it. I told her that we could just have our thing, and her sister and me could have our thing, and she agreed. This is a sister that she was raised up with, and they was close, but that's how good I was. I hit it hard and then bounced back to Mississippi at three o'clock in the morning.

"A few weeks later, I was just sitting at home because my car was in the shop for repairs, and she called me. Her sister, with her big mouth, had told her about the night we'd spent together and how many orgasms she'd had, so now she was thinking about me. She called me and asked me what was up, and I told her I was just chilling, my car was in for repairs, and I was getting ready to head over to the pool hall with a buddy of mine.

"She was like, 'You don't want to get down?'

"I was like, 'Yeah, but what are you talking about?' because I hadn't slept with her yet. She was the one I was trying to get. She said, 'We'll be there in a few hours,' and I was like 'Who is we?'

"She said, 'Me and my friend,' so an hour later, I was in the pool hall and her and her friend showed up. Her friend was fine too, but she was a white girl, so she didn't really excite me. We played pool for about two or three hours, and then we went back to my place, and it was on.

"When you got one guy and two girls, the sex can get wild. It goes into the other side of things, you know what I mean? If you got two women and one guy, the guy only got so much to do so your mouth is here, your dick is there, and their mouth is here and their coochie is there, so it's like a big love triangle.

"I was going down on the girl I really liked, and I was fucking her friend at the same time, but I really didn't care for her friend, because I wanted to fuck her. So this woman is kissing on me and loving on me, and she's the one that I want to fuck in the first place, and she's coaching me on how to fuck her friend. That was probably the most erotic thing I've ever done—it was nice. It was fun because it was my fantasy, and I think my boys got more of a kick out of hearing about it than I got out of actually doing it. They were like, 'Did you tape it? You didn't take pictures or nothing, dog?'

"After it happened, I realized that having a threesome was over-rated because it's meant for one man to be with one woman, and I re-alized that you got the same exact pleasure coming out, so it was more of a mental rush. I'm finally getting a chance to have sex with two women at the same time, but once I was doing it, I was like, *Oh, this ain't all that*. What are the chances of you getting two girls that you re-ally, really want to be with? There was one that I didn't really want to be with, but she was all right, and there was one that I really really wanted to be with, so my focus was on her, and the other woman could tell, so it was kind of messed up."

G.G.

"The most erotic evening I can recall is one I spent recently with the young lady I'm currently involved with and a couple we'd invited over for dinner. We had Caesar salads, grilled steak, and lobsters outside on the patio near the pool, and all during dinner we laughed and indulged in some pretty risqué conversation, and before long, we had drank way more than we had eaten. By our fourth or fifth drink we ended up in-side the house, sprawled out naked on the carpeted floor of the living room floor, making love to our respective partners; then the young man suggested that we switch—man to man, and woman to woman—and it was pretty sexy to watch the women put on a show for us and for one another. They hugged and kissed and slowly nibbled up and down each other's body and as we watched them bring one another to a cli-max, I couldn't wait to experience the same thing with him, but with-out the kissing, of course.

"The women had never seen two men have sex in person, and told us that it was something they wanted to view firsthand, and watching the two of us have sex only served to get the two of them even more excited, which led to us switching partners again, and this time I was with the other woman, and he was with my lady. I think the experience actually brought me and my girl closer because now we have a bond.

We have a trust that no one can break through, no matter what, and that's special. We don't have any secrets from one another, and I feel like that's the type of relationship all couples should have."

SIMEON

"I think the wildest shit I ever did was hooking up with this chick who took me to a Janet Jackson concert. When I first met this woman, I was hanging out with the fellas at a bar one night, and I was young and naïve as hell. We exchanged phone numbers, and I called her a few days later to ask her out for lunch—and to tell you exactly how naïve I was, when I asked her what she did for a living, she said, 'I dance,' and I didn't think anything of it. She had a nice body, it looked like she could easily be a dancer, so I said, 'Oh, you in ballet, folk dance, or what?'

"She said, 'No . . . I'm a stripper.'

"I was like *Whoa!* Then I thought, *Yeah, we can do this, we can hang out together.*

"This girl was renting a house for like fifteen or sixteen hundred a month, plus she was driving a Mercedes, and I had no clue women could make that much money dancing. I'd always thought you dance and the men give you a few dollars, but that sure is a lot of dollars if it allowed her to live the way she did. She also had a new SUV, but my pay wasn't too shabby either, so whenever we'd go out, I'd be like, 'I'll pay for this,' and she was like, 'No, I'll get it.' We were fifty-fifty pretty much on everything, but when I started working in corporate America, I finally learned how those dancers really made their money, and they don't make all that money dancing. She might get it from giving some old man a blow job after they go out to dinner. It's all about the sex, and I don't know for a fact if that was what she was do-ing back when I was kickin' it with her, but she damn sure did make a lot of money doing something.

"But back to my story: She bought third row center tickets to the

Janet Jackson concert as a birthday gift to me because she knew I was in love with Janet Jackson. I still am—I ain't lying. The night of the concert she showed up at my house along with this fine girlfriend of hers. I opened my door to let them in and offered them a drink and outside, parked against the curve under the streetlight, I see this gleaming black limousine. She never did anything halfway.

"I had the time of my life, during the ride to the concert, at the concert, and during the ride back. The limo was stocked with beer, champagne, Courvoisier, and light appetizers like smoked oysters, caviar, fancy crackers, cheeses, nuts—you name it. We partied in that limo all the way to the concert and all the way back. My friend had on this slamming outfit—a white leather halter top and a matching skirt, and the skirt was short. Man, she was showing all kinds of thigh. And her friend, who was a dancer too, was dressed in the very same outfit, but hers was red, and you should've seen the looks we got from people when we stepped out that limo. I felt like I was a celebrity myself.

"That was one crazy night, and it got even crazier on the way back because we could drink as much as we wanted since we weren't driving. She told the driver to take us riding around the city for a couple of hours. Then she closed the privacy window—the one that separates the passengers from the driver—and you know how every man has this fantasy about being with two women? Well my ménage a trio's fantasy was fulfilled that night. The limo had mirrored ceilings, and you could dim the lights, and we had the music playing and everything. Man, I had the time of my life.

"My friend was strictly into women, but her friend was bisexual. The two of them started stroking each other's thighs. Then they started stroking each other's breasts and their halter tops ended up on the limousine floor. By the time they started to kiss, I felt like I was watching the best porno movie ever. I was a total voyeur. My friend stretched out across the leather seat and spread her legs wide, and I soon found out that neither one of them were wearing panties, because when my friend flipped up the short skirt to offer easy access, nothing was left to the imagination. She was clean-shaven, wide open, and ready. Her girl went down on her right there in front of me, and when my friend started to moan and toss her head from side to side, I could tell she was being satisfied. She wasn't even trying to muffle the noise, and I was thankful for the dark window that separated us from the driver and the jazz music that diluted her screams.

"My friend opened her eyes while her girl was still going down on her, fumbled in her tiny purse, pulled out a condom, and between gasps said, 'Come on, sweetie. Why don't you join us? I want to give you a little something special to help you remember your birthday.'

"Her girl raised her head, licked her lips, and smiled—then took the condom from her hand and all in one fluid motion unzipped my pants and guided the rubber onto and over my penis then slowly turned her fine ass back in my direction before she once again commenced to licking and sucking at my friend's pussy like it was the sweetest thing she'd ever tasted. All of that Courvoisier I'd drank allowed me to lose any inhibitions I may have had and go with the flow, and as I slowly entered her friend, who was as moist and wet as any woman I'd ever been with, all I could think about was that this night was a dream come true."

10

ORAL, ANAL, AND
EVERYTHING IN BETWEEN

QUINCY

"I ain't into no anal sex, and I don't want nobody messing with my ass either. That's what I was talking about when I said some women try to get freaky and end up being nasty. I'll tell them quick, 'Don't be touching my ass. You know they say any man who will let you mess around with his ass needs to be watched because he probably goes both ways.'

"Now, as for oral sex, I feel like if you're married, it's wonderful. But if you're single, you've got to be careful because you don't know who's been where. That's not something you do with everybody. Nowadays, you'd better go to the doctor and take the person you're dating with you so you can both get checked out before you even start having sex, because there's a lot of stuff out there that's not detectable to the naked eye, and I'm not taking any chances. Otherwise, you're having sex with all the people she's had sex with *and* all the people *they've* had sex with, and that can add up to a lot of people. I know I sound like a commercial, but I'll be damned if I'm eating someplace where ten other men have been laying. I don't eat in everybody's kitchen, 'cause everybody ain't clean.

"One of my friends is a nurse, and she said you'd be surprised at who has what. She said the doctor she works for treats people with herpes, AIDS, and everything else, and a lot of these people are pastors, doctors, lawyers, people you would never think had something like that, just because of who they are. But looks can be deceiving."

GREG

"I like to receive oral sex, but I'm not giving it. I feel I'm less than a man if I get down and do something like that, and I've never asked a lady to do it to me, because I know I'm not going to return the favor.

"Now if she wants to give me a blow job, that's fine. I'm not going to stop her, but I make it a point to let her know I don't do anything like that. I just don't do it. And I don't want to kiss her afterwards either—hell no. I'm not a person who likes to kiss a lot anyway, because people just do so many things with their mouths these days. I mean, I could meet a woman I really like, and she's pretty and fine and all that, but God only knows who she's been giving face to and what's been happening with him. If I kiss a woman, it's basically on the cheek. But in the mouth—French kissing—no, I don't like that. There are other places you can kiss, like on the neck, behind the ears, and other sensual places during foreplay, and I don't think that hinders me from getting intimate, because I let a woman know that I'm not a kisser up front. I'm just always thinking about what or who else she's been doing after knowing what she does to me. If she gives me a blow job and she's really good at it, then I can just imagine how many others she's done it to."

XAVIER

"I keep hearing all this talk about young people having oral sex and that they don't consider oral sex real sex. I think that's a white-people thing because from what I've heard, white women tell their daughters to have oral sex in order to maintain their virginity and to keep from getting pregnant. Most sisters I know don't feel that way: sex is sex to them, even if it is oral. And oral sex is much more intimate for black women, so I know they don't feel that way."

MALIK

"I've tried oral sex a couple of times, and I'm not real keen on it, giving or receiving. My wife doesn't really like it, and I'm sure that's because we weren't really exposed to it too much as we were growing up. We've talked about it, I've tried it, and she's not really interested in it. She's never tried it on me, and that's fine with me because I don't have to have that. I prefer being inside and using different positions, so I don't feel like I'm missing anything at all.

"The big deal with men when it comes to getting a blow job is, if you can come, it is one of the most erotic feelings you can have. It feels very, very different from coming inside of a woman's vagina, because it's almost an uncontrollable type of orgasm. It's not like that warm, pulsing sensation you get when you're inside of a woman, it just jumps out and goes all over the place, it's more intense, but it takes too long, especially if a woman isn't experienced at it. I'm not saying I'm one who wants to rush into something like that, but for me it's not as good a feeling as being inside of a woman.

"And anal sex is out of the question for me. It's something I've never been interested in. I had an ex-girlfriend who wanted me to—that was her ultimate goal for us—but I just wasn't interested. Even if I'd been thinking about it, she got to be the kind of girl who really wasn't my type because of some of the things she started doing, so I knew that it would never happen. She kept saying, 'You just don't know what you're missing,' but I don't see what all the hype is. Maybe it's because I have an issue with homophobia. I feel like anal sex is too close to crossing that line. If you can run up in a woman's butt, you can probably do it with a man too. There are some guys who think it's okay for a man to give another man a blow job, and the one who's receiving is still straight, but that's bullshit to me. I don't want to do nothing close to what homosexuals do, even if it is with a woman. That's just the way I feel about it."

PIERRE

"I enjoy oral sex, giving and receiving, but I like to give it more because I think you can control a person that way, and I'm all into control. I like the fact that I can just make a woman lose her mind. You can make her lose her mind, you can break her down, even make her cry. I didn't know that was possible so the first time I did it, I was shocked. I knew I could make a female cry if I fucked her right, but with oral sex? The first time that happened, I was like, 'Damn, am I that good?'

"On the other hand, I can't say I've had a lot of occasions where a female gave me good head. Different men like different things, so you have to really know what he likes. It's just like when a man is giving a woman oral sex; you have to curtail it to what she likes. You have to ask her, 'What's your fantasy, what do you like, what do you dislike?' things like that. You need to know what a person likes before you become intimate with them so that you'll know what they want.

"Let me address the issue of women who like to swallow, or better yet, men who want to come in a woman's mouth. That's very personal because if a woman will take me in her mouth, and allow me to come, that's not something she's going to do with just anybody. That's special.

"One time Gina came on my job and did me. I couldn't believe it. She called and said, 'I'm on my way up there, I've got to taste you, *now*,' and hung up before I could say anything. When she got there, we went into the stairwell, she pushed me against the wall, sucked me off and swallowed, then got in her car and left. I was just standing there with my mouth open thinking, *Damn! I never had no one do that to me*. I swear she had me totally out there. She's the one who helped me to develop into the sexual person I am now because she did things to me that I could never imagine. We'd watch flicks together all the time.

I could call her names while I was doing her. I didn't have to be saying, *baby* or *sweetie*. I could say, 'Bitch, this ass is mine,' and she loved it. I could say whatever I wanted to say with her. I could be myself.

"I like anal sex too, probably because it's taboo. Especially if she has a nice ass. Like I said, I'm a freak, so if a see a woman with a fine ass walking by and I'm in the mood, I'm thinking, I'd like to run right up in that motherfucker 'cause I *know* it's good! It feels tighter, but if you know what you're doing, it shouldn't hurt real bad. You have to use a lubricant, you *must* use a condom, and you have to take your time. I'm not bragging or anything, and I can't say I've had anal sex with a lot of women, but most of the ones I have done it with had never done it before. It's very important that you take your time and be very gentle, and I think after a woman actually tries it and finds out it's not that bad, she won't mind trying it again if she's with the right guy.

"You have to go about it the right way. It's not just as simple as slapping some lubricant on and running up inside. There's a method to the madness because you've gotta go in there semi-hard and go slow. If there's a certain spot that turns her on like on her back or her neck or whatever, you've got to kiss her there or do something to take her mind off of it, at least until you get the head in, because that's the biggest part. You may have to go halfway in and then wait and let her relax while you talk to her, but whatever you do, you must take your time. If you do that and you do it right, she can really enjoy it.

"Gina liked to do it. She would actually make me pull out of her vagina and go there instead. Used to blow my mind, and she could even come that way. She'd be like a faucet, and I thought she was peeing because I'd never seen a woman come like that before.

"One time she told me about a girlfriend she had who was a lesbian, and she said she used to let her go down on her. She asked me how I felt about that, and I told her it didn't bother me none. I did want to know if they kissed, but she said they didn't. I don't have a problem with it, because to me you're not a lesbian unless you're the one doing the licking. Now with a guy, that's a totally different situation because with guys one actually goes inside the other. I just can't get into the whole dude thing."

ANTONIO

"As far as oral sex goes, giving or receiving is all good, and I'm good at giving, but oral sex isn't sex to me. It's not as intimate as penetrating a woman. As long as she's clean, I don't mind going down on her. I don't mind it as long as it ain't nasty. The trick is to always take a bath together and clean it up yourself and make sure it's trimmed. That little Latin girl, Julie—I would never have sex with her. I wouldn't penetrate her, because I'd have to deal with the responsibility of getting her pregnant. She's a young woman in the prime of her childbearing years, and I knew I wasn't into her like that, but I wanted to please her. So I would please her orally, and she would please me orally as well. When you're skilled at it and you can make a woman come two or three times like that, then she's happy.

"I think part of the reason men think receiving oral sex is such a big deal is because we watch porn. The conclusion of the oral sex act on most films is for the man to ejaculate in the woman's mouth or on her face or her breasts, so we're conditioned to think that's how you finish up—that's the best sex act ever. The truth is, especially in marriage or a long-term relationship, oral sex is just effortless sex. All you got to do is sit back and let somebody else do all the work until you ejaculate, so that's another reason men like oral sex. I ain't got to get up on you, I ain't got to work hard, I ain't got to do all the licking and rubbing on you. You just going to please me, all right, okay, cool. It's like getting a freebie. Just sit back and enjoy.

"The majority of women I've been with aren't very good at giving oral sex, but the bad thing about getting oral sex from women who are good at it is that you find yourself not wanting them to do it, because you know they done sucked so many dicks. You can't help but think, *If she's this good at it, how many dicks she done had in her mouth?* Ain't no such thing as being a natural at sucking a dick, trust me. When you start thinking that way, you just want to stop her and say, 'Naw, that's enough.'

"When you're in a committed relationship with somebody, you'll ask, 'Do you like this? Do you like that?' I play a game called one to ten. You do different things, and she calls out one to ten, ten meaning that feels the best and one means she don't like it. You lick here, you kiss here, you grab there, and when you can get a bunch of tens—'*Ten, ten, ten, ten, ten, ten!*'—awww, you're in a good spot, you stay there. That's how you find out about your partner: you ask questions, you listen when she talks to you about sex and about everything else.

"I like anal sex because it's so tight. It's like getting with a virgin. That's why most men like anal sex, but then again it's scary because it's also the best way to get AIDS. White women love anal sex, but most black women are like, 'Hell, naw—uh-uh, that ain't for that. You ain't sticking nothing bigger than your finger in my ass, and you're lucky if you get to do that.'"

EDWIN

"I was having a party in Galveston, and there was this woman there who was a friend of a friend, and I'd seen her around here and there. Her dad was a prominent minister with a very large congregation. She had a nice little body, so I couldn't help but go up to her and see what she was all about. We were standing in the kitchen surrounded by people, and I started flirting with her, and she started flirting back, and then I started bullshitting and made a few suggestive comments to her, but I was just talking so I was surprised when she asked if we could go somewhere private.

"We got to my bedroom, and she started unbuttoning my pants before I could close the door good. She was very intent on what she was about to do. She said all she wanted to do was give me a blow job. We made it to my bed, and I was laying there on my back and she was getting busy. She was sucking my dick like crazy, and this friend of mine, this guy, walks into my room looking for a needle and thread because a button had popped off his shirt, and he's like, 'Oh, damn. Excuse me.'

"I guess the exciting thing about that whole situation was the fact that she didn't miss a beat. She just kept on about her business like we hadn't even been interrupted. After I'd ejaculated, she sat up, dabbed at the corners of her mouth, and asked what time it was. I told her it was about three in the morning, and she jumps up and says, 'Shit—I got to go pick my husband up from work,' and I didn't even know she was married.

"I was thinking, *Boy, I sure hope she doesn't give him a kiss.*

"Oral sex has its time and place. Hell, it's just like anything else— sometimes it's fine, and sometimes you don't want to be bothered with either giving or receiving, but it's got to be somebody I'm really committed to if I'm giving. A lot of women don't know what they're doing when they're giving a man a blow job. She may be timid, so the feeling just isn't there. If you get with a freak who loves doing it, you're like, *Oh shit, this is great,* but I don't want a woman doing it just to please me if she isn't into it as well.

"I've had anal sex just for the hell of it, just because I could. It's not something I'll be sitting around fantasizing about, though. I don't sit here and think, *Boy, I'd sure like to have anal sex.* It's not like that, but when the offer comes up, I've never said no. The women I've done it with had no reservations about it. That's what they wanted, so I don't imagine it was their first time doing it either.

"There was one woman I dated who only wanted me to fuck her in the ass, so I was like, 'Hell, yeah—I'll take care of you, baby.' She was from Philly, and she would come to visit me every now and then, and she was a nympho. She even told me she was. She was into everything. She'd go to adult toy stores and buy nipple clips and handcuffs and shit. She liked to explore, so I took her up on it. I'd first met her at a business conference in Philly, and we had exchanged phone numbers.

I was talking to her on the phone and told her that my birthday was coming up on the weekend, and she put me on hold, got on another line, and made reservations to come be with me for my birthday. That was one wild weekend, and I had no idea she was going to be like that, because she looked and dressed so conservatively. She also directed the choir at her church, but she had a lot of freak in her. She was a nice-looking lady, and she loved having sex, but I don't know if one man would ever be enough for her, so there was no future for us at all."

LANDON

"I like going down on a woman—and I'm damn good. I've even had women pass out on me. For me to become an expert at going down on a woman intensifies the pleasure for her because I can do more with my tongue than I can with my dick. I'm all into oral sex. I like the smell, I like the taste, the whole nine, but she got to be clean.

"I had a woman one time who was so funky, it was a shame. I was drunk, and I still smelled her coochie, and it wasn't a pleasant smell. Usually, when you drunk, you don't smell shit. I said, 'Oh my God. I'm drunk and this shit still stank. I know good and well you don't think I'm kissing that. You must be crazy.'

"If a woman can perform oral sex right, it's good, but a lot of women don't take the time to ask how. If I'm going down on a woman, the things that I would do when I go down on this woman might be different than the things I would do if I went down on another woman. If you going down on a person you should be comfortable enough to ask, 'Do you like it when I do that?' or 'What can I do better?' so you can learn, especially if it's your soul mate. You should be trying to learn, but a lot of women don't want to do it. They just want to do what they do, and you get the vibe that they're really not into it. Some of them use their teeth, and some of them use their lips, and some use their hands, but honestly, the best is a woman who can use her hands and her mouth well, she doesn't use her teeth, and she's willing to ask you, 'Do you like it when I do that?' or 'Do you like it when I do this?'

"When a woman is just barely circling your dick with her tongue, you can't really feel that because a man who's circumcised only has a small section of the penis that has a lot of sensation, and it's right where it's been cut, right under the head on the backside—that's where all the feeling is. So if a woman is just barely licking around on the tip, I can't really feel that.

"It's different with each man, and if that's your partner for life, then it goes both ways. He should be asking you what's better for you, and you should be asking what's better for him. The whole point of making love and being with your partner is to make sure you know what pleases one another, because if you don't please them, they're going to look for it somewhere else. If a man ain't happy, he'll go and get happy. That's a man's mentality; that's our nature. We are a carnal people, which means, 'I need this, so I'm going to get it,' and as a married person, you should strive to please that other person mentally, physically, emotionally, and spiritually.

"I've tried anal sex many times, but I have never run across a woman who could actually take it. I had one experience where we were trying and there was just a little bit too much of that K-Y jelly going on, and my dick popped up in her ass too quick. She screamed, '*Stop!* Leave me the fuck alone!' You got to remember, the head is bigger than the shaft, so once that head gets in, if you're applying pressure, it's like *bam!* And that shit obviously hurt, because she was like, 'Get up off me, leave me the hell alone.' It felt good even though it only lasted for ten seconds, but it was probably the best ten seconds I ever had. I ain't going to lie, that shit felt good."

11

AFFAIRS

JOE

"I've had affairs with lots of married women. A couple of times those relationships lasted for over one or two years, and one in particular lasted about six. Sometimes I was seeing a single woman and a married woman at the same time, and sometimes the married woman was the only one I was seeing, but I always put it out there at the beginning of the relationship that I was single and reserved the right to see whoever I wanted to see, no questions asked.

"See, most of the time when a married woman has an affair with a single man, he feels like she's the one in a situation because she's the one who's committed to someone else. He's just there on the side to have some fun with her and make her life more exciting, especially if she ain't doing nothing but going to work and coming home to her family every day and doesn't have anything else going on in her life. He's not wanting to fall in love and all that shit—he's just involved with her because of the thrill of getting some other man's pussy and, besides that, it's free pussy. There are no strings attached, because he's single, and he knows there ain't a damn thing she can do if he decides to stop seeing her, even though some married women will act a pure fool when you break it off.

"Tamara, the girl I was involved with for six years, was a really sweet girl. She was pretty, had a sexy-ass body, and good pussy. Her husband was much older than she was and took for granted that she was content because he made good money and she didn't have to want for anything. She had a huge-ass rock on her finger, they lived in a gated community, the whole nine, but she was miserable because her husband was never there because his job required that he travel a lot, and when he was there, he didn't give her much attention. He basically married her so he could have a showpiece, but they had no marriage to speak of.

"One time I called her and told her I wanted to see her and she said, 'Good, I want to see you too, and I'm feeling kind of bold tonight. I want you to come over to the house. He's out of town until next week.'

"I was like, 'Are you sure, 'cause you know I ain't no punk. Say the word, and I'm on my way, but there's only one stipulation, since you're feeling jazzy. I don't want you to have no panties on when I get there, and I need to see that you don't have any on before I get out of my car.'

"Shit, homegirl was all for it, so I drove over there and called her from my cell phone, and sure enough she let the garage door up so I could pull my car in, came out, and lifted her dress to show me her freshly shaved pussy, and it was on. We fucked in every room of that house except the master bedroom. That's the kind of stuff married people should do, but they're too busy being married to handle their business.

"I can remember one week when we had good, hard sex for six days straight, but on the seventh day I didn't want no more. It was good, wet, tight, and all that, but for some reason after six straight days of it, I didn't want no more. That doesn't mean I didn't go back and get it again or that we stopped seeing each other. It just means that after six days of her good pussy, I wanted somebody else's good pussy. I can't explain it.

"The only thing I can say to a man or a woman who's having an affair is don't lose your head. It's wrong to mess around in the first place, and I wouldn't tell anybody to do it, but if you're going to do it, be selective and be discreet. Don't be messing around with somebody who would use you or jeopardize your marriage, because it's not worth it. I'm not the kind of guy who feels like a woman has to buy me things or cater to me just because she's married and I'm not. I'm in the relationship for the same reason she is: I like her, and I enjoy her company as well as the sex. But she doesn't owe me anything, just like I don't owe her anything. But there are a lot of dudes out there who expect a lot from a married woman.

"He might expect her to take him shopping, get him a cell phone, pay his car note or his rent, even take him on trips, just because he's spending time with her or giving her good sex. It's the same way when a married man is dating a single woman, but the difference is, I don't believe in women paying for those kinds of things for a man. Sure, it's nice if she gets me something for Christmas or my birthday, but I should do the same for her if it's possible. I can't tell you how many times I've had a lady friend tell me she's having an affair with a nigga and he don't even think enough of her to remember her birthday. If he likes you enough to get between your legs, then he can show some respect and at least buy you a gift, and you're a fool if you keep sleeping with him when he doesn't. If I was a woman and a nigga treated me like that, I'd be through with him; he wouldn't even need to dial my number again. But for some strange reason, women put up with shit like that.

"That's what I mean when I say you can't lose your head. Why would you allow some nigga who ain't giving you nothing but good sex, if that, to treat you in a way you wouldn't allow your husband to treat you? He ain't paying none of your bills, there really ain't no future for you and him, so if it starts turning into a one-sided relationship where he expects you to do all the giving while he just sits back grinning and shit like he's the man, then you need to step, and don't even look back. Let him find another fool who wants to put up with his bullshit. You must remember to keep things in perspective. Remember that the person at home is your spouse—that's permanent. The other situation is one where there is no real commitment, just lust, wonderful sex, and a lot of fun and laughter. It's what your marriage started out like.

AFFAIRS

"Women tell me all the time that the affair is the only thing that keeps them coming back home because it helps them deal with the reality of marriage. When they're with their lover, there are no bills to discuss, no arguments, no holding out on sex, none of the day-to-day bullshit you have to deal with in marriage, but that's why it's called an affair. If you were to leave home and get with that other person on a permanent basis, you'd eventually get into the same situation and have the same issues to deal with—that's just how marriage is.

"But if you want to stay with your spouse, remember that the person you're having an affair with may seem perfect, but also think about how that person would react to some of the things you and your spouse have been through together, like sickness, money problems, problems with the kids, weight gain, all that stuff. And if that person has shown any indication that they only like being with you as long as things are all fun and good, then you know right away that there is nothing permanent about the relationship, because all relationships will hit rough spots sooner or later. Enjoy it for what it is while you have it, and when it's over, move on."

KEN

"Zonora and I have been married for six years, and I love being married to her. She continued to work full-time when we first got married and only went to school part-time because she wasn't used to being dependent on anyone, but I was finally able to convince her that she'd finish a lot faster if she just quit her job and went to school full-time, so she did, and unfortunately that's when our problems started.

"She started taking some heavy class loads, like fifteen and eighteen hours a semester, so she didn't have much free time to spend with me, because she was always in the books and I wasn't used to being ignored. And when I say I was being ignored, I'm talking about in and out of bed. If she wasn't studying, she was in class, and if she wasn't in class, she was sleeping. There was never any quality time for us as a couple, and the times we did have sex were few and far between. It got to where I felt like I was more of a roommate than a husband.

"See, that's a major problem in most marriages: women don't understand how important sex is to men. Just 'cause a woman can go without sex for months on end doesn't mean that a man will, especially if he's young and used to getting some on a regular basis. If he isn't getting it from his wife, he's going to get it from somebody else—believe that. I love my wife, I'm crazy about her even to this day, but after the first year or so of marriage, she became totally uninterested in sex, and I got tired of having to beg her for it, so I started thinking with that other head and stepped out on her.

"Zonora had a study group to go to on Wednesday nights, and I'm a movie buff, so I would go to the movies because I didn't have to worry about it being crowded during the weekdays. One night I went to the theater and ran into this attractive woman at the concession stand. She had a banging body and a sexy short haircut. We introduced ourselves to one another. Her name was Angela, and she said, 'So, it looks like you're alone too.'

"I'm like 'Yeah, my wife's Wednesdays are all sewn up for the next few weeks, so I treat myself to a movie on Wednesdays.'

"She asked if I minded if she sat with me since her husband was out of town on business and she was by herself for the evening too, and I said no problem. We sat there, watched the movie together, made a few comments here and there, and when it was over, we went our separate ways. We didn't exchange phone numbers, didn't stop for a coffee or a snack or anything afterwards. It was totally innocent.

"The next Wednesday, I show up at the theater, and who do you think I see? Angela, and I'm like *Damn, this can't be a coincidence*, so I spoke to her, got my popcorn and cold drink, and found a seat, but she came in and sat down next to me again. We got to laughing and talking, and whatever, and right in the middle of the movie, she whispered in my ear, 'Have you ever gotten a blow job in a theater?'

"And I was like, *I know she didn't say what I thought she said.* I was like, 'Excuse me, what did you say?'

"She goes, 'You heard me. Have you ever had a blow job in a movie theater?'

"I was like, 'You know I'm married, right?'

"And she said, 'So, I won't tell your wife if you won't tell my husband.'

"So me being weak minded and using the excuse that my wife wasn't catering to my needs the way I felt she should've been and figuring nobody would find out, I let Angela unzip my pants and suck me off. It was mind blowing because my wife hated doing that. All she was interested in doing, when she had the time for sex, was the missionary position, and maybe on Valentine's Day I could hit it from the back, but a blow job was out of the question. But Angela was doing her thing like she was enjoying it. She sucked and licked and squeezed until I was about to come in her mouth, so I kind of grabbed her head to let her know I was about to come so she could ease up and just use her hand, but she kept on sucking until I exploded in her mouth. It was the most erotic experience ever.

"The next Wednesday, I went to the theater and stood out front and waited for her to arrive because even though we hadn't discussed it, I knew she would show up just like clockwork. We didn't say one word to each other. I bought the tickets, and we went straight inside and found two seats at the very back. Twenty minutes into the movie, she unzipped my jeans. She starting sucking me again, but this time she didn't let me come in her mouth.

"She said, 'This time I want you to fuck me.' She unwrapped a condom and handed it to me then hitched up her skirt, straddled my lap and, facing the screen, she guided me inside her. We fucked for about five minutes, and I could tell she was really into it because of the way she moved and because of how slippery she was, and she didn't make a sound even when she came.

"Afterwards I asked her if we could meet somewhere different because I didn't want the people who worked there to start noticing a pattern, but she couldn't meet me the following week because she had plans but said maybe we could get a room the week after. I was like, 'Cool, give me your cell phone number, and I'll call you,' and what I liked about this woman was the fact that she didn't sweat me. She didn't ask for my phone number in return, didn't want to know about whether me and my wife were getting along, didn't want to know why I was fucking around—nothing. All she wanted was the dick, and as long as we were using condoms, that was fine with me.

"That following Wednesday, my wife was having the study session at our house, so I prepared the food for her and the group and was looking forward to actually watching a movie, since I wouldn't be seeing Angela. I was getting ready to head out the door when my wife called out to me. She said the people in her group wanted to meet this great husband and cook that she had bragged so much about, so I went into the living room where they were sitting. There were two guys and four other women besides Zonora, and one of them was Angela, standing there looking at me like she'd never seen me before in her life. I almost shit my pants.

"My wife said, 'I just wanted you to meet the people who've been occupying my time these last several Wednesdays, excluding Angela with her trifling ass, since she's missed the last three or four meetings. The only reason she's here tonight is because we threatened to kick her ass out, and she knows she needs help with that big test we got coming up.'

"I was thinking to myself, *The reason she missed those last meetings was because we were sitting up in the theater fucking.* I shook everybody's hands, briefly met Angela's eyes, kissed my wife good-bye with Angela looking on, and was out of that house so fast, it would've made your head swim.

"The very next day I called her ass up and asked her what the hell she thought she was doing. She didn't even try to deny that she'd known all along that Zonora was my wife. She said she wasn't able to talk just then because she and her husband were meeting for lunch and he was due to arrive at any minute, but she'd still meet me at the hotel just like we'd planned. I was like, 'All I want is an explanation. I want to know what you're up to.' But she had to hang up because she said her husband was walking up.

"The following Wednesday we met at a hotel as planned. I'd left a key for her at the front desk, and I was inside the room just pacing because she was about thirty minutes late. I finally heard the card in the slot, and when the door swung open, she stepped inside looking sexy as hell, but I was too pissed to let her get to me like that, so I just stood there and stared at her real hard to make sure she knew exactly how pissed I was. She didn't say a word, just closed the door and leaned against it while she unbuttoned her coat. All she had underneath was a sheer bra with matching panties, a garter, stockings, and black stiletto heels, and damn if I didn't feel myself getting hard. I turned away from her and headed to the mini-bar and poured myself a whiskey straight up while I attempted to gather my thoughts and rein in my dick.

"When I asked her if she'd known all along that Zonora was my wife, she didn't bullshit me. She told me straight up that she knew I was married to Zonora because she'd seen me when I picked her up from school once. She said that before she'd even seen me, she would listen to Zonora brag about me at their study groups and say things about what a good man I was and how lucky she was to have a man who would never mess around. Angela said she thought to herself, *Any man will mess around, given the chance,* so once she saw me and liked what she saw, she set out to prove my wife wrong.

"I asked her what she planned on doing now that she'd proven her point, and she told me it didn't have to go any further than this room.

"I was like, 'Cool, so I'll see you later because I don't like it when things get messy, and I'd hate for either one of our spouses to get wind of this,' to remind her that both of us had a lot to lose if this conversation ever got back to either spouse.

"She goes, 'You don't need to worry about that,' and came up and stood behind me and rubbed her body against my back as she hugged me around my waist. 'So now that we've discussed that, why are we wasting a perfectly good bed standing here talking?'

"My dick was totally erect by then because she'd started to stroke me through my pants. I don't know how I summoned up the strength to move away from her, but I did, and I told her that I didn't plan on seeing her any longer, so she shrugged, said it had been nice, buttoned her coat, swiveled on her heels and left, slamming the door hard behind her.

"I sat on the bed for a few minutes in total shock, hoping like hell that she wouldn't tell my wife what had happened, and then I heard the key in the slot again and was thinking, *This woman has a lot of nerve. I just told her I was through.* I stood up to head towards the door, getting ready to read her the riot act, and when the door swung open, there stood Zonora looking at me like she wanted to kill me. I was like, *Aw hell, what the fuck am I going to do now?*

"Zonora stormed into the room like an avenging angel, and she was shaking, she was so mad. I was standing there thinking, *How the hell did she get a key, and how the hell am I going to get out of this?*

"She goes, 'Don't think I didn't catch the look that passed between you and Angela at the house last week. Even though you did your best to hide it, I got this funny feeling in the pit of my stomach, and I noticed that you've been acting really strange since then. I started thinking about how she'd missed our last few Wednesday meetings and then thought about the bitchy little comments she'd make when she'd see me in class like, "What has that nice husband of yours done for you lately?" I knew you always went to the movies on Wednesday, and I thought back to how she hadn't made any of our Wednesday-night study sessions except the one at our house, so tonight I decided to follow you.

" 'I watched you check in and then sat in the lobby for a minute to get my bearings, and who do I see coming in five minutes after you but that bitch? I watched her go up to the desk and heard her ask for the key, and by that time I was so pissed, I decided I'd better go over to the bar and get a drink and calm down. There was no point in my trying to follow her, because I would've given myself away, and I didn't know what room you were in, so I really had no choice but to wait until you came down.

" 'Then when she came back so quickly, I was confused but I approached her anyway, and do you know what that bitch had the nerve to say? She said that she was tired of hearing me brag about what a perfect man you were, and she was tired of hearing about all the things you did for me and how lucky I was to have a man who wouldn't mess around on me, so she had simply set out to prove me wrong. Then she handed me her key and walked off, and it was all I could do to keep from jumping on her and beating her ass, but then I thought, *She didn't drag him in here kicking and screaming. He walked up in here on his own free will.* Now what I want to know is did you fuck her?'

"I was like, 'Zonora, you can look around this room and see that nothing happened. She was only up here for a good five minutes if that.' I know how crazy my wife can be when she gets mad, so I wasn't even about to go there with her. I did what any red-blooded American male would do, and lied. I was like, 'Baby, once I found out she knew you and had set this whole thing up out of spite, I was through, so I ended it before it even got started,' and that's when Zonora flew across the room like a bat out of hell and knocked me upside my head with her heavy-ass purse before storming out.

"After sitting in the room and staring at the door for what seemed like hours, I finally got up and went to my favorite sports bar to have a drink before heading home. Both of us needed some time to think, and I especially wanted to give her a chance to cool off before she saw me again, but when I got to the house, Zonora was waiting up for me. She was sitting on the bed, arms folded across her chest, and with tears in her eyes she asked me how could I have even contemplated fucking around on her. I talked to her for a long time and just poured my heart out. I explained how I'd been feeling neglected because she was so busy with school, and surprisingly, she agreed that she'd had her priorities all wrong lately, but said that still didn't excuse what I'd almost done.

"She said as far as she was concerned, I'd already had the affair, even though I hadn't slept with Angela, because I'd taken the time and enjoyed the whole process of secretly talking to her and setting the whole thing up. I still didn't confess to anything, 'cause I ain't no fool, but we talked things over, and I promised that I wouldn't be that stupid and selfish again, and she promised to remember to put our marriage first, before everything else.

"That was a wake-up call for both of us, and it was rough for a while after that. We had plenty of conversations about whether or not we should stay together, but we worked through it, and things have been much better since then."

ANTONIO

"It was difficult to remain monogamous when I was married, because I wasn't happy. Since I own the sports bar, I'm always out there. I had an affair with a woman I met at the bar, and again, going back to my Catholic upbringing, it devastated me. I felt terrible. I wasn't getting any kind of support at home even though I was giving and giving, so it was bound to happen, but I still felt bad.

"We had a Super Bowl party at the bar, and this white girl came up to me. I'd seen her before. She was what we would call a club bunny because she was at the clubs all the time, and we started dancing and drinking and got too high. I took her to her house afterwards, and she begged me for it. She pulled off my pants, pulled my dick out, put it in her mouth, and sucked it for a while then pushed me back on the bed and straddled me. I was *almost* fighting it, but I'm a man, and it's hard to argue with a stiff dick. Afterwards, I was like, *Oh God, what have I just done*. It took me a long time to get over it. I even stopped going to church because I didn't feel right until I finally went to confession.

"There were other times where I got into that situation and never actually penetrated a woman, because I said, *I can't do this*, but the things we did do were just as bad. I had girlfriends I would go out with, and at the end of the evening we'd go to her house and cuddle and hug and kiss because I wasn't getting that at home, but I never had sex with anybody else. I just couldn't do it.

"I think it's wrong for anybody to have an affair. If you're in a committed relationship, that's what it means. If you want to be with somebody else, then you should leave. With me, even as a single person, I only like to have sex with one woman at a time. If I were to have sex with two women, that's just like having an affair because I'd be cheating on both of them, and that's just not right."

EDWIN

"I had an affair with my second wife while I was married to my third wife, but it was just a one-time thing, and it was in the early stages of the marriage, during the first six months. I tried to avoid putting myself in situations like that afterwards; I'd go talk a lot of shit, but most of the time I'd walk away.

"I think men have more affairs than women because men are more doggish. There is something about a man doing it that makes him feel like he's more of a man, but that's just my opinion. I know having an affair isn't right. You have a conscience, and you have to live with the fact that you've done something like that, and it doesn't feel good to sit around thinking, *Damn, I hope she doesn't find out.* The reason I cheated on my wife with my ex was because I just wanted to go hit it one more time to see if it was still good, but that doesn't make it right.

"I wouldn't sleep with a woman if I knew she was married. It's just not right. If you got a commitment with somebody and it isn't working out, you need to look inside your house and straighten out the situation. Really, I don't have a lot of respect for a woman who has an affair. I would tell any friend of mine messing with a married woman to cut it loose and leave it alone."

RUBEN

"When a man wants to make love and his woman tells him no, he takes that personally. Why does a man stray? Because he's not getting his needs met at home. If a man is doing everything he's supposed to do for a woman, she ain't going to say no. She's going to give him everything he wants. It ain't about giving; it's about sharing. When you start throwing around the word *giving*, saying, 'How come she won't give it up?' she ain't got to. If you're handling up on your business, she'll handle up on hers. But see, a lot of men think all they have to do is bring home a paycheck to get sex anytime they want it, and that's wrong. If a woman works outside the home—well, hell, even if she's a stay-at-home wife—she can't work, cook, clean, take care of the kids, the bills, et cetera, et cetera and still be expected to have the same energy he has if all he does is go to work and then come home and chill.

"You can't allow boredom to creep into your relationship, and we bring boredom upon ourselves. I can be at home all by myself and be bored. I can be in a relationship with somebody and be bored. Once again it goes back to that plant—remember that you have to fertilize and nurture that relationship. Life is precious—why be bored? All relationships take work. You're not going to grow a tree from a little seed without work. And if you don't prune it, it's going to grow wild, and once those branches are set in place, you aren't going to change it."

LANDON

"An adulterous relationship doesn't always have to consist of sex; it can be done in other ways. I used to go to this particular Wal-Mart, and every time I went, I saw a very beautiful black lady there about a size two, perfect body, everything, and when I saw her, I would always stare at her because I thought she looked nice. After a while she started looking back, and then it got to where she would wave to me. I've never gone through this woman's register, never knew her name or anything, but every time she'd see me, she'd say hi, and that's cheating. You know why, because any time you let anybody in, it's an emotional tie. Now every time I walk into that store, she expects me to say hi. Every time I see her, I expect her to say hi. Now when she's working, she's looking for me, and every time I walk in that store, I'm looking for her. That's an emotional tie I have with another woman, so that's cheating. Remember, you're not only tied to your husband physically; you're tied to him emotionally too. Anytime you step outside of that, it's cheating.

"If you're flirting with a man at work, it's cheating even if you don't sleep together. It's an emotional tie you have with that person, because now you and him have that expectation of what could happen. The only thing left is to do it, have a conversation and do it. You've already gotten to that point. You've already tied yourself to that person in some kind of way.

"I've been on military bases where the husbands would go on a temporary duty assignment for a few months, and the same day those husbands left, you could go to the club on base and find a lot of the wives there looking for some young man to keep them company for six months. They'd even be wearing the squadron shirt, letting you know exactly where their husbands were. I've had women come up to me and say, 'You know what, baby—I'll buy you whatever you want as long as you just keep me company for these next few months.' They'd buy me clothes, whatever. I'd go to her house, I'd see his picture on the fireplace and recognize him, and then remember that I went on an assignment with him before and saw him out there doing his thing too, so it's like, whatever.

"A young man like me, I was trying to get everything I could. I probably hit a couple of men's wives because they came to me straight. It was like, 'Look, I'll get you whatever you want, all I want you to do is sleep with me, spend time with me, stay next to me while he's gone, and when he comes back, it's over.' So I did.

"That's a whole different degree of love. A woman will wait, a woman doesn't even have to love a man much to wait. But a man is not going to wait for a woman unless she's the one. If she ain't the one, he ain't waiting, I'll tell you straight up. It ain't happening. Do you know how long it takes to cheat? Five minutes, clock it. Five minutes. I can say, 'Baby I'm going to the grocery store.' I can see my ex-girlfriend at the grocery store, get in the backseat of the car, and hit it in five minutes and be back home, and my woman will never know. She'll only think I went to the grocery store. It don't take that long."

SIMEON

"Have I ever had a relationship with a married woman?" Simeon chuckled. "I ain't never been involved in no affair. Why?" He glanced around the room like he was looking for a hidden camera. "What you know, you know something? You got tapes or what?

"Seriously though, even if a woman is married and I'm single, it's still an affair. Cheating is cheating. I get approached by more married than single women, but I think marriage is very sacred and it shouldn't be taken lightly. The first thing I run across from married women in day-to-day conversations is, 'He just doesn't do this and he just doesn't do that, and he's this and he's that' and you think she's just using you as a sounding board. But nine times out of ten, she's softening you up to consider getting involved with her.

"She wants you to turn the tables and say, 'Well, since he's dogging you out, why don't you give me a chance?' As I said, game recognizes game. Normally when a woman is married and she comes at me like that, I know where it's going. It may not happen that day, but she's feeling you out to see if you may be willing.

"The big problem with men is this: when a man cheats, he can't keep his damn mouth shut—but if a woman cheats, you're never, ever going to know. She'll go and lay in that bed with another man, and her man is never going to know. When I say a man can't keep his mouth shut,

I mean he's doing things like coming in late at night, the phone starts ringing, his wife answers and the person on the other end hangs up, he may get perfume or lipstick on his clothes, and that, to me, is not keeping your mouth shut. He's putting himself out there. I've even seen married guys out at social events all hugged up with their other woman, and to me that's totally disrespectful, not to mention stupid.

"Cheating is not right. In my opinion, the worst thing that could happen to a human being is to be embarrassed, especially when everybody knows my business and I'm the last to find out. That's what I'm saying. Don't cheat on me, because you're going to embarrass me, because you don't know who I know. You never know who you're going to run into—you really don't.

"When you go into a place and you don't know who's there, sure enough someone you know will see you and go, 'Isn't that Simeon's wife? Isn't that Simeon's girl?' And it may be somebody who doesn't like you. It may not get back to you, but they're feasting on it. They'll look right in your face and ask, 'Oh, how you and your girl doing? Why don't y'all come on over,' knowing all along that your dumb ass doesn't have a clue about what your girl is doing. It could be a very embarrassing situation.

"That brings me back to the shit my ex-girlfriend did with the baby. When those DNA tests came back, all I could think about was how she could have been cheating on me without anyone in our close circle of friends knowing about it. Needless to say, I ended a couple of those friendships behind that because I found out they had known but just hadn't told me. What I wanna know is, How you gonna say you're my boy and then let me get played like that?

"In hindsight, I now realize that some of them tried to make me aware that she was screwing around by some of the things they said or did. You know how on TV when that lightbulb comes on over the cartoon character's head? You get to thinking, you hit this rewind button, and you go back over all the conversations, and suddenly everything becomes clear. Out of the blue your friend might say something like,

'You know, man, it's about twenty percent for child support.' And after all of this has happened, you're sitting there thinking, *Why was he talking to me about child support back then? Was this his way of saying, 'Hey, man, we need to talk about something?'* But I still think they should've just come right out and told me what was up. I felt like a fool when the truth came out.

"If one of my friends was being cheated on, I would tell him. I've done it before. Friendships are sacred, but they're always tested. If I'm your friend and I know your wife is out cheating on you, you explain to me why I *shouldn't* tell you. Why should I allow you to go through that? Why shouldn't I tell you?

"Sure, some people don't want to know. Some people feel like, *If you hadn't told me, I wouldn't have to make a decision.* Well, what about facing up to responsibility? If I had a friend who was going through stuff and I didn't know about it, and then I saw him at a party and he done lost thirty, forty pounds, I'm supposed to wonder, *What the hell's going on with him?* If I find out that he caught his wife cheating with the guy I saw her eating lunch with a few months ago, I'd feel bad because I could have said something.

"On the other hand, there was a situation with one of my boys and his wife, where one of our frat brothers pulled him over to the side and said, 'Look, man—I saw your wife in Dallas, another man was driving the car, blah, blah, blah,' and the guy shook it off. After that, he was never allowed back in their house. That was almost ten years ago, and they're going through a separation now, but the pitiful thing is that we'd tried to tell him that his wife was cheating, but he didn't want to hear it. He didn't want to know the truth; he just assumed his frat brother was after his wife.

"I'm not a psychiatrist, but a friend should be able to tell a friend anything. If that same friend can come bail you out if you get a DWI, why can't he tell you your lady is messing around without you thinking he has some ulterior motive? That doesn't make any sense."

3
SELF

CRAWFISH ÉTOUFÉE

MAKES 20 (4-OUNCE) PORTIONS

1 cup chopped onion

2 ounces red bell pepper, diced

2 ounces green bell pepper, diced

2 ounces celery, diced

1 cup olive oil

2 teaspoons salt

1 teaspoon freshly ground black pepper

1 teaspoon cayenne pepper

2 tablespoons paprika

¼ cup (½ stick) butter

1 pound crawfish tails

½ cup dried Italian-style bread crumbs

2 cups water or crawfish stock

½ cup chopped green onions

2 cups cooked rice

Sauté the onion, red and green bell peppers, and celery in the olive oil until translucent, about 5 minutes. Add the salt, black and cayenne pepper, paprika, and butter, stirring until blended with the vegetables. Add the crawfish tails and combine. Allow the mixture to cook down for 5 to 7 minutes in a covered pot. Add the bread crumbs, stirring to mix the ingredients together for 2 to 3 minutes. Add the

(continued)

(continued)

water and simmer for 15 minutes. Serve in bowls over the cooked rice. The étoufée will keep, covered and in the refrigerator, for two days.

12

MATURING

ANTONIO

"I feel great about getting older. I had a physical recently, and the doctor told me something I thought was hilarious. He said when you get older, you can't keep up the pace that you did when you were younger. He said, 'A tired man has a tired penis—remember that,' so I try to get as much rest as I can."

EDWIN

"You're only as old as you think and old as you feel. I work out almost every day or I'll go to the track and run. I really haven't seen a downside to aging. I receive more respect as I've grown older, and I don't rip and run like I used to, but I still do a lot of the same activities. I stopped playing basketball just last year because I couldn't hang with the young kids anymore.

"Physically I usually don't have the desire to have sex every day. Then again, I might want it every day and sometimes twice a day. It just depends on the mood. I still process things quickly, but I don't remember like I used to. Just like a computer—you have to have it backed up or you're going to push aside things that are less important. I went to my doctor and got my checkup, and I said, 'Hey, man, I need a pill to help me remember things.'

"He said, 'Yeah, and when I start taking it, I'll give you some because I'm forgetting a lot of stuff too.' That's just all a part of it.

"I'm getting a little tummy now, and I'm self-conscious about that, so that's why I work out. I watch what I eat, and I don't do a lot of fried foods. I bake just about everything now, or I might throw something on the grill, and I make sure I have the veggies. I don't do a lot of drinking; I do smoke cigars occasionally, but for the most part, no booze, no smoking, and no drugs. I think the biggest thing of all is being at peace with yourself, and I don't have any worries."

QUINCY

"As I get older, I feel like I'm becoming more settled. Certain things I don't think about as much as I used to, like sex. Sure, I like sex, but it doesn't drive me like it did when I was young. I'm more into things like my finances and my future; I want to always be stable and comfortable. Like Chris Rock said, 'I don't want to be the old nigga up in the club.' I want my comfort and my peace of mind, I want to go to work and enjoy it, and I want to come home and relax. It's almost like everything is slowing down for me, but it's a good thing. I used to drive fast and always be in a hurry, but now I don't have to do that. I'm not in a hurry to live my life, and part of that is because of my kids.

"My ex-wife can act a fool if she wants to and try to keep the kids away from me, but one day they're going to need me to do things for them, and I want to be able to help them, in spite of her. I can't afford to react to the stupid stuff she does, because in the long run, it's not gonna hurt her—it's gonna hurt the kids, and that's what I'm concerned about. If she wants to party all the time and not save anything for a rainy day, then I already know they'll have to depend on me. What am I gonna say, 'I ain't giving y'all shit, go ask your mama what she did with all the money I gave her when y'all were kids?' I can't do that. Those are my kids too, so one of us has to act like an adult."

MALIK

"I don't mind getting older at all, I just feel that as I do get older, I have to take care of my body and become even more knowledgeable. There are people who have not and will not make it as far in life as I already have, so I try to enjoy each day that I've been blessed with.

"I have noticed changes in my mental state as I get older. I make wiser decisions than I did in the past, and I tolerate some things now that I never would have tolerated when I was younger. Physically, it's harder for me to keep my weight down, so I really have to work on it, but I feel more distinguished in stature and carry myself with more respect than I did when I was younger. I watch what I eat, get regular checkups, and I have a personal trainer. All these things tend to help with the stresses in my life concerning my wife, my job, my kids, money, even the unknown things I sometimes worry about. I hope to age gracefully and retire someday without having to worry about money."

NEAL

"I'm not getting older—I'm getting better, I'm getting wiser, and I'm more willing to share with others. Whatever I can do to assist others in enjoying life, and to help them be successful, productive citizens, that's what I want to do. I try to share everything I have whether it's finances, food, clothing, or transportation, if it's going to help another individual. I believe in setting the example."

COLLIER

"Let me tell you how I feel about getting older: I don't. I don't feel anything about getting older. I mean, naturally things are supposed to happen as you get older, but it ain't nothing to shock me. In my mind, I'm fine.

"There is a saying that goes, 'I walk by faith, not by sight' and I'm a true witness that it's possible to live that way. The surgeries I've had affected my sight somewhat, so I see more with my mind now than I do with my sight because everything is already here."

Collier pointed to his head.

"I shouldn't drive, but I do, and you know what, God is taking care of me. He ain't gonna let nothing happen to me. I told somebody the other day that I'm gonna live a long life—I feel it. I don't know what is supposed to happen to me but whatever it is, it's already been written, it's already there, so I don't let anything faze me. I can do just about anything that anybody else can do, and maybe do it better, regardless of my age."

13

SELF-IMAGE

SIMEON

"You mentioned dating outside my race, so let me address that. If I was to say race didn't matter to me, I would be lying. Relationships are hard, period, and dating outside of your race is adding a complication that wouldn't be there if you dated within your race. Relationships are about you and the other person and maybe both of your families, but when you date outside your race, you need to recognize the fact that you are bringing society's opinion into your relationship. Going out to dinner, going to a movie, taking a trip, being part of this particular organization—all of those things factor in. I would be wrong to say I don't like you because your husband's white or I like you better because your husband is black or Hispanic. It's wrong for me to put my opinion out there, because what you're doing has nothing to do with me, but people still do that anyway. In the business world, you may lose a contract when you show up at somebody's house for a dinner party and they see that your wife is white.

"Our parents grew up in a time when things weren't so nice, and it wasn't something they had to read in a book—they lived it. A great many of our black youth today have no idea what went on, because they're living in a different culture. Black, white, Asian, Hispanic—you name it—these kids have grown up together and hung out together. It's kind of hard for a white kid to say, 'I don't like you because you're black,' to his black friend if they grew up together and they know each other really well. Kids in this generation don't usually dislike someone because their skin is a different color. But back in the day, that wasn't the case. Back then, a person might not like you just because their parents said they shouldn't like you.

"My mom never said, 'Don't date no white girl,' but I'm sure she would prefer that I dated and married someone of my own race. With my dad, it was a little different, and I knew it was an issue when I started dating this white girl and he bought me a gun. He told me, 'Son, you must be a fool if you think you can ride around in your car with this white girl with nothing to protect yourself.' He gave me a twenty-five automatic and said, 'You keep this on you at all times if you going to be dating that white girl.'

"That's when I found out the truth. I was like, 'Aw, Dad, people ain't like that.' But then we took a trip—it was my girlfriend, her daughter, her sister, her sister's husband, and I. We went to a small town in Texas for the Fourth of July, where they specialized in selling antiques. We were walking around the stores, and they had all of these little posters of black people jumping the broom, Aunt Jemima with the head scarf wrapped around her forehead, and all that, and I thought, *Man, that's kind of racist*, but I let it go.

"Later that day, we went to the lake to go swimming, and I noticed that I was the only black guy out there, and I was like, *What the hell?* Then we finished swimming and started to walk back to our car. My girl was behind me, and all of a sudden, she started cursing this white guy out, saying, 'You know you need to get out of here with all that shit.' I was thinking he must've said *motherfucker* or something like that around her daughter, so I told her to ignore him, 'cause people were out there drinking and stuff, and you know how they get.

"She said, 'He asked me how did I like my nigger boyfriend,' and I was livid. He walked to his truck, and his friend and some girl were telling him, 'Come on, let's go,' but he walked around to the bed of the truck and reached for something, and I'm like, *Oh hell no.* So I went to my car and opened my trunk. It was about to be *on*, right there in the park. But see, if I'd been dating a black girl, that shit never would've happened.

"You need to be able to understand when dating outside your race that other people's opinions will factor in and affect your life. I'm not saying don't do it, but you need to understand that you're going to have to deal with that, and if you get married and have kids, your kids are going to have to deal with it too.

"I think there is a difference between dating black women and women outside of my race because there are some things you're not going to say to someone outside your race that you would say to somebody of your same race. You may be a little bolder, but to me, it's just understanding racism. You got some white people who will just walk on eggshells because of the prejudiced things that have happened to blacks in the past. Then you got some white people who are like, 'Look, I ain't responsible for what my ancestors did, so don't expect nothing from me.' You got some white girls who date a black guy just to be rebellious towards their family or because they think he has a bigger dick—people have their own reasons.

"If I dated Janet Jackson, I would treat her differently than I'm going to treat the normal woman off the street because she's Janet Jackson. Probably for the first couple of weeks or first couple of months, you're going to put the difference up on a pedestal, and that doesn't mean put it on a pedestal and treat it better. You may put it on a pedestal and say, *Well, this is a white girl—I can just run all over her. I'm going to date her and somebody else at the same time, but I won't do that with a black girl.* Or you'll say something like, 'You're just saying that because I'm black,' which is not something you'd have to say to a black girl. So, because that person is so different from you, you tend to do things differently. Some things are worse; some things are better. If someone says dating a person outside their race is no different than dating a person inside their race, they're lying to you. It can't be the same.

"Now, the sex is all the same. There's good sex and there's bad sex, and race ain't got nothing to do with it. Sex can get boring after a while with the same person, but that's because people start taking each other for granted. You get in a rut like, I do this, then you do this, then you do that—and that's your sex life. You get in that routine, and sex can become boring, no matter what color the woman is."

ANTONIO

"I think I'm a good person, I'm a quality person, I'm one of a kind, and I think highly of myself. Everything I'm saying must sound like I have a huge ego, but this is all the truth. I think I'm a good catch, and if a woman doesn't realize that, it's her loss, not mine. When somebody says, 'I like bigger men, I like men with no kids, I like this, I like that,' it's like they don't know what a great guy they're missing, so okay, *bye*. Next. That kind of stuff used to hurt me, but not anymore.

"I know some people do think I'm arrogant, but I'm the go-to man. Everybody comes to me—my friends, my family, and my employees come to me—I'm the guy that can make things happen, and I'm dependable. I try to say it doesn't matter what other people think about me, but truthfully it does. I don't mope around saying, *God, they don't like me*; it ain't like that. It's gratifying to help people and to have people say good things about you, so I like that.

"I've succeeded beyond my wildest dreams already, and my problem now is that I've set my goals high and I've hit them all. A friend of mine told me that I need to reassess my life and set some higher goals, because everything that I ever dreamed of, I've achieved. I'm living the life I dreamed about; I'm really blessed. I worked hard and I sacrificed a lot to do it, but success to me is making a living at doing something you love. They say if you do something you love, you'll never work a day in your life. So I can honestly say I've never worked a day in my life."

JARED

"I have a serious issue with dudes who go out there and make babies all over the place like they don't have a care in the world. They go out there and have unprotected sex without a thought as to what will happen if the girl gets pregnant, and she's just as much at fault as he is. I mean, *damn!* How difficult is it for a man to wear a condom, and that being said, how hard is it for a woman to tell her man he ain't getting none unless he wraps it up?

"There is this one chick I went to high school with who had four kids by four different men before she was even twenty-five. I don't get that. I can understand making a mistake, but I don't understand how you can make the same mistake four different times. Why didn't she learn her lesson after she had that first child? And she ain't getting child support from either one of those men.

"I knew this other chick that dropped out of college when she got pregnant. She had about one year left to go before she got her degree, and she was a smart girl—she would always get the highest score in the class on our calculus tests, but then I found out she didn't have much common sense at all. The guy she got pregnant by already had two babies by two different women, and he was still living at home with his mama, and she knew all of this. And I just can't quite understand how a woman who *knows* that her man already has two children that he isn't taking care of can lay up and get pregnant by him with baby number three. What makes her think he's going to treat her any different?

"I absolutely refuse to date women who have children, because I don't want the drama, and I always use a condom when I have sex. I use a condom not only because I don't want to catch something I can't get rid of—"

Jared grimaced and motioned to the waitress for another Corona.

"—but I also don't want to take the chance of having a child with a woman I don't plan on marrying, and I don't want another man raising my child.

"I dated this one woman for about six months before I found out she had a child, and I found out by accident because she made it a point not to tell me. Whenever I went over to her house, I noticed that she never had any family pictures out, which I thought was weird, but she explained it by saying she was a neat freak like that, so I guess that's why the small picture frame that was laying facedown on her fireplace mantel caught my attention. It looked like it had fallen over and she just hadn't noticed it. I picked it up, and damn if it wasn't a picture of her and this cute little brown-skinned girl who looked just like her. When I asked if that was her daughter, she said yes, so I was like *Well, why didn't you tell me you had a child? We talked about everything else.* She explains to me that some men don't usually like to date women who have children. And I'm thinking to myself, *You got that right,* but I'm also thinking, *How long were you planning to hide this from me? Maybe one day after I'd started to have some real feelings for you and maybe even asked you to marry me? Were you going to introduce me to your daughter at our wedding when I asked who the cute flower girl was?* When I asked where the child's father was and she told me he was in prison but about to get out in another year or so, I was too through.

"My mom made it real clear when we were growing up that she did not want us to date women with kids. She would always tell me and my brother, 'If a woman already has a child, you don't need to be trying to date her. Have your children with your wife so that you don't have to be raising no other man's child, because nine times out of ten, that's just trouble waiting to happen.' Now I'm not saying it's right or wrong, but personally speaking, I don't have children, so to me it's only fair that I expect to fall in love with and marry a woman who doesn't have children either. That way we start off on an even keel.

"That may offend some women, but I'm just being honest. If she can pick and choose whether she likes tall men, short men, pretty men, or whatever, then I have the right to decide if I want a woman with or without kids. It's simply a matter of choice."

EDWIN

"I don't have a role model. I've always been the one to push myself to succeed. I've had the opportunity to work with a number of successful people, like senators and governors, but I wouldn't necessarily say they were role models. I'm the kind of person who sees somebody at the top and says to myself, *How did he do that? I want to get there too.* I'm extremely self-motivated, and I've just worked hard to get where I am.

"My dad would always tell me and my brothers. 'You people are almost grown, so you need to get a job and get on out of here. Don't be sitting around, waiting for a check to come in.' He's been known to say this more than once, especially if he'd had a few beers. I think he and my mom were part of my motivation. I saw how hard they worked every day. That was expected, especially in those days. Kids who grew up in the country *knew* that it was up to a man to find a job and work, and when he got married, he was *expected* to take care of his family. It was like this—"

Edwin used his fingers to count off the points.

"You got a job, you got your family, and you took care of them. You didn't depend on a woman to go to work and take care of you. And today, that is *still* my philosophy. If my woman wants to work, that's fine, but we don't depend on her income.

"Heading home with a sense of accomplishment is success to me. If I leave work feeling good about the day, then I'm successful, but I always feel like I have to have something to strive for, so I'm constantly raising the bar. I've achieved the goals I set for myself, but I've quickly established new goals because I don't want to get complacent.

"I'm extroverted in my business life but introverted in my personal life. I like a lot of time by myself; I like having positions of leadership and being involved in the community and making a difference."

TERRENCE

"I'm glad you asked how I feel about my self-image because that's a big issue for me. You know, you've got guys out there who were raised by their mother and father in a nice neighborhood with everything they wanted, and they still turned out bad. Then you've got a guy who doesn't even know who his dad is, or maybe his dad was in the streets dealing drugs while Mama raised the kids, but he turned out to be okay. So I think it's all in the choices we make, and we can't always blame somebody else if we make a bad choice.

"I could sit around and feel bad because my parents gave me up for adoption. I could use that as an excuse to be another angry, bitter black man, but I choose not to because I'm not going to waste my time moping around about something I can't change. My parents taught me that every day when I wake up, I have to make a choice; I can choose to dwell on my past and what may have been, or I can be thankful for who I am and what I have, so I choose to be thankful because there are so many people who are less fortunate than me. I think highly of myself, and I set goals for myself because I always feel I can be a better man.

"My boy back home who grew up right next door to me came up in a really good home, but he decided he wanted to get out there and sling drugs because he said he didn't want to work hard all his life just to make thirty or forty thousand a year. Well, of course, he got locked up, and now he wants to blame everybody except himself. I went to visit him a few times when he first got incarcerated, but all he ever talked about was how the man had made these crack laws to target minorities and how it wasn't fair that he was a first-time offender but still got five years even though they only caught him with two little rocks. I told him, 'Man, how the hell are you going to blame *the man* for what you did, and who is *the man* anyway? Nobody told you to go out there and sell drugs—that was a choice that you made, so stop whining and do your time like a man.'

"He got mad and called me a sellout and all that, telling me I thought I was better than him just because I was in the military. Then he said I shouldn't have joined the *white man's military* and started telling me about how he's going to become Muslim, and that pissed me off. Not because he wants to be Muslim, but because he's sitting in prison and still hasn't realized that he's the one who sold out when he sold drugs to kids in his own neighborhood. I hope the Muslims teach him something about being a black man because he can get all the religion he wants, but if he doesn't learn to accept responsibility for his choices, he'll probably spend the rest of his life in and out of prison.

"I'm a black man just like him, and I could have sold drugs or did a number of things that would generate more money than being in the military, but I didn't want to spend my life looking over my shoulder all the time. I'm tired of hearing brothers talk about *the man*, and I'm tired of all that bullshit about how I ought to 'help a brother out.' Brothers need to help themselves *out*, just like our ancestors did. We already know we can't expect *the man*, if you will, to give us any hand-outs, so why are we even looking for one? Sure, racism still exists, but I decided I was not going to let that be a deterrent for me, no matter what it takes, and I don't feel sorry for a brother when he's had more opportunities than the average person and he was just too sorry to take advantage of them.

"My wife has a younger brother who just turned twenty. He's working part-time because he says he can't get a full-time job, he's not in college because he says college isn't for him, and all I ever hear him and his boys talking about is women, sex, clothes, and cars, even though none of them has a means to acquire any of those things. I cornered him one day and asked him what was he going to do with his life and tried to tell him about the opportunities in the military. This boy—and that's what I call him, since that's what he acts like—told me he doesn't want to go into the military, because he doesn't want anybody telling him what to do, and I didn't even know what to say.

"You can't tell me that his manager at the grocery store where he works stocking groceries part-time, for minimum wage, doesn't tell his dumb ass what to do every time he walks through that door. I told him, 'Man, even if you don't want to go into the military because we're at war, that's cool. I understand. But damn, don't just sit around on your butt every day and wait for opportunity to come to you, because it's not going to happen.'

"I know the black man has always had to work harder and be better than average just to get what he deserves even when others don't, and I agree that it's not fair. We should be much further advanced economically and financially in this day and age, but until we get some more brothers like Magic Johnson and others like him who know what's up and are trying to create opportunities, we're going to have to struggle. So quit complaining about it, and do what you got to do. That's what being a man is all about: you've got to make your own way because nobody's going to give you anything."

XAVIER

"I like people, and I'm comfortable around people, but then sometimes I can be very quiet and distant. The majority of the time I'm very sociable, but I'm never the life of the party or anything like that, especially if I'm around a lot of people I don't know. I used to live in Dallas and I partied a lot, but once I moved back home, I settled down, and I don't party too much anymore, because it's boring. Everybody knows everybody else, everywhere you go, there's always the same people there, doing the same old thing, so there's no reason to go out."

MALIK

"I think I'm a very honest person. I really try to treat everyone fair, the same way I would prefer to be treated. I would rather tell you up front what's on my mind than hold it in. I have very high self-esteem. I'm the type of person who feels that a job or classification is not what makes a person; it's what the person makes of the job. I have high expectations of myself. I have been told quite often that I have a likeable personality. Guys who work with me have said that if I ever made supervisor, they could work for me because I require just as much of myself as I do of others around me. Their overall opinion of me is pretty good. I tell my kids all the time that it doesn't matter what others think, but when it comes to how I feel about myself, it does matter. Sometimes what others think of you can help you get ahead in life, depending on the circumstances."

NEAL

"After high school, I went to enroll in college at Florida State University, and the registration process was so slow and the lines were so long out there in that heat that I got discouraged. I was about to get in the car and go home when one of my partners we used to call T-Mac, who was a big football player, hollered at me and said, 'Hey, man, where you going?'

"I told him, 'Man, I can't fight that line,' so he said, 'No problem, come with me,' and he walked me to the front of the line and I registered, and nobody said a word. Within four years, I had finished college and got a job at Florida State, but the Vietnam War had also begun.

"I had an education waiver, which kept me from being drafted, but as soon as I graduated, rather than waiting for that little brown envelope to come in the mail telling me I was going to be drafted into the Army, I joined the Air Force. They wouldn't have accepted me if I hadn't had a degree, but I still didn't go in as an officer. Once I got in, I took the

Officer Candidate School exam, and I passed it and there was a white guy out of Texas who flunked it, but they gave him a twenty-five-point waiver—for being white, I guess. When the two of us went in for our interview, they asked which Officer Candidate School I wanted to attend, I told them I wanted to attend Pilot Training. They said that career field was closed to me because my score was two points lower than it needed to be, but it was open to the white guy who'd flunked the test, because he had that twenty-five-point waiver. So I made up my mind then and there that my four years in the Air Force would be just a good experience, because I wasn't going to deal with that for an entire career.

"I had some wonderful experiences, but I had some bad ones too, like brothers who seemed to have no purpose in life and because of that, they were really abused and mistreated. I saw white guys put rifles in these brother's mouths, make them do push-ups out on the hot asphalt on their knuckles and knees when the temperature was about ninety-five degrees, and I couldn't take it. One day I went out there and told them, 'Get up. You don't have to do that,' and the squadron commander came and asked me, 'Who do you think you are? You're no different from that other airman.'

"I told him, 'Sir, I realize that I'm no different, but I'm a damn man, and I'm not going to stand here and see you abuse my brothers.'

"So he went up to my captain and told him what had happened, and the captain called me in. I told him, 'You know, we are citizens of the United States, we are honorable men, and they're not going to do such things to me, nor will I stand by and see them do it to someone else and not say anything about it. That's wrong, and that's why I told them to get up.'

"After that, I gained the respect of my senior officers because I had stood up for myself and the other men in a respectful way. I didn't get loud and start cursing or acting like a fool; I simply stated the facts and left it at that, and I didn't have any more problems with anyone.

"Everything was going along fine until Martin Luther King Jr. was assassinated. We were on our way to Incirlik, Turkey, and while we were loading pallets, we saw them lower the flag to half-mast. There were about five hundred men in my squadron, and about one hundred of us were black. Since they looked up to me, I went and asked the captain what was going on, and he told me to have a seat.

"He said, 'We need your help on this. Martin Luther King Jr. has been assassinated by a white man, and we need you to go out and meet with the other black guys and give them the news and try to keep them calm.'

"It was about one p.m. on a clear, beautiful, sun-filled day, but when he told me that, everything turned dark. I got up and got all the guys together and told them what had happened and also told them the captain was concerned that we would cause problems. Then I said, 'I've told you guys what the captain said, and you can handle it how- ever you want to,' then I went out and *started* the riot. I went out and kicked plenty butt because I was so hurt and angry. It was like it was the end of the world. Martin Luther King Jr. was our hope for a brighter future, so we were all pissed because we felt we had nothing else to live for. We felt that his death meant that all the progress mi- norities had made was for nothing.

"That was probably the worst thing I can remember happening while I was in the military, but I managed to finish my tour and got an Honorable Discharge. Back then, there was a policy that if you held a state job prior to going into the military, you could return to that job once your military time was up, so when I got out, I was prepared to go back to my old job at Florida State, but then I got a call from one of the high schools because I'd applied for a counseling position. I went in for the interview one morning and started working the very next week, and after thirty years I'm just about ready to retire."

COLLIER

"I'm a positive person, even through the negative. I've been in low places in my life where I felt like I couldn't see how I'd make it through the day, but I always kept my face towards the sun. When you've got your face towards the sun, your shadow falls behind you, not in front of you. If you think negatively, nine times out of ten, negative things happen. Just like right now—I'm not at my best as far as my health, but I think I'm doing fine, so I am."

14

SPIRITUALITY

JOE

"You know, I was raised in church—just about everybody in my neighborhood back in the day was raised in the church—but I hate the way some of these preachers have turned church into a business. I believe in God, I believe in the Bible, and I believe you should pray every day and have a relationship with God. But the problem is there's so much corruption in the church.

"I know guys who used to be out in the streets just like me when we were younger, and now that they're saved and sanctified, they try to get all brand-new, like they forgot how they used to live. I'm not saying people can't change, but damn, don't be trying to preach to me when you used to be a bigger whore than I was and all you've done now is changed the environment you're whoring around in. I think that if you're living the life of a Christian, all you have to do is live it and people will recognize that. People don't want to hear about how you're living—they want to see it, they want to know that it's possible for them to change because they know your past and see that you've changed.

"I can't stand these people who get saved and then every other word out of their mouth is, 'God is good. Praise the Lord. Be blessed brother, be blessed.' The Bible says, 'Of whom much is forgiven, much is required,' and that's probably the reason some of those new Christians are always trying to quote Scripture to other people. They know how bad they were when they were out there in the world, and now they feel guilty. I don't believe true salvation is meant to make you feel guilty—at least that's not the way I interpret the Bible. If God has forgiven you, then that old life you used to live is nothing for you to be ashamed of because now you're a new person. But that doesn't mean you should forget to the point that you start judging other people, and that's the mistake a lot of people make when they get saved, because they don't know any better.

"Things are gradually getting better, some of the up-and-coming preachers who are educated and have really studied the Bible are teaching people the truth and actually have requirements before members can be active in church, but all these preachers who go around telling people, 'I been called to preach,' and are allowed to get up in the pulpit without any formal education from a theological seminary need to go sit down somewhere. All that old guilt, hellfire, and brimstone preaching should be outlawed because you can't scare people into being saved, especially when they know what kind of life you've lived.

"The other thing I don't understand is why some black churches still hold church from eleven in the morning until two in the afternoon, take up three offerings, and then spend fifteen minutes reading the weekly activities and the sick and shut-in list when people can read it on their own. It's almost like once some of these preachers get an audience, they're afraid to let them go. And I've actually heard preachers say, 'If y'all do right and pay your tithes like the Bible says you should, I wouldn't have to get up here and beg.'

"Well, let's be realistic about that: it's hard for a man and his wife to commit to paying tithes and give to all these other building funds and stuff when they're struggling just to buy their kid a pair of shoes.

Many people do pay tithes out of obedience and continue to drive around in a broken-down car while the pastor is driving a Cadillac Escalade, his wife who hasn't worked in five years is driving a Lincoln Navigator, and both of his rude, spoiled kids are driving new cars, but the roof on the church still hasn't been repaired after that last hailstorm. Does that even make sense? I know people are supposed to pay their tithes and let God deal with these preachers who misappropriate the church's funds, but be for real—people aren't blind. Why would I pay tithes and struggle while you live like a king?

"So, with all of that said, I go to church when I feel a need to go and fellowship, and I have a relationship with God, but I'm not going to go and sit there and act like I don't know what's really going on, and I'm not going to join a church if I have to come home and complain, because then I'd be a hypocrite, and there are more than enough hypocrites in the church already. You know there is another Scripture that says in so many words, 'Everybody who says Lord, Lord, ain't going to get into heaven,' so they might as well stop perpetrating. I think God has a lot more respect for an honest man than he does for one who calls himself spiritual and then acts a fool the minute his church members ain't looking."

DANTE

"I don't really like the word *spiritual,* but I guess it's okay to use that to define how I feel about God, since I am a very spiritual person. For me, it's just knowing that there is an almighty power, and recognizing Him as that. I love God, I respect Him, and I know He's there, but I also treat Him like a friend. You gotta talk to Him because He has the key to your future, and you've got to read the Bible to know His word.

"I feel like the Bible has been tainted over the years, even though there's a Scripture that says we are not to add or take away from it, but I don't worry about that, because God will take care of those who twisted it. You should read the Bible as it is and don't try to read more into it, because God also said that our thoughts are not His. The world is His Monopoly game, and we're just pieces in it. We ain't running nothing, and we need to remember that.

"As for church, it's been corrupted, but you go to hear the Word and to fellowship with other Christians. Just be sure you don't go for the wrong reasons, like to see what Shantay is wearing this Sunday, or to see if the usher and the deacon are making eyes at each other. That's none of your business. Your business is to hear God's word and try to live by it, not get into or start any mess.

"That doesn't mean I'd go to a church that has a gay preacher or a preacher who's a whore. I just can't do that, because that's immoral. How's he gonna tell me about morality when he's a whore? Or if he's gay, how can I have any respect for him as a leader? That just doesn't make sense to me—that's like the blind leading the blind. As a matter of fact, I don't even see how they can preach around that in the Bible, because it's in there and not just one time. What's he gonna say if I ask him what the Bible says about being a whore—is he gonna say, 'That ain't in my Bible'?

"I'm not a perfect Christian myself, but come on, where do you draw the line? I know I need to make some improvements, like I'd really like to stop lusting, but I just can't seem to do it. That's the only thing I have in my life, and in my heart, that needs to go, and it's rough on a brother out here with all of these beautiful women around. I know I have a beautiful wife, but it's not about that. It's like this: I could own the finest car on the block, but if my neighbor has nice car, I want his car too, just because it looks good, and that's lust, so it's wrong. God made the game, but I gotta play it, and I gotta play it His way, and that's not easy. I'm trying to do things His way, and I'm not saying I'm jumping off the path, but I'm damn sure leaning.

"The thing is, you can't walk the line. Just because it's in our nature to lust and be sexually immoral or do whatever else, that's not a good enough excuse for God, even though He knows how hard it is to walk the straight and narrow. I think He's really going to judge us by our hearts when everything is over and we come before Him. He knows straight up that it's too hard because we're human and temptation is hard for us to resist sometimes. I'm not saying that God makes it hard. Satan is the one who does that because he knows what we like just like God does. Men are hunters, and I think that's the reason so many of us have affairs. It's because once a man gets married, he misses the thrill of the chase. Men aren't scared of commitment like women think they are. They're afraid of losing that freedom to chase.

"When I got married, my being horny all the time went away because I could get sex whenever I wanted it, from a woman I was in love with, who was safe. But it was almost like the tiger in me was caged up, like someone had put a muzzle over my mouth and said, 'You can only have what I offer you, and only when I want to offer it to you.' In all reality, that animal nature in a man should be targeted towards his wife, and he should lust after her all the time, but when you see a thick-ass fine woman out there and you know she's willing and available—man, it's hard. I'm not saying all men feel that way, but the majority of us do. That's just the way men are. Life can be complicated sometimes, and it's hard to stay focused unless you're really committed to your spirituality.

"If you walk the way God wants you to, and keep your focus on Him, then the other stuff that gets you sidetracked won't be so hard to resist, because you're not even letting it faze you. But for me, that's hard. You know, it's like, *God, I want to be good, I really do, and I need you to help me. But before you do, can I have a little bit of that over there? Just a little taste of it, just let me hit it one time, that's all I'm asking for.* But God knows that if He lets us have a little taste, it won't be enough. Sometimes we do things we know are wrong because we also know that we're going to ask for His forgiveness, but that's playing with God, and I just don't want to play with Him like that.

"Even if I did get busy with some woman I was lusting after, I'm afraid that as soon as I got ready to come, He'd make me have a heart attack right then and there. And then my wife would be hurt when she found out that not only did I die of a heart attack, I was actually lying up between some other woman's legs, trying to knock her shit out the frame when it happened.

"On the other hand, I could mess around and come home with no evidence of what I did, but my conscience would bother me, and I'd get cancer, or a tumor from worrying about it every day, so hell, it's not even worth it for me to act on my lust. That's my worst sin, and I guess I just have to live with it until I die."

XAVIER

"I'm still young, so I feel my options are open. There are certain things I'm not going to do, but there are still some things I need to work on. I'm a Christian and I believe in Christ, but my girlfriend is Muslim. I don't have a problem with her beliefs, and I really understand their perspective in that they think God can't have any partners. That means they don't believe that Jesus was anything more than a prophet, because to believe otherwise would make Him partners with God. Now, just because I understand that way of thinking, that doesn't mean I believe that for myself. I believe that Jesus was more than a prophet. My belief is that he was the human form of God because God, knowing all, can still never feel like a human unless He is one, and that's the reason for Jesus. I believe I should walk as closely in that spiritual path as I can."

MALIK

"I think being spiritual means that you understand who you are, and why and by whom you were put on this earth, and I feel that each person should have a connection with this spirit who put us here on earth, and I choose to call that spirit God. I believe that I am a spiritual person, but probably not day in and day out like I could be. I believe in

God, the Bible, and church, but I don't feel that you have to be in church every moment of your life to be saved, and I definitely don't believe that all who attend are saved anyway. Overall, I feel that I'm a good person, but as a father and head of my house, there are times when I need to let my spirituality determine my actions, especially around my children."

NEAL

"Spirituality to me is believing that there is a higher being, and I believe in the birth, death, resurrection, and ascension of Jesus Christ. My spirituality is not where it needs to be, but there have been some changes, and even though I'm not what I should be, I'm not what I used to be.

"I'm currently reading this book called *Forty Days of Purpose: Why Am I Here on This Earth?* It's heavy, and it reminds me of when I took my first course in counseling, when I thought that we were perfect individuals and that there were other folks who were abnormal—only for me to find out that we are all abnormal, we all have obsessions. It's the same thing in my spiritual life; I'm always striving to be where I should be. One thing I'm eager to do is learn to remember more Scriptures so that when I talk with individuals, I will be able to tell them where to look in the Bible for themselves. I have not reached that point in my life yet, and even though I can complete a Scripture once someone begins to say it, I can't tell you what book and verse it comes from.

"That's important to me because I really believe that when you get into trying to help someone come to Christ, you need to be able to back up what you say. The Bible says we should all study to show ourselves approved, and I deeply believe that if I can tell someone something out of the Bible, but can't tell them where to go find it for themselves, then I'm somewhat stating it, I'm not actually doing it. Just like I take the time to do everything else that I do, I need to take that same amount of time and put it into studying the Bible more. I read the newspaper every day from front to back, and I can go back and tell you what each article was about and then tell you what section to find it in, but I can't tell you to look in John or Matthew for a certain Scripture, and there's no excuse for that."

G.G.

"I am a son of God, but I still have human challenges that I have to deal with on a daily basis. The one thing I dislike about myself is my low level of self-confidence and total faith in my God. I am very spiritual and have been involved in the church all of my life, and I honestly believe that God loves all of us unconditionally and heals us through his Holy Spirit because He knows no sin. The Bible is, was, and always will be interpreted by men who have misinterpreted many things, so I'm not always sure how much confidence I can put into it. I feel that the church should bring us together as a community by reaching out and bringing together all people, no matter what their differences—be it race, sexual orientation, or whatever.

"If God created you and I with all of our differences and all of our hidden sins and still loves each of us in spite of those things, why is it so hard for us to love one another? Why do we continue to think the next person should feel, think, and live as we do when we are obviously all different even though somewhat the same, since we are made in God's image? We should spend more time learning to be tolerant and to love and forgive because only then will we be able to truly *live* in God's image. Until we stop looking at each other with eyes of condemnation and judgment, none of us will ever fulfill our purpose. Life is short, so we should spend more time doing those things that make others feel good because then we are sure to make God feel good as well."

COLLIER

"Christianity is a belief. I carry on a lot of foolishness, but that's just my personality. Deep down inside, I know that I could have been one of the best ministers out there had I chosen to take that path. I could have been anything that I wanted to be, and when I made the decisions I made, it wasn't like I didn't know what I was doing, but sometimes when you try to help someone along the way, it holds you back.

"My mama used to say, 'As sure as you live, surely you will die.' Don't expect that you're gonna live on earth forever—you got to go just like everybody else. You've never known anybody to leave here and come back and tell you how it was, so everybody got to find that out for themselves. Let me tell you what happened to me—I dream a lot, and I dreamed that I'd died. In my dream, people were passing by me, looking down in my coffin, and I was telling them, 'I ain't dead, I ain't dead,' and they just kept passing by shaking their heads and crying because they could not hear me. That has a lot to do with the soul, and I think God gave me that dream to help me to understand that your body has to leave and people won't see you anymore. But the soul, the inner you, never dies.

"It's like somebody giving you a shovel or a hoe and telling you to go out there and scrape up that grass in your yard, and you go scrape it up. In a little while, in a moment of time, that grass is gonna come back, and so is your soul. If you're not present here, you're present somewhere else. Let me go back to Kahlil and his book *The Prophet* again. They were talking about death, and somebody asked the prophet about death, and he said something like, 'Death is a moment in time, and after a little time upon the winds, another woman shall bear you.' That means we all will live again, but in a different realm.

"Have you ever wondered sometimes why things happen the way they do? The night my mama died, it stormed. The wind was blowing and it was thundering and lightning, and I felt something was going on because I kept tossing and turning in my sleep. Then the telephone rung and woke me up, and it was my brother calling to say, 'Collie, Mama just passed.' But you know, it was her moment in time. I was hurt because I didn't want her to die, but what could I do about it? She'd had her moment in time.

"You hear people who believe in reincarnation talk about what they're gonna come back as after they die. I heard one guy say, "I'm gonna come back as an animal." How are you gonna come back as an animal if you didn't leave here as an animal? If you plant an apple seed, ain't no banana tree gonna come up. An apple tree is gonna come up. If you plant some collard greens, ain't no mustards gonna come up. Collards are gonna come up. So when you leave here, you leave as a human, and if you come back, you're coming back as a human, otherwise relativity is all wrong. What you plant is what's going to come up."

ANTONIO

"Spirituality means having a personal relationship with God, so I pray all the time. I'm in a crisis with my religion right now because a divorced Catholic is an oxymoron, and I was raised Catholic, so I don't have a church. I'm an Easter and Christmas Catholic. I pray to God, and God talks to me, but I have to be quiet and listen.

"I have faith but it's not like I want it to be. I'd like to have a more solid faith, a more unwavering faith. I want to be one of those people who absolutely know where I stand with God. I do have a strong, strong faith, I won't even take the Lord's name in vain but I wish it was stronger, I wish it was unshakable."

EDWIN

"I go to church sometimes, but I think spirituality comes from within. If you have respect for others and if you're doing the right thing and you've got your God, then all is well. Being spiritual to me is treating others fairly, being respectful, and not committing adultery. It's when you can truly look at your conscience and live with yourself and say, *I did the right thing. I didn't screw anybody out of anything.* In the past, if someone gave me too much change back, I would say, *Shit, too bad,* but now I turn around and say, "You gave me too much money." Being spiritual is when you can truly say you're being a fair person.

"I believe in God and the Bible, but I think some of it is skewed. I think the Bible is something that helps bring people together to help them want to do the right thing. You need that because there are just as many hypocrites in church as there are out of church, and I'm fully aware of that. I'm a strong believer, but I take in and evaluate what's being said in church just like I evaluate politicians on the big screen—I see what fits for me. I do need to go to church a little more, and I would like to get involved with some of the youth committees—that would make me feel good. I was youth director once before, and it was a good feeling to try to do something for the children."

WARREN

"A spiritual person is a person who has Christ in their life, a person who fears God and has set goals and principles for himself in life to live accordingly. Everybody who claims to be spiritual ain't. Growing up in the church and going to Sunday school and stuff made me a more spiritual person because I would've done things a whole lot differently if I hadn't been raised up in the church. I see people do things and I'm like, *How in the world could they do that? How could they do that?*

"When my mom was living, I used to go by the house and discuss things with her. We'd talk about the news and all this crazy stuff happening in the world, and she'd say, 'You have to look at people and how they're raised. You all were taught to fear God, and you were also taught to fear me and your daddy, but when people grow up and never go to church, they don't have that fear of God, so there's nothing that they won't do. Life means nothing to them.'

"They taught us in officer training at the prison that young people are more dangerous than older people. For instance, you go into a situation where older people are involved, and there is a thought process about death before firing a gun. You go into a situation with young people, and they don't even think—they just pull the trigger. They don't have no fear, none at all. You'd be surprised if you just watch some of these younger guys out there on the street, these little gang members and stuff. You know when they see a church? When one of their homeboys die, and you can spot them a mile away. You can tell they never sat in a service, they've never known what none of that was about, because that's the only time they've gone to church. They grew up raising their parents, they grew up like brother and sister with their parents, but you can't be friends with your kids.

"I look at it every day—me and my youngest son, we go at it all the time, because he can't understand life, but I can. His mama says, 'You're arguing with him too much.' But I'm gonna argue with him. I don't want to be his friend. I'm his daddy, and if he don't hear it from me, who he gon' hear it from? So when he hears it, whether he does it or not or whether he likes it or not, somewhere down the line he's gonna say, 'Daddy said that.' That's when it works because even now my mom and dad are dead and I look at some of the things they told me while I was growing up. Just about every day, a situation comes up that reminds me of something they taught me.

"I think there is a lot more I can do for my spirituality. As the old people would say, I think there is something in life God wants me to do, and I've been running from it. Both of my brothers are deacons at my church, and my mom always said, 'You'll preach one day,' but I don't know about that.

"I don't think that's what God has in mind for me, but I know that it's something He wants me to do that I'm not doing. I'm just waiting, and I feel like He'll reveal it soon enough. My wife says all the time, 'You need to quit drinking,' and I say 'Well, you know what? One of the best ministers I know in this area is Reverend Davidson, and I remember when I was a kid he used to come to our house on Saturday morning, and they'd play bid whist all day long and drink.' He's a minister now, and he don't drink no more, but he stopped when he got ready to stop. Well, I won't say when he got ready, when God got ready for him to stop, all that stopped. I believe that God shows you what he wants you to do. You might run from it, but when He gets ready for you to stop running, He gon' call you, then you gon' have to listen—you not gonna have a choice."

RUBEN

"It was put to me this way when I was growing up, 'If you put your faith in man, you're going to fail. If you need a role model in your life, look to Jesus Christ.' And my dad always told us, 'There are men in this world who are good men and great men, and you can learn a lot from successful people, but don't put your faith in man.'

"For example, say you know somebody who became successful by pulling himself up by his own bootstraps—like, look at Colin Powell. You can learn from somebody like that, but you still wouldn't put your faith in him. It takes dedication, hard work, and commitment. Those are all positive attributes that you can see. I have never put my faith in any man, not even my dad. He retired at fifty-five, and he's financially secure, we never missed a meal, we never lacked for anything, and we always got what we wanted, but we had to work, and we had to learn to look to God. He worked through Dad to provide for us.

"I've always been spiritual, but the Catholic Church doesn't teach the Bible. They read to you. They have three readings, but it's not like you have Bible study. Now my mom's take on all of that is, 'That's up to you. It's not the church's responsibility to teach you to read the Bible. The church can't be with you all the way. Those readings tell you how you are to live your life, and those readings are for you to reflect on this week and study.'

"That's what I try to tell kids: pay attention to the readings. I've had some come back and say, 'You know, something that the priest said when he was explaining the Gospel about Luke or Matthew, that happened to me during the week, and I was able to utilize it.'"

LANDON

"I'm very spiritual. I've read the Bible from cover to cover at least twice, and that's not much, but some people haven't even read it once, and I believe in the Word. I'm not the perfect man, and there are a lot of things I do and have done in my life that He will probably frown on, but I also believe that we go through experiences and hardships so we can learn from them and become better people. I believe that He allows those obstacles in our lives to make us stronger."

15

ADVICE

JOE

"There's an old saying, 'if you find an ass, sit on it,' and that's what men—or women, for that matter—tend to do with people who they feel are just crazy about them. If you go around acting like you can't do without a man or you don't want him to go anywhere or do anything without you, then you're acting like an ass. You're acting like your whole world revolves around him, and he's gonna sit on your feelings and think nothing of it because you're acting like that's acceptable.

Another word of advice I have for women, especially single women and women involved in affairs is, after the nut, he don't give a fuck."

SIMEON

"My advice would be to create a solid foundation. If you have a solid foundation, you can go in a lot of different directions. You can construct virtually anything as long as you've got a strong foundation. If your foundation is weak, you tend to have to repair it a lot because it crumbles. So whatever you want to get into, whatever venture you want to take on, have a strong foundation.

"In order to have a strong foundation, you have to be prepared and have plans. You have to investigate the environment—is the soil kind of shaky, is it going to shift, is it going to crack? A young man should say, *Okay, what do I want to do with my life? If this is what I want to do with my life, then I need to investigate and prepare. If I want a military career, then going out and selling drugs may not be the thing to do. I may need to be in the ROTC, I may need to decide whether I want to go in as commissioned or non-commissioned. I may want to talk to people who are already in the military, I may want to see if I can get into the Academy.* If you build a solid foundation, then everything else should just fall into place."

ANTONIO

"The golden rule, 'Treat others how you want to be treated,' was the best advice ever given to me, and that's how I live my life. I'd tell younger men to learn respect. Respect for other people, respect for yourself, and respect for your environment. Young men don't respect shit, not even themselves. How can you go and do some of the stuff you do and respect yourself? How can you get a woman pregnant and leave her and not take care of your child and respect yourself? You got a little boy out there who don't know his daddy, so he's getting punked everyday, probably going to get raped and sodomized because he's so weak because he don't have a father in his life, but you don't care, that ain't your problem? That ain't respect. Respect the woman, respect what a woman has to offer, and when a woman gives you something, respect it.

"The biggest thing I would like to tell women is before you get involved in a new relationship, wipe that chalkboard clean. Let me write my own paragraph. Let me put my own story on there. Don't write it for me, and don't give me somebody else's story and just add mine to it. Give me a fair chance to prove myself. All that baggage—all that shit you drag into each relationship—that's what causes a relationship to end before it begins. As soon as you start in with, 'Well, my ex-husband said' or 'My man said,' it's already over. Why would I want to hear that? I'm not him.

"I had so many female friends that I used to mix up their names. That's something women should know; if a man is calling you baby and sweetie and *never* calls you by your name, that's because he has a lot of women.

"The other advice I would give to women is, 'Listen,' because a lot of women do not listen. They talk and talk incessantly about every-thing from taking a shower when they woke up to the minute they went to bed; they think everything they do is fodder for conversation. 'Oooh, let me tell you, child. I got up this morning and I was out of toothpaste.' And I'm like *Okay I can think about something else right now.*

"I've tuned her out because I know what she's saying; it's the same shit she said yesterday. 'I went to my job, and I told that bitch, I said, "Girrrrrrl, I ain't putting up with that shit, I don't need all that stuff, I'm just not a corporate person. I just can't be working in corporate America."' And she said the same shit yesterday. I might have heard when she said it the first time, but after that, I'm tuning her out. I want to tell her, 'Shut up. Just shut the hell up—don't be talking just to be saying something.'

"You know you're really comfortable with somebody when you can just sit there and be quiet. Ain't nothing more wonderful than to have a woman in your arms and it's just quiet, you can hear her breathing, you can hear when she sighs—that's a wonderful thing. But all this, 'Yeah, baby, you know . . . that woman in that cubicle next to me . . . .'"

Antonio pretended to be pressing a remote control and turning the volume knob up. "I'm looking for a game on TV or something be-cause she ain't saying shit."

EDWIN

"When I was younger, my grandmother pointed in the direction of my privates and said, 'That thang's going to get you in trouble someday.' I was about sixteen or seventeen when she said that, and I wasn't even fooling around with anybody, but she was right. If I could've kept it zipped up a little bit longer and met the right person and done all the right things, then I wouldn't have gotten involved with women who were inappropriate or who weren't a good match for me.

"Some of the worst advice I've received was a guy telling me, 'Boy, you're a fool if you don't hit that,' so the advice I'd give to younger men is to be cautious in their affairs with women. Don't try to move too quick. A young man needs to get himself together first before getting into a serious commitment. Find out who you are first.

"I would tell young women to be independent and self-sufficient. Get into a position where you can stand on your own without having to depend on a man, but also understand that it's nice to be part of a loving relationship. Don't be so dependent, where you got to wait for a guy to bring his check home so you can go put groceries on the table. You need to know how to make it on your own if you have to. I've seen situations where when the guy walks away from a woman, she's just there; she doesn't know what she's going to do because he's always been the one to bring home the paycheck. Then you have women who are financially able to take care of themselves, and when the sorry-ass guy she's married to walks out, she doesn't know that's the best god-damn thing that could've happened to her, and she's standing there crying her heart out.

"An independent woman understands that a job doesn't necessarily work around a nine-to-five position, they understand that, *Hey, when my man calls me and says he has to be at the office until eight or ten at night, that's part of making it happen in his career.* When I was married, that was a big issue with my third wife. 'So-and-so next door comes home at three forty-five every day. Why can't you come home like that?'

I don't have a job that pays by the hour; it's whatever it takes to get my job done. Some days I may be at the golf course at ten in the morning, and some days I may be at the office until ten or twelve at night, but typically an independent woman understands that life doesn't revolve around a nine-to-five commitment. Sometimes it goes beyond that.

"You've got to have that balance, and the woman I'm dating now is pretty close to that balance. She's independent, she understands that life isn't wrapped around a fixed schedule, and she understands that giving a man space is important and so is having respect for one another."

WARREN

"Women should be more affectionate, and they should be more aware of what their man likes. So many women mess up good relationships because once they get what they want, they forget about what it takes to keep it going. They'll do anything in the beginning, but once they get him, it's like, *Oh well, my work here is done,* things become routine, and that's something a lot of men can't handle. Women don't realize that they still need to work at the relationship. Just because she's got this man to commit to her and she's been with him for a little while, she still needs to do those things that keep him happy, and if she makes that man happy, he'll always try to make her happy. So many women don't understand that. I notice that more than anything, especially when women get kids, they totally change.

"Her main concern is the kids; the man doesn't mean nothing anymore. Whatever the kids want, she takes care of, and he's left out in the cold, and it causes jealousy and it causes bitterness because he's thinking, *Hey I had you before we had these kids, what about me?* See, when it comes to the children versus your spouse, you need to be supporting your spouse, you need to be together on things because kids will use you. They will play one end against the other, and if you stick together, you can raise a stronger, more responsible kid. You can raise that kid to be just like you are because he's going to look back at the decisions you made together as parents.

"I would also tell a man that the same thing it took to get that woman—it's going to take that and a lot more to keep her, and I would tell a man to spend time with his woman and don't let your relationship get to a point where you're doing one thing and she's doing another. Keep it together. Even if it's nothing more than going to church on Sunday morning, you need to go together. If it's going to the store, go together, if you're going to a party or going out, go out together. You'll find out you can be friends with your wife just like you can anybody else, and it makes a difference. That's one of the reasons men get into trouble. They tend to run off and leave their wives at home, but I think you should keep your woman with you, do things together. Become each other's best friend, be lovers, don't just be husband and wife. There are things she ain't gonna like, and there are some things you not gonna like, but if you don't take time to learn each other, you not going to know what those things are, and it's never going to work out.

"Young men need to get an education. Stop making babies before you get an education and establish yourself. You don't have to have a woman. I started young, at twenty years old, and I been working every day of my life since then. If I had it to do all over again, I would still marry the same woman. I would still do the same thing, but I would've waited. I would've waited long enough to finish college and buy a house so that when I decided to get a wife, I could just put her in it. It wouldn't have been so hard then. Nowadays, it takes everybody in the household to work and pay the bills. That's the thing young people fail to realize. They don't think about what it's going to take to make it down the road; they just think about what's happening now. I tell my boys, you can't buy everything you see. You got to save some of your money. You got to have some money in the bank. Without money in the bank, you can't do nothing. You struggle your whole life, and you never get on top. We always sit back and look at the white folk and say they always doing this and that and having a good time, but that's because they spend their money wisely and pass that wisdom on to their children. We should do the same thing.

"I also tell young people, get life insurance. For some reason, we as black people don't like to get life insurance. We don't like to pay for life insurance because we don't want to leave nothing to nobody else. But when the white man dies, he's left his family two or three hundred thousand dollars at least so everything is paid for. They're set. But when the black man dies, the family members got to scrape money from everybody they know just to bury him. These young black kids think they going to live forever, but they don't realize people are dying young. You got to have that insurance; you got to set your family up."

RUBEN

"Let me tell you what I learned at an all-male retreat I attended; I remember one of the lectures given to us by a priest, who was truly a man of God, and I know he was a man of God because when he walked past me, goose bumps just raised up on my skin. He said, 'Every night you go home, act like you're a director or a movie producer. When you're a director, you cut out things in the movie that you're filming because not every scene goes right. When you live your life, not every scene goes right. You need to give yourself time before you've said your prayers and gone to bed to reassess that day. You need to take those things that weren't right and ask, *God, how can I become better?*'

"You need to do that every night, and that's what I've done since then. If I'm at work and somebody pisses me off, which happens all the time, I have to go back and ask myself how do I get stronger to be able to deal with these idiots, because they are idiots—there's just no way around it. But you're the director of your own movie. You're sitting in that chair, and you go back and make that scene better. It might not be the next week, it might not be the next month, but you're gonna have the opportunity to grow through that and be able to respond better next time."

LANDON

"Never do anything you would live to regret. Find your purpose in life, and make sure that whatever you're doing is not just a senseless waste of time, because even as a twenty-six-year-old, I realize that one day I'm going to be old. After I turned eighteen, the years just started to fly by. You got one life to live, so make it happen. If you're a procrastinator, like a lot of people my age, you're going to see life pass you by, and you'll never become anything. Don't keep saying, 'I'm gonna do it.' Do it. Don't talk about it; be about it.

"A butterfly is what I would call a woman who won't let a man between her legs. A man like me, being the player I am and being able to maneuver and get between any woman's legs I want to at any time, I would respect and appreciate a woman who would make me wait until we got married. I've always searched for the woman who would make me wait. If a woman would make a man wait, he would wait, if he really loved her. That's a true test.

"Even if I was going home and had to hit myself off every day, I would still fall in love with that woman because you know what, when you get into marriage and you get to making love, the heat is on. That emotional relationship ain't there if she didn't make you wait, because you probably got in the drawers before you even got to know her. I've always wanted a woman who would just say, 'Let's not do that,' just tell me no, or make me wait because you know what, now for me the challenge is there. That's the point of my whole existence now, just being with you. I'm telling you, the second a man gets it, he's gone if he don't love you, so make him wait."

QUINCY

"The mistakes we make as men are going after women for their looks first rather than getting to know them, not knowing them long enough before getting too serious in the relationship, and not listening to what they have to say. If you really listen, it won't take long to find out if you want to go any further. Believe me, I've made the mistake of moving too fast in more than a few relationships, and it was a big waste of time.

"The attorney I used when I got my divorce told me something that I'll never forget, and that is you need to learn to love yourself first. Don't get involved in a relationship if you think that's the only thing that will make you happy. If you get divorced or if you've been in a long relationship and break up, try to stay single about half of the amount of time you were in that relationship because you need that much time to get over what you've been through. If you don't believe me, just listen to people who were with someone a long time, and you'll see that they still talk about that other person every chance they get. I divorced my wife eight years ago, and I still talk about her from time to time. It takes time to get over that person, and it takes time to learn to love yourself. Another person can't make you happy, especially if you aren't happy with yourself already.

"She also shared this bit of advice with me. She said, 'A woman can walk on her hands for a year or a year and a half, maybe even two years if she's good, but after a little while, the truth will start coming out. If she wants you bad enough, she'll act like what you're looking for, but she can't put on that act for too long.' My best advice to people who are out there dating is don't ever tell the person you're dating what you're looking for, because they will become that. That's something you should keep to yourself because people are good at morphing into what you tell them you're looking for.

"I got some good advice from my father too. He said never get involved with someone who isn't your equal, because that can cause problems. I don't think he just meant material things when he said that—he meant physically, mentally, financially, everything. All of those things play into a relationship.

"The best advice I can give to men specifically is that some women grew up watching their mother argue and fight with their father all the time. If you get with a woman who you feel is always trying to pick a fight with you, you need to leave, because you will eventually end up knocking the hell out of her, and you're the one who's going to end up going to jail. Some women want you to get mad, and they will test you and try you and push every damn button you have until they find the right one. But domestic violence is a very serious issue, and police and lawmakers are not playing around with it, so if you're dating a woman and start seeing that side, you need to leave her alone.

"Let me also say this: don't be going on blind dates with people you meet on the Internet and all that. The Internet, phone chat lines, and all that stuff is for losers, and that's what you'll find there most of the time. People using these services don't tell you who they really are. They tell you all this stuff that sounds good, but it's not all true. Probably ninety-five percent of them are nothing like they say they are, and it won't take long to find that out."

GREG

"I think it's important for young men to stay focused and positive. If you believe in yourself, you can do just about anything you want to. If I was giving advice to a young man about a woman, I would tell him to take the time to respect and understand her. He should be as honest as he can be, and he should also be aware of where he stands in the relationship, so he won't get hurt by being too honest.

"I don't think I'd give a woman any other advice except that she should never believe anything a man says, because we lie, and we're very sincere in our lying. We can look you dead in the eye, lie, and not even blink. A woman needs to use her own judgment, don't depend on anyone else to tell you anything about the man you're involved with, follow your own intuition. Men are good liars, and we don't even have to have a reason to lie. We sometimes do it just because we can, and some women will believe a lie before they'll believe the truth. Women are so used to hearing lies that it's hard for them to accept that a man would tell them the truth. Even about something simple.

"The advice I would give to married men is that they need to stop messing around because it's not fair to that woman. Sure, I've done it—and that's why I can say that. If you're always gonna cheat because one woman isn't enough, let your wife know, and move on. Really, that outside relationship is not going to work anyway, and I feel like if you're cheating with her and she knows you're married, then there's no telling what she's doing when you're not around.

"The most important thing black women and black men need to do is sit down and talk and get to know each other. Most people today just want to jump in the bed without getting to know each other. That's the reason we have so many problems in relationships, because once the sex is gone or once you've tried everything and it's not exciting anymore, there's nothing left. We can't talk, because we never talked in the first place, so the relationship has nothing to fall back on.

"The person I'm dating now, we were friends first, so she really knows me. I'm moody, and she knows my moods, so she knows how to get me to open up and express my feelings when I really want to just shut down. I'm very aware of how moody I am, and I'm working on it, but when she knows I'm in a mood, most of the time she won't bother me because she's understanding and she lets me have my space. That's what makes our relationship work.

"It's also important to me that my family likes her, and my mother really likes this lady. I've dated a lot of women, but my mother called me last week and told me if I ever left this woman or hurt her that I'd have to answer to her, and I always try to listen to my mother where women are concerned because I know she wouldn't tell me anything wrong. If my mother didn't like her, I don't think I would want to marry her, because I'd end up in the middle of two opposing personalities, and it would be hard for me to work that out. If I want to see my mother, and my lady doesn't want me to go, then I've got to deal with her feelings, and my mother would be mad because I didn't come to see her, so I just wouldn't marry that person, because there would be too much drama."

G.G.

"The worst advice I ever received was, 'Always work the system because the system will work you.' The best advice I've received always included the word *L-O-V-E*. It's very simple: love, and you will receive love in return and have a wonderful life.

"The one piece of advice I'd like to give a woman looking for a man, or a woman who already has a man but is worried that he might be on the DL or that he's bisexual and not telling, is this: Be cautious. Take your time, and get to know a man before becoming sexually involved, and use protection, because, sweetie, it's wild out here, and most of y'all don't even have a clue. Just because a man is big and fine don't mean a damn thing—he could still be DL. And just because he's thugged out and acting all hard don't mean nothing either, because you've got the homie boys running around fooling young girls—it's everywhere.

"I don't give a damn if brothers read this and get pissed off at me because they need to make a choice or at least make a statement. If you want to have your cake and eat it too, just say that. Be a man. It's a shame that black women have been given yet another thing to worry about. It is truly unfair for brothers to be creeping with other men and keeping women in the dark. When you take into consideration all of the things that black women have had to endure throughout the years and how they've had our backs when we couldn't turn to anyone else, the least we can do is give them a choice. Let them decide if they want to share, especially if it's another brother she's sharing you with."

DANTE

"You might not believe this, but the best advice I ever received was when an old man told me, 'Don't stick it in if it stinks.' When I asked him what it was supposed to smell like he, said, 'Oh, believe me, son, you'll know,' and he was right.

"There's a woman I know who used to smell bad. All you had to do was walk near her, and you could smell her. She always smelled like she'd had sex before she left for work and then didn't wash her monkey. It was pitiful. We work on the ramp at the airport throwing luggage, and it gets hot out there, so by the middle of the day, homegirl would be humming. The odor would almost make you pass out.

"One day it was almost a hundred degrees, and I walked past her and thought I might be smelling myself. I went around the corner and sniffed my clothes and sniffed under my arms, but I didn't smell nothing. I asked another brother to step over that way with me and tell me if he smelled anything, and he didn't even try to be polite about it. He stood right next to this woman, started looking around like he had lost something, then got all loud and said, 'What the hell is that smell? Damn, somebody is stank up in here, and I sure hope it ain't no woman, 'cause if it is, baby, your shit is rank.'

"Supervision finally had to call her on it because she smelled so bad. They told her to go home and not come back smelling like that, because it was offensive to her coworkers. So if I had to give a young man some advice, I'd tell him the same thing. 'If it's humming, keep stepping.'

"As far as the worst advice I've ever received, 'Just Do It' fits the bill perfectly. That's a slogan I've never liked, because people got it twisted. First it was, 'Just Do It,' and then our people got a hold of it and changed it to, 'Do the Damn Thang.' That's almost as bad as 'shit happens.' I don't believe in that. I believe that life happens, and I'd advise anybody who wants to listen to handle their life carefully and think about the decisions they make before they act on them. When you don't do that, that's when 'shit happens.'"

XAVIER

"I would tell young ladies to hold out for as long as possible, for real. The guy who really waits for you should be your pick. The ones who just give you enough of their attention to keep you on that string while they go and do whatever they want to do, with whomever they want to do it with, aren't really waiting on you. They're just biding time, and it's easy to do that when he has other women on the side to meet his needs. If a guy really cares about you, your body is a gift he shouldn't mind waiting for, because a relationship is about more than sex.

"You really should try to wait until you're married because if you at least shoot for that as a goal, you'll come somewhere close to it. Young ladies should treat their bodies as something sacred because it's special, and once you give it away, you can't get it back."

MALIK

"Some of the worst advice I ever received was from my mother's husband before he left home for the last time. He was so ignorant that he told me, 'In this life, you just have to take what the world gives you,' and for a long time, I actually thought that was true. But now that I'm older and I know better, I wonder how much further and how much more successful I would be if he hadn't said that to me. It's horrible to receive bad advice like that from someone you're supposed to love and trust, because unfortunately as a child we believe the things our parents tell us, positive and negative. But I try not to focus on what *could* have been or what *should* have been. I have to move past that and better myself, regardless of the negative things that have happened to me.

"The best advice I received was from my English teacher when I was a senior in high school. She said she saw something special in me, and that one day, if I worked hard, I'd find out where my talents lay, but I was kind of lazy back then. I'll tell any young man out there: stop talking all that shit about how 'the man' is trying to keep us down. Only you can keep you down. You have to get up, get out there, and do for yourself. Stop sitting around waiting for reparations, because it probably ain't ever going to happen. If it does, great, but go out there and get your own. And if you have children, be responsible. Be a man like the man you thought you were when you laid between that woman's legs and made that baby, and stop bitching and complaining about how you got tricked or how you weren't ready to be a daddy.

"The best advice I can give to women is this: Most men don't understand relationships or how to make them work. Look at the role model that man had when he was growing up—like his father, his brother, or uncle—and what you see there is probably a lot of what you'll see in your man. Maybe you won't see it at first, but somewhere down the road in the relationship, it's going to come out. If you're interested in a man, talk openly and honestly with him about what it is you want and expect in a relationship. Once you've done that, listen with your head and your heart while he tells you what it is he wants and expects before you jump up and decide you want to take the relationship any farther. If you don't know what it is you want in a relationship, you shouldn't be in one, because all you're doing is wasting your time and his."

NEAL

"The advice I would give to young women and men is the same advice I received from my parents: You must first have love and respect for God, your country, and yourself because if you don't love yourself, you can't love anyone else. Also, respect the elderly and be unselfish in your ways. Don't always think about yourself. Think about others, and you will have a more fulfilling life. And lastly, get an education because it opens many doors. Nowadays, you can't get a decent job and take care of a family without some type of formal education. There are all types of grants, scholarships, even technical schools for those who don't want to go to college. But whatever you do, get something in your head that no one can take from you. Take advantage of every opportunity presented to you that will help to make you a better person."

PIERRE

"My advice to females would be, don't be so sensitive, don't take things so personal, and guard your heart. Don't always be looking for a husband; have some fun and just roll with it because usually when you're looking for something like that, you're not going to find it. Stop looking and just focus on yourself. Nobody can like you if you don't like you first, and nobody can love you if you don't love you first. If you don't like yourself, it's evident in the way you carry yourself and the way you do things. If you haven't taken time to work out the issues you have from past relationships and if you haven't been able to bury those old feelings, then it's always going to come up as a problem later in your relationships. It's going to keep raising its head until you deal with it. Accept you for who you are, and then somebody else will be able to do the same.

"I would tell younger men to be careful. Take your time, and don't have any babies before you're ready. Focus on your career instead, and establish yourself because women will always, always, *always* be around. Men stay virile longer than women do, so when you're young there'll be older women, and when you're old, there'll be younger women, if that's what you want. Just when you think you've got the finest woman alive, there's one being born somewhere who will be finer than her. Pay attention to taking care of yourself, and establish your life before you even worry about that.

"Women can be trouble. They can get you off track and get you caught up in a whole bunch of other stuff that you don't need to be worried about. Even if you get involved with a woman you really care for, if she starts saying you're too career oriented, you're too selfish, or you don't love her, let her walk if she doesn't like it because there will always be another one."

COLLIER

"Live happily and positively. Avoid all the negativity. If you live positively, you'll live longer. I'm like this—I love advice. I can get advice from a fool, but what makes him a fool is he has this knowledge that he don't know how to use. I use that knowledge—you know what I'm saying. A fool preaches good, but he don't practice what he preach, and that's what makes him a fool."

SHRIMP BOIL

SERVES 4

3 gallons water

6 lemons (halved)

12 cloves garlic

5 tablespoons kosher salt

5 tablespoons Zatarain's Crab Boil

12 drops Tabasco pepper sauce

6 bay leaves

3 tablespoons freshly ground black pepper

5 lbs shrimp

Ice

In a large stockpot, place the water, lemons (squeeze out the juice and put both it and the rinds into the pot), garlic, salt, Crab Boil, Tabasco, bay leaves, and pepper. Bring the mixture to a boil for 3 minutes. Add the shrimp, and boil for 2 minutes. Turn off the heat, and pour ice into the pot to stop the cooking process. Let the mixture stand for 15 minutes. Strain the shrimp after 5 minutes, and keep it in the refrigerator until needed, but for no more than seven days.

AUTHORS' NOTE

Mister Gumbo proved to be a challenging and interesting project because, as we all know, men are not so eager to discuss their issues with women. Especially when they're talking to women about women. Although many said they wanted to discuss or respond to some of the things women talked about in *Sister Gumbo*, some were apprehensive about exactly what they would say, or how detailed they wanted to get. It's often said that men brag and tell stories in the presence of other men, but it appears they still care what women think because with us, they did more talking than storytelling. As a matter of fact, one prospective interviewee cancelled on us because, as he said, "I would love to answer some of the questions women want the answers to, and I could tell you about a lot of stuff I've experienced, but then I probably couldn't look at you the next day."

We applaud these men for what they did tell us because once they became comfortable and opened up, we could see and hear that they spoke from the heart. We found that no matter how big, how tall, how deep their voices, or how proud they may be, men experience love, pain, joy, hurt, and disappointment the same way women do. Their gumbo includes many of the same ingredients as ours, only they stir theirs a little differently, and maybe with a different size spoon.

They may keep their game face on when times get tough, but they do get emotional. They may not demonstrate it in the same way women do, but they love their children, and are often devastated when divorce or a failed relationship separates them from those children.

In no way does this book represent the experiences, views, and opinions of all men, as it would be almost impossible to write such a book. But we did our best to include a variety of men, and to create an atmosphere in which they could honestly discuss their issues and concerns, including those that some women may find controversial.

Just as we did not seek to judge the women in *Sister Gumbo*, we wanted to give these men the same consideration. Therefore, it is our hope that readers will be able to appreciate what these men were willing to share. Whether positive or negative, their life experiences make them the men they are, and as long as they're still willing to evaluate the ingredients in their respective pots, there's still room to get the flavor right.

ABOUT THE AUTHORS

Ursula Inga Kindred has a bachelor of business administration degree in finance from Texas Christian University. She is employed as a senior cost analyst for a large aeronautics company and has future aspirations of becoming a full-time author. She resides in a small country town outside of Fort Worth, Texas, with her family.

Mirranda Guerin-Williams spent six years in the U.S. Air Force; worked as a licensed cosmetologist and is now employed by the federal government. She is pursuing a bachelor's degree in sociology and plans to become a full-time author and speaker. She resides in a small town just outside of Fort Worth, Texas, with her family.